The
Fractured
Dream

BY ROBERT F. DRINAN, S.J.

Stories from the American Soul: A Reader in Ethics and American Policy for the 1990s (1990)

Cry of the Oppressed: The History and Hope of the Human Rights Revolution (1987)

God and Caesar on the Potomac: A Pilgrimage of Conscience (1985)

Beyond the Nuclear Freeze (1983)

Honor the Promise: America's Commitment to Israel (1977)

Vietnam and Armageddon (1970)

Democracy, Dissent, and Disorder (1969)

Religion, the Courts, and Public Policy (1963)

Acknowledgements

The author gratefully acknowledges the assistance of Gregory T. Moffatt, who researched several topics for this book and helped prepare the manuscript for publication. Thanks are also due Mary Ann DeRosa, Jennifer Fairfax, Pamela Green, Sheila Johnson, and Frank Tam, who coordinated, typed, and proofread the manuscript.

THE FRACTURED DREAM

America's Divisive Moral Choices

ROBERT F. DRINAN

CROSSROAD · NEW YORK

1991

The Crossroad Publishing Company
370 Lexington Avenue, New York, NY 10017

Printed in the United States of America

Library of Congress Cataloging-in-Publication Data

Drinan, Robert F.
    The fratured dream : America's divisive moral choices / Robert F. Drinan.
        p. cm.
    Includes index.
    ISBN 0-8245-1087-9 (hard)
    1. Religion and state—United States.   2. Religion and politics—United States.   3. Church and social problems—United States.
    4. United States—Politics and government—1989–   5. United States—Religion—1960–   I. Title.
    BL2525.D75   1991
    261'.0973—dc20   91-12633
                                                                                            CIP

Contents

Preface

The history of religion reveals that when religious groups enroll a significant or substantial number of the citizens in a country, they almost always seek to transform the laws and the culture of that country so that the institutions of the nation reinforce, support, and perpetuate the religion in question. This tendency is present not merely in religion, it is endemic to every cultural and ethnic group which believes so ardently in its way of life that it feels almost compelled to share it with others.

This approach to things has characterized Christianity as much as, and perhaps more, than other religions like Judaism, Islam, and Buddhism. The message and the mission of Christianity probably make Christians more desirous to share their faith with others. Indeed, the urgency of that desire has prompted Christians to do things through the centuries which contemporary Christians would like to forget.

The Protestants who fashioned America from 1620 to 1787, when the Constitution was accepted, did not differ in their approach to church and state from the Christians who preceded them in both the Catholic and Protestant nations of Europe. Religious freedom, or the freedom to be liberated from a church established by the state, was a right yet to be born. Christians in Europe and Christians in the American colonies did not differ in their basic belief that the state should be friendly to religion because its values and its ideals derive from religion. Governments, on the other hand, sought to be friendly and favorable to religion because the inculcation of virtue was deemed to be the joint undertaking of both the church and the state.

That approach to the relationship between church and state was more and more accepted in the pan-Protestant atmosphere of nineteenth-century America. The memory of those years—and illusions about the alleged harmony during that period—is one of the persistent delusions of those who today want to improve public morality in America. Churches can make a powerful argument why the government should follow and enforce their viewpoint. Many, but not all, religious leaders sincerely feel that it is their right and their duty to insist that the truths that they teach be accepted, at least in part, by the government.

But for at least a generation, the notion that church groups should somehow dictate the policy of the government has been fading away. Some ninety million Americans have no affiliation with any church. The churches, moreover, are divided on some important issues. And the issues are often much too complex to be capable of resolution by any simple action, positive or negative. But the erosion of the important role granted in American tradition to the opinion of the churches has left a vacuum, which is troubling to everyone concerned with the state of public morality in the United States. Even if people are no longer believers in Christianity, they have to feel that the civilizing and humanizing role carried on by the churches is an enormous contribution to the state. Everyone has to realize, furthermore, that basic rules have to be made in a society, and no one feels very comfortable in America if the government, and the government alone, is fashioning and enforcing the rules about morality.

The picture is further complicated by the rejection of coercion by religious groups. That rejection is now a part of official Catholic theology. In an epoch-making declaration in 1965, the 2,300 Catholic bishops at Vatican II, in their "Declaration on Religious Freedom," condemned coercion in the name of faith, whether done by individuals, churches, or governments. A ban on coercion in all its forms is now an essential part of Catholic teaching.

The words of Vatican II are very relevant:

> It follows that a wrong is done when government imposes upon its people, by force or fear or other means, the professional repudiation of any religion, or when it hinders men from joining or leaving a religious body. All the more is it a violation of the will of God and of the sacred rights of the person and the family of nations, when force is brought to bear in any way in order to destroy or repress religion, either in the whole of mankind or in a particular country or in a specific community. (Paragraph 6)

Even though there are several restraints placed on religious bodies in America, they are nonetheless expected to be active, articulate, and aggressive in promoting what they feel is best for the people of the United States. Churches are expected to carry out their role in a Christian manner—with courtesy, kindness, and forgiveness. But they *are* expected to be prophetic. In that capacity, they are expected to be persuasive. Their persuasion can sometimes become pressure. It can on occasion become political, but at that point the consensus among the churches as to what should be done comes to an end. There is a point—ill-defined and difficult to locate—beyond which the churches may not proceed.

It goes without saying, when this book refers to "churches" or "religious bodies," it includes all groups—Jewish, non-Christian, and secularist. Jewish groups have contributed enormously to the development of the public morality of America. No reference or expression in this book should be taken as suggesting anything to the contrary. America is a delicate distillation of Judaism, Christianity, rationalism, and secularism. All of these ideological groups—and others—have the right and the duty of seeking to influence America's position as a nation that cherishes basic moral values which America believes are good for the United States and for the world.

The boundaries separating the prophetic position of the churches from their political posture are never clearly defined prior to the arrival of a new and urgent legal/moral issue. But the appropriate boundaries can be defined—at least in a general way—by an analysis of America's role in the world, its spiritual traditions, and its moral aspirations. But no permanent new set of commandments for the role of the churches can be discovered, because the problems get deeper all of the time and the understanding of America's mission as a nation in the world continues to evolve in ways that are hard to predict, or even imagine.

The greatest temptation for those involved in a church which seeks to try to restructure the social order is to neglect the essential spiritual, supernatural, and mystical nature of the church. If a church can be perceived as simply another agency working for humanitarian objectives, it loses a good deal of its credibility. It is true, to be sure, that those who disagree with the message of the church will impugn the motives and attack the character of the messenger. Those who benefit from the social order which the churches criticize clearly seek to undermine the authority of the spokesman, by denying to it the moral authority of its origin and its mission. And if the church has drifted away from its spiritual moorings, such attacks can carry weight.

Putting it more strongly, it can be said that if a church is carrying out its prime function of sanctifying souls, the transformation of the social order into a just society will take care of itself. But in a sinful world, the church hardly ever faces a situation where it can bring sanctification to an entire community or nation and expect to see that society adopt a social system that is just. Almost always the powerful, the strong, and the wealthy have already taken control of a society by legitimate or illegitimate means. Consequently, the churches must seek to inculcate principles of social justice into congregants who, either as a minority or a majority, must struggle against the principalities and princes who control the levers of power. The task of the Christian is almost always to depose tyrants and to exalt the powerless.

For Christians in the modern world, that task is enormously complicated, frequently baffling, and often discouraging. As a result, not a few Christians retreat to a spirituality that is essentially pious and private; they feel that their spiritual strength is distracted and diminished by participating in struggles that involve political and economic forces which often offer no bright lines between good and evil. Sometimes indeed, in their frustration, those who have retreated into a personal piety, with few involvements in social issues, attack the social activists as imperfect or confused Christians who dilute the faith by identifying it with a wide variety of social and political issues on which Christians have different opinions.

Despite all of these difficulties, this book is an attempt to analyze the clashing and competing moral visions in which the churches and the governments in America are involved.

CHAPTER ONE

The Role of Religion in Formulating America's Public Morality

S hould religious groups in America speak out more forcefully or more specifically about those issues in America which clearly have a moral dimension?

That question is of deep concern to believers in America. It is also a concern to those nonbelievers who are troubled by several abrupt departures from customary morality by large numbers of persons in America.

The question may be clear but the answer is complex and contingent.

Questions concerning the origins and roots of the public morality of America have always elicited diverse and ambivalent answers. While there has been a pan-Protestant orientation to many of the attitudes which the nation has adopted, the legislatures and the courts of America have fiercely resisted any shadow of theocracy while always looking for some moral standards for which there is a consensus in public opinion.

It has consequently always been difficult to pinpoint the exact theological or philosophical root of a new or old attitude that has been accepted as a part of the public morality of America. But the longing and the quest for some unifying moral ideal has not diminished. Indeed it has grown as the moral opinions accepted in America have multiplied and become more inconsistent with basic traditional values.

There is, of course, a moral core of belief and conviction in America which no one is challenging or even criticizing. Theft, lying, rape, bribery, arson, assault, homicide, and comparable evils are forbidden and punished by severe sanctions. The level of morality expected of all citizens is moreover being elevated all of the time by new laws; it is forbidden, for example, to discriminate on the basis of race, sex, age, or handicap. The standards expected of public officials have been raised. There is, nonetheless, a deepening feeling that there has been an erosion, a withering away, a decline in those moral standards on which the nation is based.

Religious groups have sought regularly in American history to make some of the views they deem fundamental a part of the nation's law. The Volstead Act prohibiting the sale or use of alcohol is one of the most visible examples of such conduct. The Moral Majority, prior to its demise in 1989, openly sought to have the Congress adopt its views that abortion should be recriminalized and that tuition tax credits should be given to parents whose children attend church-related schools. Neither view has been adopted.

Still, religious groups and others sense that there is a new crisis in America, and as a result they feel more compelled than ever before to try to change the public morality of America. But the churches are hesitant to utilize religious teachings as the basis for some change in civil law. They are also anxious not to impose their views on a citizenry that may be divided or uncertain about the advisability of accepting guidelines derived from religion.

The anxieties of religious groups about changes in American life are well-founded. Some three million couples now live together without the blessing of an ecclesiastical or secular official; such widespread disregard of the laws regulating marriage is a very new phenomenon and one totally unprecedented in American history. One estimate, moreover, suggests that up to 50 percent of all couples live together for a period prior to their marriage.

Other deviations from customary moral standards are also visible everywhere. There are 1.6 million abortions each year, meaning that every third child of those conceived each year dies before birth. The divorce rate—now approaching 50 percent of all marriages—is totally new in America and is one of the highest divorce rates in the world. The incidence of crime is shocking and the number of persons in prison has doubled in the last generation. The number of persons who indulge in narcotics is also amazingly high and the problem of AIDS leaves religious observers stunned, although they seek to be compassionate.

Does all of this indicate a reversal and a decline in public morality? Have the churches neglected their duties? Should they be more articulate and aggressive in seeking legal sanctions and civil punishments for those evil deeds which clearly violate traditional moral standards?

There are other less startling but still serious departures from tradition and accepted moral standards. America has suddenly lost its aversion to gambling, a practice that was banned by severe laws from the birth of the republic until the recent past. In a majority of the states citizens gamble billions of dollars each year, indulging in the potentially immoral hope that they can get something for nothing. Less specific but still egregious is the gross materialism of millions of persons who are at least nominally religious, who are involved in greed and avarice in ways which any traditional Christian morality would have to condemn.

What should religious bodies in America do about this deterioration in the public morality of the nation they seek to serve? It is expected that the churches will speak out on those issues on which there is agreement among religious groups and on which there is some consensus in America. Religious bodies of almost all ideological orientations agree in their condemnation of apartheid, their opposition to narcotics, and their ban on racism. But as soon as the problems get complicated and the consensus doubtful, religious bodies retreat and are silent.

One could argue that religious bodies should be more prophetic in their approach. But the people of America are leery of religious spokesmen who clash with some widely held views. Religious bodies are consequently caught in a difficult situation; by the truths they hold and the traditions they revere they are required to denounce evils. But they are not expected to substitute their morality for what the government or the people have decided upon as the appropriate approach.

Because of this clash of expectations the churches in America have been tempted to become private bodies, taking positions on moral issues but declining to make these issues binding even on the members of the congregation. Religious officials would be reluctant to admit that their pronouncements are not binding. But they are simultaneously hesitant to insist that the faithful are disloyal if they reach an opinion which is contrary to the official position of the church.

Despite all this ambiguity and ambivalence, religious bodies in the United States will and should continue to take positions on public issues where there is a relatively clear moral question involved.

But there are few firm guidelines which can be applied to all religious groups. Americans are acutely aware of the fallible judgments of religious bodies—especially after the failure of the Eighteenth Amendment and the exaggerations of the Moral Majority. In addition, situations change rapidly, requiring a high degree of flexibility and adaptability on the part of all groups wanting to make recommendations which will enjoy some credibility.

Although it is difficult to formulate generalizations about the role of all religious groups in America, the new situation in which America's fifty-four million Catholics find themselves calls for some comment. Catholic leaders have, until recently, been hesitant to proffer recommendations which might clash with those of mainstream Protestants. Indeed, it is remarkable how much agreement there has been among all religious groups concerning the basic legal/moral issues over the past two generations. Catholic, Protestant, and Jewish groups have found themselves in substantial agreement on issues related to refugees, immigrants, social welfare legislation, educational benefits, civil rights, and related topics. The major issues on which Catholic spokesmen have differed from non-Catholic legislative representatives center on abortion, Catholic schools, and some sex-related topics.

The National Council of Churches expressly endorsed the result and the reasoning of the Catholic Bishops' 1985 pastoral on nuclear war. Jewish groups and Catholic bodies have had a remarkable parallelism in their positions and priorities on most socio-economic problems.

Although Catholic organizations do not expect to depart from the areas of agreement which they have enjoyed with most non-Catholic groups, they do have a sense that they should be more "prophetic" in their message—as well as in the way they present it. Catholics are told by Reverend Richard Neuhaus, a neoconservative Lutheran pastor, that this is the "Catholic moment" in American history. No one is certain what "the Catholic moment" means, but Catholics do have a feeling that they should be more creative in communicating their message and more compelling in the ways they seek to advance it.

In addition Catholics have the benefit—and the burden—of centuries-old philosophical and theological teachings that justify metaphysically those traditional values grounded in the natural moral law which, until recently, were accepted and followed as a part of America's public morality. Catholics are as hesitant now as they have always been to impose their views on a majority or a minority of Americans. But they feel nonetheless, that they have inherited in their tradition many of the basic teachings from which America's public morality derived. There is therefore a sense among some of America's best-educated Catholics that the Catholic Church in America should speak out and reinsert into the public ethos those moral values without which America's moral and legal institutions could not have been established. They are anxious to reverse the decline of America, a nation which, they fear, is forgetting some of its finest and noblest moral values.

Catholics are also possessed of a new sense of self-confidence. They are 22 percent of the population and are probably the highest-educated of any social group in the country. Furthermore, the pastorals of the 300 Catholic bishops on nuclear war and the economy brought the spotlight of national and international attention to the moral traditions, the intellectual heritage, and the uncommon courage and faith of America's largest religious denomination.

But the new status and the self-esteem of Catholics makes the role of the church in the formation of public morality not more simple but more complex. If Americans are to be more articulate and aggressive in making known their convictions, does that mean that one religious body can go to elected officials or to the electorate seeking to have them enact or reenact into law those measures on which there is substantial disagreement?

The very suggestion that there should be a Catholic electorate instructed to vote a certain way on designated measures prompts resistance by everyone—including Catholics. At the same time churches are expected to speak out on behalf of their positions. Americans do not want their government to be the ultimate source or origin of the moral positions it takes. Americans are not entirely comfortable even when the government creates or advances a position with which most persons agree. The government has been so wrong on so many occasions that the people of America want it to be reined in—by the churches and by comparable secular groups. The wholesome approach of the American electorate is that they do not fully trust the churches or the government—or even the people themselves. Americans want an ongoing reexamination of the policies and the positions which the government has taken or should take. And the American people welcome every voice in the babel of voices from which eventually a public policy will emerge.

This may sound like a definition of chaos but it is creative chaos. America has no royal family, no established church, no permanent government, and hence no abiding source of its moral standards. That is both the strength and the weakness of this nation. America is always searching for new or better moral values but it has no one authority or any platonic guardians from which it can receive its moral code. It is a unique approach, never really tried before in history. If one knew nothing about America and was told of the above scenario, he or she would almost certainly conclude that such a scheme would never work.

But somehow that scheme has "worked"—at least until the last generation or so. Has it broken down? Does America need to adopt some new or old moral guidelines which will correct the lunging and lurching which seem to characterize America's present search for a good and just society?

Religious groups in America—and perhaps Catholics especially— wonder and worry about this question all of the time. The believers in these groups are divided; some want to be assertive and bold in proposing political initiatives. Others want to inculcate an intellectualism and a deeper spirituality, feeling that the infusion of such qualities will produce better leaders and a more moral government. But most, wanting to be better citizens, are puzzled and perplexed about what they can or should do. For better or for worse there are no clearly stated overarching principles as to what believers or Catholics should do to improve the public morality of the United States. The situation involves enormously complicated social and moral forces that are moving rapidly and unpredictably. In addition, there are millions in the Protestant and Catholic communities who are unaware of the social teachings of their church and who would resist or ignore any declaration by their religious leaders contrary to the status quo. And, last and most important, there are officials in all religious groups who do not have the convictions or the courage to assert that the teachings of their church collide with the tenets of any government.

Is it feasible to prescind from the virtual impossibility of formulating any overall conclusion as to what religious bodies in America should do? Let us talk, for now, about those issues on which there has been or could be types of collaboration that might result in the adoption of policies that would make America a country more compatible with the Judeo-Christian tradition.

Some will undoubtedly resist such an approach and suggest that if the churches follow this path they are likely to reduce themselves to the level of nonreligious bodies that lobby for social causes. But there are others who will say that the churches have succumbed to the sin of silence and that America needs their voice—loud and clear—prophetically recommending a way out of the wilderness.

I am not sure where I would come out exactly among these differing opinions. All I know is that America has deep, deep moral problems as to its national and international policies. And I want everyone with a viewpoint to join in the chorus of voices as to what America should do as it enters its third century as a nation. Its fate and its future in that third century are not at all clear. It could emerge as a great moral force as it did during and after World War II, when it was the prime force behind the formation of the United Nations and the establishment of the Marshall Plan. Or it could flounder as it did during the Vietnam War when it had no clear or coherent moral objective. The future of America beyond the year 2000 depends upon the spiritual vision and moral mission embraced by its leaders and the predicted 300 million persons that will live in the fifty states in the year 2000. By that time the world population will have increased from 5.0 billion in 1988 to 6.2 billion. Global environmental disasters, millions of refugees, and massive malnutrition will be only a few of the problems confronting the United States as a new century opens.

I want to outline some of the moral dilemmas and the spiritual challenges that religious groups face now in the United States. Church-related groups have worked on some of these problems but have been unable or unwilling to work on some of the more complicated. None of the problems will go away, and all cannot be resolved without the active and abiding participation of all religious and nonreligious groups in America.

CHAPTER 2

Religion and America's Foreign Policy

O ne of the most difficult questions for believers to confront is this: were they too silent during the forty years from 1948 to 1988 when the United States armed itself with unbelievable military might and threatened to annihilate the whole world with nuclear weapons? The cold war is over—according to Margaret Thatcher. The tyranny of the Kremlin is crumbling in Eastern Europe. Soviet imperialism, never very successful around the world, faded into oblivion after the withdrawal of Soviet troops from Afghanistan.

History may judge harshly of the theory and the tactics with which the United States pursued the cold war. After America defeated the Nazis and the Japanese, it suddenly saw a new adversary arise—the Soviet empire. The United States assumed somehow that military might could defeat the Soviets, just as military devices decimated the Nazis and the Japanese. But the United States, for a thousand different reasons, never used and possibly never came close to using its massive military might against the Soviets. The one exception is the occupation of South Korea by the United States—with the blessing of the United Nations. The attempt by the United States to keep South Vietnam separated from North Vietnam failed for a wide variety of reasons.

As one looks back on the four decades of the militarization of America and the sustained attempts to intimidate the Communists, one has to conclude that the policy was dubiously moral, wasteful, and ineffective. As the East-West divide dissolves and as communism as a system crumbles, the question has to be asked: did the foreign policy of the United States delay or accelerate that process or was it just irrelevant?

Religious groups were silent or ineffective in the 1950s when the United States began its colossal military build-up. Little analysis, moreover, was done at that time by anyone concerning the fears and anxieties of persons in the Kremlin. Before and after the death of Stalin in 1953, it was just assumed that massive military strength was needed in Europe in order to prevent or stop an invasion of Western Europe by Soviet forces. Little thought was given to the possibility that the build-up of the Warsaw Pact nations came about because the Kremlin honestly thought that the United States and the NATO nations intended to invade the USSR. It was the fear of the West that impelled Soviet leaders to occupy Eastern Europe and retain the Baltic nations under their dictatorship. The Russians had many reasons to think that the West would invade again—as the West had done from the age of Napoleon up to the death of Hitler.

The United States, after the Truman Doctrine was announced, and especially after the Eisenhower presidency, became wedded to the concept that tremendous military superiority was essential if the "free world" was to survive. As the cold war fades into history it becomes more evident every day that the United States adopted policies based on surmise and speculation. The paranoia about the Soviets led to a collective mind-set about the Soviet Union which in retrospect can only be regarded as wrongheaded.

Some will argue that massive military might has in fact induced Mikhail Gorbachev to change the basic approach of his country toward the modern world. But these commentators cannot really prove their case. Gorbachev changed the approach of his country because he understood that his people could not obtain the consumer goods they yearned for as long as the government spent immense sums on armaments. In addition Gorbachev saw what millions see more and more—the stupidity, the futility, and the cruelty of spending hundreds of billions of dollars on weapons which the Soviets would in all probability never use. Gorbachev's predecessors were captivated or obsessed with the same fear and paranoia that gripped the Pentagon beginning in the early 1950s.

In the United States some church and religious groups began to say in the 1950s what Gorbachev realizes today—the folly of a mighty military build-up with weapons which could not be used in any way which would be consistent with the fundamental moral beliefs of the American people. Indeed the use of the weapons could not be squared with the mandates of the four Geneva treaties governing warfare agreed to by the United States in 1949.

But the religious voices that protested the militarization of America were drowned out by the rhetoric of a devout Protestant churchman, John Foster Dulles, secretary of state in the Eisenhower administration. He and his associates created the ideological framework by which the crusade against communism became the foremost element in America's foreign policy. Dulles sincerely felt that this crusade was also allowed, indeed required, by America's relationship with Christianity. He also believed that the policy of "massive retaliation" against the Soviets could be reconciled with a foreign policy grounded at least ultimately in Christian principles.

As the confrontation between the United States and the USSR diminishes and even ceases, religious organizations have to look back and examine their consciences about the way in which they have thought and acted in the last four decades. Have they acquiesced too much in the transformation of America into the most powerful military power in the history of the world? Have they failed to preach the basic Christian doctrine that every person in every nation must seek reconciliation with all opponents and enemies? Have Christian churches in the United States accepted the cold war as inevitable and unavoidable?

The judgment of the new millennium after the year 2000 may be very harsh on the United States—and on the Christian churches in America. As the year 2000 dawns, the cold war may be just a memory. The forces of democracy and the moral power of the idea of human rights will have triumphed in most places on the earth. Will the United States get credit for this evolution or will history record that the United States from 1948 to the year 2000 was blind, deaf, arrogant, militaristic, and unchristian?

But the second question is even more difficult: did the churches abdicate their duties during the forty-year cold war? If they had spoken out vigorously and persistently, would the world have followed a different path?

It is clear that in the 1990s and in the new millennium the churches in America and Europe have to be as honest and as forthcoming as they can in responding to the question, "Where were you during the decades of the cold war when we needed you to preach love while the American government was preaching hatred?"

The habit of demonizing the Communists began with President Truman and continued through the 1980's when President Reagan called the Soviet Union the "evil empire." There were obviously terrible things done in the Stalin era and thereafter. But at least in retrospect we have to ask ourselves the question whether the military strength of "the West" led to the termination of some of the barbarisms of the Soviet leaders. If the United States had followed a different approach would the results have been different? The United States has always been convinced that America must tell its story to the world and attract people to its positive features. It invented the Voice of America, the Peace Corps, the emphasis on human rights as a part of U.S. foreign policy, and a wide variety of other pro-democracy measures. But the funding for these programs has been minuscule compared to the fantastic sums spent on the military. In 1988 the United States spent about $300 billion dollars on the military—or $812 million per day! If some substantial part of that sum had been spent in arousing the people of the "captive nations" to rise up against their masters, would the despotism of the Soviet Union in Eastern Europe have ended a lot earlier than it did? If the United States had concentrated in the 1950s and thereafter on helping the peoples in the Baltic nations—Lithuania, Estonia, and Latvia—to reclaim their sovereignty, would they have been successful? Could the United States have so captured the minds of the citizens of these three nations—along with those in Poland and others in Eastern Europe—that they would have been ungovernable by the Communists?

The United States tried to do that over a number of years. But the efforts were feeble, intermittent, and underfunded. The adoption of the Helsinki Accords on August 1, 1975, by the United States and thirty-four European nations demonstrates the immense impact which that recommitment to human rights has had. The acceptance by the USSR and all of the nations of Eastern Europe of the wide range of human rights set forth in the third part of the Helsinki Accords has been one of the major factors that led to Solidarity in Poland and comparable liberation movements in those nations seized by the Soviets immediately after World War II.

The almost exclusive concentration on military means to combat communism over the last four decades has to be reexamined now that the enmity between the United States and the USSR is fading. That reexamination will, however, be very difficult because voices are now being raised alleging that it was the military strength of the United States and NATO nations that brought the USSR to its present position. And, these voices will insist, the United States must continue to be militarily strong to prevent any recurrence of communism in the Soviet Union or elsewhere.

It may be that the superficial appeal of this line of argument will be so strong that it will be impossible to bring about any significant diminution of the military might of the United States. But those who want the United States to be a moral nation, based at least ultimately on the Judeo-Christian tradition, are required to reassess all of the major premises of America's foreign policy. For the pure pacifist, that analysis will be easy. But for a person who is not pacifist like this writer, the task will be quite difficult.

The bottom line for everyone in the world after the cold war is this: if America wants to be, and be perceived to be, a moral nation, what should be its attitude toward nations that are or were deemed to be its ideological rivals?

America's answer to that question has been clear and constant since 1948: The Communists must be deterred and contained because somehow—and here the anticommunist approach gets blurred—the Communists will conquer the world and eventually endanger the freedom and independence of the United States.

That black and white approach to the world has dominated American political thinking for forty years. It was modified somewhat by the flowering of detente. But the hard-line, no-holds-barred anticommunist approach has been the core of America's policy from the Truman administration up to President Bush. Any politician who raises serious questions about the major assumptions behind that policy will be vulnerable to the charge that he is "soft on communism," and therefore he is un-American and even disloyal to the United States.

As the cold war eases and the next millennium approaches, we will become more aware of how the anticommunist syndrome has dominated the minds and hearts of the American electorate. It will be enormously difficult—perhaps impossible— to change that mind-set. The fear of the Communists—drilled into the minds of Americans in

a thousand different ways—will make the abandonment of the possession of nuclear weapons very difficult; this will be true even if mutual
nuclear disarmament with the Soviets is attainable and verifiable. The
American psyche, in short, is so conditioned to believe that we have a
permanent worldwide treacherous enemy in the Communists that a
sea change in attitudes will not be easily or rapidly forthcoming.

Christians in America have always been troubled at the belligerence, the animosity, the hatred, and the distress which have been a
part of America's foreign policy since 1948. Such attitudes are new in
American thinking. From 1787 to 1948 America had no permanent
long-term enemies. Americans spoke out against tyranny and fought
against an aggressive Germany in World War I. But the United States
tolerated the aggressions of the European colonial powers as they
dominated and exploited peoples in Latin America, Asia, and Africa.

More and more, scholars will be examining what happened to the
United States in the years after 1948 when, for the first time in its
history, it adopted a policy of hostility to a group of nations because
they were controlled by Marxists or Communists. America emerged as
the world's principal military power after World War II. Did the
presence of a very large military establishment in America after World
War II—a phenomenon never present in American life before—help
to induce the President and the Congress to go on an extended,
incredible, and unprecedented military expansion? What subtle forms
of national pride, or arrogance, or blindness led America to proclaim
that it would "contain" communism? And of equal importance,
whoever said that the bundle of ideas we call Communism could be
contained by assigning American military forces around the world?

It has been possible, and pleasant, up to the present time to forget
about these questions—indeed not even to make them thinkable. But
now these questions are not merely thinkable: they are crying out for
answers. And Christians in America are expected to have some of
those answers. At least Christians are expected to want some answers.

We are beginning a period when we shall be assessing what the
militarization of America has done to the United States over the past
forty years. It is of course premature to think that there will be some
substantial shrinking of the military. Few if any commentators are
declaring that we do not need 2.1 million men under arms. This
figure, however, had never been scientifically or empirically validated.
There are, to be sure, some voices urging that with the end of the cold

war, the $303 billion for the military budget for 1989 should be slashed.

The militarization of America has done several things in the United States for the first time in its history. We now have a standing army in peacetime. This goes against the traditions and the thinking of all of those who have made America great during its lifetime. The fact has to be faced that a standing army, in all probability, makes war more likely. Would the United States have sent over 500,000 soldiers to Vietnam if the Pentagon had not had two million men in uniform and many more available through the military draft?

After Vietnam, the Congress and the country are very reluctant to send American soldiers into wars in the Third World. The Reagan administration did not dare propose that American soldiers be sent to El Salvador to help the government, or to Nicaragua to battle the government of the Sandinistas. The White House sent fifty-five U.S. military advisors to El Salvador and some $3 billion in eight years to defeat the alleged Communist insurgents; the contribution of $1 million a day to El Salvador, continued into 1990, has not enabled that nation to curb or control the rebels. The Congress lost faith in the mission of the Contras. The Congress terminated funding for this group, which was designed to topple the government in Managua. But no one is urging that American boys be sent to "contain communism" in Central America.

What then is left of America's policy of containing communism? Clearly the time has come for an agonizing re-appraisal of where the nation has been for forty years in its foreign policy.

In all discussions of these issues this question keeps recurring: where were the Christians during the four decades when the United States followed its policy of containing communism? Some Christians, of course, joined the crusade against communism, giving it a religious dimension by calling the Communists the "Antichrist." On the other side of the spectrum we have had a large number of profoundly peace-oriented groups who were opposed to using the threat of force to achieve ideological objectives. But in the vast middle, most religious bodies went along silently with the policy of containing communism. Many church groups opposed America's intervention in Vietnam, but it cannot be said that there is any overwhelming consensus among the churches since Vietnam that containment as it has been traditionally defined must go. The churches have temporized—opposing military intervention in Central America and favoring nuclear arms reduction, but not openly and flatly calling for a complete repudiation of the whole idea of containment.

It may be that reexamination of containment is no longer postponable. One of the most terrible features of containment as it has been practiced is that it is not really a policy on which America will act. The United States refused to help when Czechoslovakia and Hungary were invaded. The United States declined to help the people of Cuba—after one abortive attempt to invade. The United States withdrew all diplomatic recognition from China after Peking fell to the Communists in 1949. But the United States did nothing to "contain" communism in China or to help the one billion Chinese to rise up against their masters. The United States did help the rebels in Afghanistan to oust the Soviet military machine. But overall one has to conclude that containment has not worked—indeed has not been employed—in the nations taken over by the Communists. Those who claim that the persistent use of containment by the United States has deterred the Kremlin have a burden of proof that is very heavy.

Although Americans on the record have not followed through on their policy of containment when U.S. military or other help could have made a difference, the policy has allowed Americans to indulge in a good deal of pompous, self-righteous, self-proclaimed idealism, and even sheer hypocrisy. The rhetoric about preserving the "free nations" from the scourge of Communism and the patriotic proclamations about the devotion of America to the rule of law have made Americans feel good about themselves. But how will all of this stand up under the analysis that will be required in the world after the cold war is just a memory?

Nations, like individuals, have a genius for not remembering; for even denying their mistakes and their sins. Any nation—indeed anyone who listens to the imperious voice of conscience—is aware of everyone's capacity for self-deception when confronted with the hard reality of one's own betrayals and negligences. But despite all of the self-deception of which we are capable, there are moments of grace when we admit our malice and acknowledge our failings. Such moments seem to come at unpredictable times and in unforeseen circumstances. The Christian knows that it is the grace of God that somehow has illumined the darkness of our minds and done away with our deafness and blindness.

Nations also have moments like that. Americans have shared together their regret over the incarceration of 120,000 Japanese-Americans during World War II, and have indemnified each of the internees with a sum of $20,000. The 101st Congress passed a bill which forbids discrimination against the physically and mentally handicapped in ways that are so generous that they would have been thought to be unattainable.

Americans are quite capable of regretting and repenting of their mistakes and their errors. Will America, as the end of the cold war becomes clearer, regret and repent some of the policies it espoused and some of the belligerence it pursued over the past forty years?

Many Americans are not prepared to change their attitude concerning the Communists. The anticommunists have set the agenda for two generations. They are not about to concede that they were wrong—or even that their adversaries have changed their attitudes. The mind-set of persons hostile to Communism is fixed in such a way that it often seems impossible to modify it. No dialogue or ecumenical approach is desired or accepted. A firm and unyielding policy of opposing Russia and other Communist nations makes the world a rational and explainable place for those people who are convinced of this view. It gives any American pride and a sense of destiny. It can be used to support one's religious faith and, of course, one's patriotism.

Can Christians alter this attitude by appeals to reason, conscience, and the universal love which everyone would agree is the very essence of Christianity? It will not be easy. Americans have been taught by their government to love to hate. For two generations, the government has tended to define Americanism in terms of a crusade against "godless communism." An informal coalition of groups of veterans, fraternal orders, civic organizations, and some religious bodies have reinforced the government's definition of the essence of Americanism as a struggle against godless forces organized under Communism throughout the world.

I have always been astonished that some of the brightest young people in the country accept all of the anticommunist crusade without questioning. Indeed, it is often impossible to raise in their minds any question which would cause them to have the slightest doubt about what they have been taught as the essential—and sacred—anticommunist role which America must play in the world.

Christians in America, therefore, who want to explain why they have the most serious misgivings about the morality of their country's foreign policy must confront generations who have accepted notions about government which cannot be reconciled with many traditional Christian concepts of what a good government should be. Indeed the Christians who want to challenge some of the fundamentals of America's foreign policy will find not a few other Christians who will accuse them of being false prophets.

The Catholic bishops' pastoral letter on peace in 1983 was, for America's 54 million Catholics, the beginning of the reappraisal being discussed here. The mere issuance of the pastoral—developed in a nuanced and collegial way—was a milestone for Catholics in America. It symbolized the arrival of the Catholic community at a point where its leaders could put forth a statement on the key questions of foreign policy—a statement which would be taken seriously by the nation and the world.

That document did not satisfy everyone since, while it forbade the use of nuclear weapons for any purpose, it did allow the possession of these weapons for the purpose of deterrence—but on the clear condition that a method of phasing them out is being developed.

For the first time the bishops called into question the underlying assumptions of America's foreign policy. The pastoral echoed the 3,500 words in Vatican II on war and peace, and arguably did not advance substantially beyond Vatican II. But the message set forth by the 300 Catholic bishops of the United States was in itself one of the most significant events in the entire history of church-state relations in America.

The National Council of Churches, representing all mainline Protestants, spontaneously endorsed the results and the reasoning of the Catholic bishops' pastoral. At a later time, America's Methodist bishops issued a statement condemning both the use and the possession of nuclear weapons.

Do all these statements form the matrix from which there could emerge a comprehensive Christian consensus on what the United States should do in the world after the cold war? It is not impossible. Ecumenical dialogues and inter-credal cooperation are at an all-time high in America. There are few basic differences between Christian and Jewish communities on issues of war and peace. Some fundamentalist groups still feel that the United States should struggle against Communism with military might. But there is a remarkable consensus of dissatisfaction among religious groups in America with America's military position. At the present time these groups do not control or even set the agenda. There is, moreover, a question as to how deep the consensus is among the congregants in the pews.

History will record in the next millennium what the churches did in the crucial years of the 1990s as the Communist world crumbled and as the United States struggled to reformulate its foreign policy in a world vastly different from the situation in the early 1950s when America solemnly vowed to "contain" communism. Nations, like individuals, are very slow to reexamine policies which have been accepted—even when it is increasingly clear that the policies are outdated and anachronistic. It is the task of the churches in the 1990s in America to induce people to think the unthinkable.

It should not be "unthinkable" to urge a greater utilization of the United Nations, or that new consideration be given to the idea of world federalism. But it is unlikely—although Christians should be prepared to deal with individuals and nations that are seeking to clarify the moral principles by which they are governed.

In 1995, the world will celebrate the fiftieth anniversary of the establishment of the United Nations. The United Nations, the first organization in the history of the world to bring countries together in a mutual quest for international peace, owes its very existence to American leadership. The finest strands of American morality and idealism went into the structures of the United Nations. The U.N. Charter refers to the obligation of living together as "good neighbors" and the duty of all to "practice tolerance" and to "live together in peace."

The Universal Declaration of Human Rights, initiated by nongovernmental groups and shepherded through the United Nations by Eleanor Roosevelt, is the quintessence of the best in America's moral and religious traditions. The U.N. declaration does not mention God expressly nor is it a theistic document, but it incorporates the basic ideas of equality, fairness, due process, and human rights which constitute the American dream. It was America's leadership which, more than any other factor, brought about the adoption on December 10, 1948, of the Universal Declaration of Human Rights. This manifesto has probably had more impact on humanity than any other legal document in the history of the world.

The United Nations Charter seeks to curb and control war by

requiring that all nations bring their grievances with another nation to the Security Council. The United States and the world, weary and frustrated after two world wars, wanted to recapture and redeem the dream of the League of Nations. American leaders knew as they structured the United Nations that it was the United States and particularly the U.S. Senate which had torpedoed the League of Nations. The United Nations Charter was ratified by the United States Senate in 1945 with only a handful of negative votes.

How the United States has obeyed or defied the United Nations over the past five decades is, of course, a vast topic. But it seems fair to state that in several important areas the United States has forgotten its own dream of outlawing war by negotiation and mediation and has followed its own course of action without consultation with or even reference to the United Nations. The clearest case is, of course, America's unilateral adventure into Vietnam.

Another instance is President Ronald Reagan's invasion of Grenada. The United Nations General Assembly repudiated that effort and reprimanded America by a vote of 109 to 8.

No one pretends that if the United States returned to its original devotion to the moral and political principles underlying the United Nations, world peace would break out. Other nations have bypassed the United Nations and followed their own selfish interests. But the chances for international peace would increase immensely if the United States revived its commitment to insisting that all nations refrain from military adventures and bring their complaints against their neighbors in the world to the Security Council.

In the late 1980s there was a surge of good feeling about the United Nations as it was able to mediate an end to the long and awful war between Iraq and Iran, and as it acted effectively with U.N. troops to finalize the liberation of Namibia. But the indifference, or the apathy, or even the hostility of the United States toward the United Nations constitutes an abiding depressant to everyone who sees the potential of that organization being frustrated.

The specialized agencies of the United Nations have done extraordinarily well; they have, for the most part, received adequate financial and organizational cooperation from the United States. The very first to be established in 1945—the World Health Organization—has transformed the world by bringing medical knowledge, inoculations, and public health measures to the underdeveloped nations. The Food and

Agricultural Organization has revitalized farming by introducing new types of fertilizer and pesticides to remote areas. Similarly, the United Nations Development Fund, UNICEF, and Unesco have brought about quiet revolutions in promoting literacy, the transmission of culture, and related fields.

The United Nations Environmental Program, established in the 1980's has already changed the thinking of the world by insisting that, for example, certain toxic substances be eliminated by the end of the century.

Why have the peace-keeping functions of the United Nations been less successful than the specialized agencies? There is plenty of blame to go around. But one of the principal reasons has to be the fact that the United States began a policy in the 1950s of establishing its own world priorities, bypassing or at least ignoring the machinery for peace established by the United Nations.

If the churches in America had insisted that the United States continue its early enthusiasm for the peace-keeping missions of the United Nations, would the history of the last forty years be essentially different? It might well have been. The churches of course might have failed to persuade America to remain faithful to its commitments, or the leaders of America could have claimed that it is unrealistic for a great power to feel bound by the strictures of the United Nations. If the government took that position, the churches would have been able to join in the substantial efforts to reform or modernize the structures of the United Nations. These efforts, fostered by the United Nations Association (UNA), a private organization, are well-developed, impressive, and indeed compelling. Unfortunately there has been too little organizational support for these measures from the churches of America.

Related to the efforts to modernize the United Nations is the emergence of a strong national and international movement for world federalism. The essence of federalism is that each nation agrees to surrender a bit of its sovereignty. The paradigm is the coming together of the original thirteen American colonies and the development of the fifty American states. The model is not perfect, but doesn't the analogy offer hope for some kind of a world union of the 160 countries which are now members of the United Nations?

World Federalists is a strong and attractive organization. Fathered by Norman Cousins and many others, World Federalists offers a vision of a world beyond the United Nations. World federalism was explicitly endorsed by Pope Pius XII and has won praise from every Pope since and from religious leaders everywhere. But again, churches in America have not focused any particular energy on the movement to bring about a federation of states which would feature unprecedented cooperation and which would outlaw war as a method of resolving differences.

Historians in the year 2050 will be required to make some judgment on the activities and the quality of the faith of the churches in America in the period from the end of World War II to the end of the cold war. They may well conclude that the churches were too timid, too silent, too little aware of the fact that a person who really believes in Christianity has to seek to extend that belief into the morality of the world in which he or she lives.

CHAPTER 3

The Churches and African Americans in the United States

Religious organizations in America may be able to suggest that they have several excuses for not being able to control or modify the ways in which the foreign policy of the United States developed in the decade after World War II. Issues in that complex area were dictated in part by world events beyond the control of the United States and church organizations in America. It is plausible to think that, even if the churches in America never lost sight of the basic themes of justice, equality, and love, they would not have been able to guide and shape America's foreign policy. That policy reflected and reacted to global developments in Moscow, Beijing, and elsewhere.

But more direct responsibility for the bleak situation of blacks in America cannot be avoided by the churches. Indeed the guilt and complicity of the churches in the terrible plight of almost 30 million black Americans should be set forth in full. Religious groups should be reminded of it on a regular basis. A collective and perduring sense of guilt and repentance on the part of the churches might bring about a change for the better in the condition of those Americans whose ancestors were brought to America as slaves. It may be in fact that a sense of profound regret on the part of churches for their attitudes toward slaves and their progeny is the indispensable component of a formula which could bring about justice and equality for the 12 percent of Americans who are black.

There is resistance in America when one religious group or even a broad alliance of several religious bodies seek to influence public policy on marriage, divorce, abortion, and comparable issues. But there is little resistance when religious organizations come forward to urge action on racial matters. The churches therefore have opportunities in this area which may not be present in almost any other field where there are legal/moral problems. The churches used the opportunity to influence race relations in 1963 when they assembled for the First National Conference on Race and Religion in Chicago; we will have occasion later to refer to the important statement that emerged from that unprecedented meeting of 1,200 of the nation's top religious leaders.

There is no recorded protest by any church group in the American colonies in 1619, when merchants brought African men and women to Jamestown, Virginia, where they were purchased like bales of cotton. Southern farmers were so anxious to acquire inexpensive labor that they resorted to a tactic which today has to be termed barbarous. Indeed it seems incredible that presumably religious people would indulge in such a practice. They could not and would not bring white people to America in the way they kidnapped individuals in Africa. If the earliest slave-owners had any intention of improving the lot of their newly acquired chattels it did not appear—except that they arranged in due course for the baptism and Christianization of the slaves.

It is astonishing that by the time the fifty-five white men were writing the United States Constitution in the summer of 1787 there were 700,000 slaves in the country, or about 20 percent of the 3.5 million persons who in thirteen newly-independent states had organized themselves under the Articles of Confederation. Most Americans do not like to think of the several ways in which the framers of the Constitution compromised with the Southern states in order to retain the institution of slavery. Slaves were counted as three-fifths of a person for the purpose of apportionment of seats in the United States Congress; as a result the slave states had a disproportionate number of seats in the Congress from 1789 until the Civil War. The Constitution also prohibited Congress from enacting a ban on the importation of slaves until the year 1808. The ban legislated in that year was not enforced very effectively. The Constitution also made it illegal for Northerners to free slaves who came into free territories; they were required to return them to their owners.

These pro-slavery provisions in the United States Constitution clearly institutionalized the prejudices of white people against those of African ancestry. The Constitution carried forward the stereotype of the slave in ways which inevitably implanted in the American psyche a hostility to blacks which is present even today.

Although the churches began to protest the pro-slavery taint of the Constitution, they were unable or unwilling to bring the slaves into the white churches. The first black American religious denomination, the African Methodist Episcopal (AME) and the African Methodist Episcopal Zion (AMEZ) were founded in 1810 and 1822 respectively. Other black churches were organized at a later date, but the fact is that blacks in America were excluded from white churches, or did not want to join them because they would not feel comfortable there.

Southern Baptists split from Northern Baptists in 1845 over the issue of slavery. The predominately white Methodist churches divided North and South in 1844, and did not rejoin to become the United Methodist church until 1939.

Although in recent years many white Protestant groups have aggressively invited blacks to join their denominations, the number of blacks in predominantly white churches is small. The important study, "A Common Destiny: Blacks and American Society," published in 1989 and authored by Gerald David Jaynes and Robin M. Williams, Jr., states that about 6 percent of black Protestants belong to predominately white denominations (page 93).

Protestant congregations lament what has happened and are seeking in several ways to become racially integrated communities. But the fact remains that the most segregated hour in American life is 11:00 A.M. on Sunday.

All of this is relevant to any understanding of the racial situation in America today. The one institution, the church, which in American tradition and mythology is destined to guide the development of the nation's public morality, has until recently condoned or acquiesced or failed to protest vigorously the formation of a Jim Crow society. The churches, alas, allowed the separation of the races to occur within the churches themselves.

The law and the courts were as confused as the churches about the status of those persons in America whose skin pigmentation was different from that of the immigrants who came from Europe. There is no such thing as race, anthropologists tell us. There is no biological or genetic difference between persons whose skin is black, yellow, brown, or red from those whose skin is without color or white. America has now presumably learned that lesson. But the Supreme Court of the United States took decades to learn it. In the *Dred Scott* decision in 1857, the nation's highest tribunal ruled that Congress could not constitutionally legislate that a slave could in some circumstances become a citizen. The Court, interpreting the Constitution woodenly, held that Congress cannot enact a law by which the property rights of the slave-owner are taken away when he takes his slave into a free state. The Civil War resulted in part from the *Dred Scott* decision.

When the Congress enacted the first civil rights law designed to confer equality and enforceable rights on former slaves, the Supreme Court in 1883 put them down. In 1896, in *Plessy v. Ferguson*, the Supreme Court legitimated all Jim Crow arrangements in the South; the Court in essence prevented the implementation of the provisions of the Fourteenth Amendment. Finally in 1954, in *Brown v. Board of Education*, the Supreme Court unanimously ruled that separate but equal cannot be equal.

From 1619 to 1954, three hundred and thirty-five years—people of African ancestry residing in the United States were by law treated as so inferior and unequal that they could and should be separated from whites in schools, hospitals, parks, and neighborhoods. Looking back, it is incredible that in a nation with profoundly Christian roots such a thing could have happened. It is equally incredible that the churches, with notable exceptions, tended to acquiesce in the legalization of keeping blacks as a society within a society. It should be noted of course that the abolitionists were largely church-affiliated, and that without them the nation would never have been delivered from slavery. The abolitionists had a double struggle—against the racism of their government and against the "heretical" strong conviction among the religious denominations that it was permissible to segregate persons because their ancestors came from Africa.

It is of course easy to look back and condemn the silence or the sins of churchmen in the 1800s with respect to slavery. But it is nonetheless egregious that so many religious people over such a long period of time should have accepted the idea of an institutionalized inferior status for the four million individuals who were slaves at the time of the Civil War.

The supreme irony following the liberation of the blacks that came in 1954 with *Brown v. Board of Education* was that it was not white clergy that led that liberation, but black ministers like Dr. Martin Luther King, Jr. Even after the Supreme Court had repudiated its errors, reversed *Plessy v. Ferguson*, and ended 335 years of state-sponsored discrimination against blacks, the white churches of America gave faltering leadership to the pro-integration forces. But even if white churches had been more vigorous, their efforts would not have been successful unless the blacks in the United States revived and restored some of the self-confidence which had been eroded or destroyed by more than 300 years of humiliation. Those who are treated as inferior often accept the classification imposed on them by their superiors or masters. The victims begin to believe the stereotype and act on it. Americans are only beginning to try to appreciate what 300 years of degradation have done to the psyche of blacks in America. The insecure structure of the black family, the large number of unemployed among black urban teenagers, and the incidence of pregnancy among black teenagers are almost certainly related to the inferiority complex and the poor self-image which blacks almost inevitably have acquired from the unspoken assumption by the white majority that blacks are inferior and unequal.

The churches of America, black and white, have been trying to erase the effects of the debasement of blacks over many generations. But apparently there is a feeling that the integration and the assimilation of white and black churches is not required or even desirable. Blacks feel at home in their churches. Even if a significant number of blacks moved from the inner city to the suburbs, their church would go with them, or they would return to their church. Protestant churches will continue outreach programs, but there is no clear indication that truly integrated churches will be very numerous in the very foreseeable future. There are only 2 million blacks who are Catholics and many of them are concentrated in black communities in Louisiana and elsewhere. There appears to be little likelihood of truly integrated Catholic parishes, since whites in metropolitan areas have either moved to the suburbs or live in residential areas within the city to which blacks do not move.

Experts on black culture remark on the centrality of the black church in the lives and careers of black Americans. There seems to be little feeling or resentment on the part of African Americans that the black churches have kept them out of the mainstream of American life. Nor is there much articulation of disappointment from the white churches because they have not brought blacks into their life and their development. At the present time the black and white churches seem to be living their lives along parallel lines. Will they ever meet? That is the question central to everything the churches have to think about as they seek to continue their efforts to rectify all the multiple injustices that are still a part of the daily suffering of African Americans.

It seems elementary that white Christian churches are required to fight for social justice for blacks—even though the blacks continue to be congregants of churches which are almost exclusively black. If the churches, it has to be asked, cannot or will not break out of a pattern of segregation, how can industries, schools, and communities be expected to do so? If the churches continue to go along with congregations divided by race, will they be perceived as condoning what they officially denounce? And will the Christian communities of black people be scandalized when the white majority, unlike civil society, fails to develop a racially integrated society by employing, as the government does, the techniques of affirmative action, goals, targets and timetables? Will the white churches be the last institution in America to be integrated?

But it has to be emphasized that the white churches of America came alive in the early 1960s and, as never before, worked for the enactment of the Civil Rights Act of 1964 and the Voting Rights Act in 1965. The 1963 National Conference on Race and Religion, noted above, issued what is probably the single most important declaration on black Americans ever published by a church-related group. The document sounds remote today, but in 1963 it was a ringing confession of the mistakes of the churches, the presence of racism in America, and the need for a profound change in the law and in the hearts of Americans.

The improvement in the lot of the blacks in America has been significant since 1965. But as the comprehensive 1989 study, "A Common Destiny," notes, "we cannot exclude the possibility of confrontation and violence . . . the ingredients are there: large populations of jobless youths, an extensive sense of relative deprivation and injustice, distrust of the legal system, frequently abrasive public-community relations, highly visible inequalities, extreme concentration of poverty and great racial awareness" (page 31).

A study authorized by the National Urban League, released in

August 1989, points out that "prospects for racial parity for African Americans are bleak." The disparity between black and white unemployment is widening. At the present pace, moreover, the earnings of blacks will not reach parity with whites until the year 2058. The proportion of blacks enrolled in colleges is projected to come to equal that of whites in the year 2040.

Other facts reported in the study, which is entitled "Stalling Out: The Relative Progress of African Americans," are grim. The racial gap in infant mortality is widening so that parity would never eventuate. In terms of home ownership, the projection is that the parity goal would not be attained until the year 3148.

Religious groups look at these foreboding statistics and wonder what more can be done to eliminate bias toward African Americans. Church personnel feel a very special responsibility to black Americans, since their plight was brought about in part as a result of the negligence of the churches, or at least because the churches failed to ameliorate a century of legalized discrimination after slavery was abolished. In addition, almost all blacks are Christians—worshipping in churches which were created because the white Christian churches did not welcome blacks.

The scene from the viewpoint of white Christians is sad. Canada never had slavery, and the attitude toward persons of African ancestry is different and better in Canada than it is in the United States. Differences between blacks and those of Spanish and Portuguese ancestry in Latin America are visible and tangible, but there has been a significant amount of intermarriage. England abolished slavery in the forty-eight Commonwealth nations in 1833; distinctions between whites and blacks in the former colonies are noticeable, but the number of whites is so small that the situation is very different from the relationship of whites and blacks in the United States. That relationship is unique in the world. No other nation brought in large numbers of slaves and kept them in a legal underclass for 335 years. No other nation had a civil war largely over the perpetuation of slavery.

In view of the fact that the treatment of the slaves and descendants of slaves by the United States has been uniquely different from the ways other countries have handled the problem, the Christian churches in America have a responsibility which churches in other nations do not have. The complexity of that problem is aggravated by the fact that 52 million immigrants came voluntarily to American shores seeking a better life; only Africans were brought to America involuntarily, not to seek a better life, but to be the property of plantation owners.

Everyone involved in the quest for social justice would like to forget the melancholy history of blacks in America. But the history is inescapable. Intermarriage, for example, was made impossible in all of the Southern states by laws against miscegnation. Those laws, not invalidated by the Supreme Court until the *Loving v. Virginia* decision in 1967, taught the nation that black women and black men are not worthy of marrying white people. A more blatant teaching of racism can hardly be imagined.

Because of these laws and countless other factors, there is no trend whatsoever toward interracial marriage. As far as one can see, blacks will not enter into any significant number of marriages with whites. Again the problem is uniquely different. The absence of interracial marriage perpetuates and deepens the non-integrated patterns of housing in America's cities; checkerboard designs will continue to characterize metropolitan areas. Schools, housing, and churches will tend to be de facto segregated. There have been some breakthroughs as upwardly mobile blacks move into the suburbs. One has to wonder whether predominantly white churches in the suburbs could be so attractive that they would be a magnet for blacks to move. But if such a phenomenon developed, would those churches experience the "tipping" factor which happens in neighborhoods when a significant number of the homeowners become black?

Church groups, like everyone else, find it painful to reflect on the mistakes America has made over a long period of time in handling its slaves and their progeny. Many people in America are able to avoid thinking or dealing with the fact that every eighth American is of African ancestry. And when they do think about the problem they have enough negative information to perpetuate their stereotypes. And the negative information is abundant. Drugs and crime in black communities are notorious. Murders in black sections of major cities, including Washington, are unbelievably numerous, with the increasing homicide rates showing little sign of leveling off. And in 1987, 47 percent of all persons in federal prisons in America were black.

Many whites have their first involvement with the black community when programs of affirmative action surface. President Lyndon

Johnson virtually invented affirmative action. It was created to carry out the provisions of the Civil Rights Act of 1964. Affirmative action has always precluded rigid quotas and the promotion of persons unqualified for the positions to which they aspire. Affirmative action does encourage outreach programs to attract persons who have never worked in a particular area. It also looks favorably on goals, targets, and timetables as incentives to bring blacks into fields where they have been severely under-represented.

Those who have been hurt or think that they will be hurt by affirmative action call it discrimination in reverse. Hardly anyone realizes that affirmative action is authorized and mandated by international law. As the white colonial powers withdrew after World War II from the nations in Africa and Asia which they had entered and governed, those remaining in these nations recognized that they had been discriminated against and held back for decades.

As a result, the laws which they adopted sometimes made arrangements by which downtrodden groups could "catch up." The Constitution and basic laws of India provide for preferential treatment for castes like the Untouchables. The theory is simple: it is unrealistic to think that individuals who have been stigmatized and deprived of opportunities for generations can suddenly attain parity if there is only an opportunity to start at the bottom.

This concept was accepted in 1966 when the United Nations General Assembly adopted the International Convention on the Elimination of All Forms of Racial Discrimination. The treaty provided that "special measures" may be undertaken to accelerate the integration of those classes or individuals who had long been repressed. The one proviso was that such "special measures" must be phased out when they are no longer required. (Affirmative action has been compared to a strong prescription drug. It should be taken only when it is absolutely necessary and its use should be discontinued as soon as the symptoms suggesting it have disappeared.) That treaty, now ratified by 129 nations, is binding on all countries since it was put in force as a part of international law. Although the United States has not ratified that document, it is arguable that the treaty imposes some obligations on the United States.

Affirmative action was spectacularly successful in America from 1964 to 1981. Hundreds of thousands of minorities were able for the first time to secure positions and promotions which had not been available to them before the enactment of the Civil Rights Act of 1964. Women were also the beneficiaries of affirmative action; they obtained positions such as bus drivers, which because of a stereotype, had not been made available to them before.

From the Eisenhower administration through the Carter era, the Justice Department and the nongovernmental civil rights groups moved forward together. There was a remarkable solidarity in the objectives and the techniques recommended by the government and by the private sector. As a result, a climate of cooperation and amity grew. The white majority became amazingly sensitized to what America had done through the decades to her citizens of African ancestry. A tangible, palpable attitude of white-black cooperation became the rule rather than the exception. For many years the federal government engaged in education and enforcement, and the results were remarkable. Formerly segregated school systems in the South became among the most thoroughly and amiably integrated in the country.

In 1981 the Reagan Justice Department for the first time declared a war on affirmative action—or at least proposed a radical redefinition of the concept. The downplaying of affirmative action by the Reagan administration brought about, for the first time in recent U.S. history, a difference in the approach to racial integration between the government and the Leadership Conference, a group of 160 public interest and church-related groups dedicated to the implementation and the improvement of the nation's civil rights laws.

It is not clear whether the attitudes of the Reagan administration— perceived to be negative to blacks by the civil rights community— made an irreversible impression on white America to the extent that the good feelings generated in the 1960s and the 1970s cannot be revived and restored. What is clear is that the United States Supreme Court will establish the future of affirmative action in the 1990s. Decisions issued by the Supreme Court in the late 1980s are not reassuring to those who feel that affirmative action is still needed, and that without some form of affirmative action the progress which blacks have made in employment and in education may be lost. The retirement during 1990 of Justice William Brennan, one of the champions of affirmative action, and President Bush's choice of unknown Justice David H. Souter as Brennan's replacement, has served only to further heighten anxiety over the future of affirmative action.

Will the 1990s see more turmoil in race relations or could the nation be on the brink of a new maturity in the way blacks and whites interact? The white majority has had a long record of self-deception and self-delusion concerning black people in America. One of the central misconceptions lingers on—the idea that blacks want to live apart. Another deeply-seated myth is that blacks, like every other minority group, will somehow "make it." There are other myths, seldom enunciated, which are kept in the subconscious. Unfortunately those myths may continue and even become more powerful unless there is a much more extensive social intermingling of blacks and whites. But the sad fact is that although there is more association of blacks and whites in the workplace, at 5:00 P.M. they go off to their own very separate private lives.

If the churches and the Christians of America had all the courage and commitment which genuine Christians should have in the face of the awful tragedy of black people in America, could the Christians bring justice to African Americans in a decade or a generation? Theoretically they could. But the prejudices and the biases on the part of both white and black Americans are now so pervasive that it is difficult to know how the whole situation can or will develop.

The core of the problem was, of course, the separation of black schoolchildren from the white mainstream of America. It is unbelievable that segregation in the public schools of the United States existed until 1954, and it is also unbelievable that school desegregation did not happen until several years after the decision in *Brown v. The Board of Education.* That means that virtually all white persons in America over the age of 40 had no black children in the elementary or secondary schools which they attended. Millions of these citizens have hardly ever talked to a black person. When persons in this category hear of blacks taking jobs as policemen or fire fighters which otherwise would go to white persons, they are open to emotional responses. Whites in these age groups were inclined to vote for Ronald Reagan in 1980 and 1984 because he subtly but clearly promised that appointments and promotions would be on merit alone. For many, that was a code word for reversing the progress of blacks. And that is why 90 percent of black Americans voted twice against Ronald Reagan and again against George Bush in his 1988 presidential campaign.

The whole world is watching to see how the struggle over civil rights in America will develop in the 1990s. Masses of people in the hundred new nations of the world—the recently liberated colonies of European nations—watched with pride and gratitude as the United States in the 1950s, 1960s, and 1970s courageously repudiated its earlier policy of racial segregation. These same millions have observed the reversal and the retrogression in some of America's bold plans to undo the economic and social damage done to African Americans by policies which were the products of bias, bigotry, and racism. Now these millions in the struggling nations of the Third World hope and pray that America will somehow return to the ringing affirmations of Chief Justice Earl Warren in *Brown v. The Board of Education* and to the unforgettable challenges of Dr. Martin Luther King, Jr.

The eyes of the world are on the churches in America. Will church groups rally as a courageous group of the churches did when a new nation in 1800 declared that it wanted to keep slavery? The abolitionists made the retention of slavery impossible.

Will the churches in America make the retention of racism impossible? One has to believe that the power of Christianity and the grace of God that accompanies it can destroy the evil and erroneous attitude that blacks are inferior to whites. The Christian churches, in their efforts to eliminate racism, will continue to have the active, articulate, and aggressive support of the Jewish community, working against all forms of prejudice. The churches will also have the power and the popularity of secular groups like the American Civil Liberties Union.

Indeed the armies of individuals and organizations opposed to prejudice are so mighty that it seems difficult to think that they could lose. But in American history, these forces have lost—systematically and regularly. Slavery existed in America for the first seventy-five years of the existence of this country. A Jim Crow society replaced slavery and existed for some eighty years. A society requiring equality for blacks has been in existence in America for only some fifty of the nation's 200 years. Bigotry and bias against blacks were the norm in America for three-fourths of the time this country has existed. Brotherhood is relatively new in American history!

Will America be on its way to a society with interracial justice and peace as the third Christian millennium opens in the year 2000?

If enough Christians love God and man with faith and hope, Americans can at last be a society that will be just to the descendants of those slaves whose ancestors were brought in chains to the shores of Virginia in the year 1619.

CHAPTER 4

Marriage, Privacy, and Abortion

I s it possible that the institution of marriage as it has been known in the Christian world for several centuries is fragmenting and dissolving? Monogamy is still a requirement of the law and of religion. But the permanence and indissolubility of marriage, insisted on by the churches and the law in England and in the United States for centuries, have crumbled and decayed at least in practice. Catholics are almost alone in continuing to insist that what God has put together man should not put asunder.

What is the future of marriage and the family in the next millennium? Is it conceivable that non-Catholic churches will reexamine the fundamentals of marriage and reestablish a firm and unyielding requirement that all valid marriages performed between two consenting adults cannot be dissolved? That was the hard and unwavering teaching of all the Christian churches until the last generation or two. Did the churches alter their doctrine in America after the states allowed divorce—first by an adversary procedure, and now virtually by consent because of irreconcilable differences? Some churches, but not all, fought against the relaxation of divorce laws. But it was a losing struggle. The churches and other moral groups have failed even to obtain adequate counseling services for spouses who wish to dissolve their marriage.

Perhaps even more significantly, the churches and the law failed to provide any adequate mechanisms to guarantee economic stability for children whose parents divorce. All of the surveys show that the children of divorce—who are now at least one-third of all young people under the age of 21—endure deprivations of many of the economic advantages which children in unbroken homes enjoy. The loss of emotional and spiritual solidarity with both parents is hard to quantify but it is real, acute, and widespread.

The churches of America feel that they are sitting on the sidelines during the unravelling of marriage and the family as these institutions have been known during almost 200 years of American history. The churches have apparently decided not to fight the civil law any longer. They have presumably concluded that the government is no longer the protector and the guarantor of the indissolubility of marriage, and that it will not assume that role again. The churches seem also to be abandoning concerns or reforms in the law which will guarantee the rights of children at and after the divorce of their parents.

Why have the churches abdicated an area which for centuries was thought to be one of the principal meeting points of law and morality? Indeed family law in England and in the United States was derived almost in its entirety from the ecclesiastical law of England—and ultimately of the Catholic church.

American law accepted most of the rules regulating marriage from the ecclesiastical courts of England. Regulations related to consanguinity and affinity, the norms for allowing separations but not divorce, and guidelines for all aspects of marriage were taken from English ecclesiastical law and practice into the law of all of the states in America. And a prohibition of divorce except in rare and extraordinary circumstances was a part of America's law on marriage from the formation of the colonies until divorces became available in the 1930s.

No one in ecclesiastical circles is suggesting that the churches should seek to reenact civil laws that preserve the indissolubility of marriage. At the same time the churches see that the very institution of marriage is crumbling. Almost everyone has at least one divorce in his or her family. That may be one of the many reasons why no one is urging that the government do something to slow down or reverse the tidal wave of divorces. The consequences of what is happening are of course enormous. It appears that the children of divorce are themselves less likely to form a permanent marriage. And the deprivations and sufferings of children who have to shuttle between two households because of a divorce are still not fully known; but by everyone's admission, they are profound.

In view of the apparent impossibility of expecting the government to lend support to the Christian and Jewish belief that marriage should be permanent, religious groups are trying almost desperately to educate their young people about the beauty, the sanctity, and the permanence of marriage as a divinely sanctioned institution. Many professionals in religion feel that they are working against tremendous odds and that the state is almost their enemy. The state has withdrawn its blessing from most of those supports for marriage which have been part of Anglo-American law for centuries. Adultery and fornication are no longer criminally forbidden in a majority of states, and where such laws still exist they are not enforced. Legal action against seduction and alienation of affections has been abolished on the contention that such actions are too likely to be abused. And most importantly, the contract of marriage has been virtually turned over to the spouses as if it were a totally personal matter.

Most churches have not recently protested the secularization or privatization of marriage, but they are increasingly realizing that the churches, and perhaps the churches almost alone, will in all probability be the agencies to resist any profound fundamental alteration in the nature of marriage as conceived by civil law.

The ongoing practice of privatizing marriage in America has almost been forgotten or accepted. Churches have put aside any desires which they might have had to stop the process. But those decisions flare up—often in emotional ways—when male or female homosexuals ask to have the same legal rights, in their unions with persons of the same sex, which go automatically to persons of different sexes who fulfill the requirements of a civil marriage.

In 1989, the Court of Appeals of New York, the state's highest court, ruled that a gay couple who had lived together for a decade could be considered a family under New York City's rent-control regulations. New York City now offers certain benefits, like paid bereavement leave, to municipal employees who live as unmarried couples. Seattle, Los Angeles, and Madison, Wisconsin continue to study benefits for domestic partners. San Francisco now allows unmarried partners to register their relationship with the city.

The nation's legislatures and courts will, it would seem, eventually have to take a position on the advisability of granting the benefits which married couples enjoy to persons of the same sex who live together on a permanent basis. It is difficult to predict the type of situation which will precipitate the necessity for such judgments. But it seems clear that the fragmenting of the traditional family structure will produce situations on which public officials must pronounce. In 1988 the Federal Census Bureau reported that only 27 percent of the nation's 91.1 million households fit the traditional definition of a family—two parents living with children. That figure was down from 40 percent in 1970.

There does not seem to be any clear or vigorous consensus among the churches as to what they should do about the request for the legalization of a relationship made up of two persons of the same sex. There is clearly an overwhelming feeling among most Christian groups that this type of union cannot be a marriage in any sacramental or theological sense. But that does not necessarily mean that the churches are prepared to lend their resources to oppose the adoption of this idea in the legislatures or the courts. Many feel that the idea is extreme, and that even if a permanent union of same-sex persons is granted a legal status, this does not necessarily mean that the exalted place given to marriage for centuries in Anglo-American law will be compromised. Churches would feel this—or hope this—because they want to accept and enhance the concept of privacy as it has flowered in American law in the last generation.

It is difficult to resist the attraction of the idea of privacy. No one wants the government to intrude into the intimate areas of anyone's life or the very personal relationship of marriage. Americans, who have resisted totalitarian and authoritarian regimes around the world, instinctively want to protect their own lives and families from intrusive conduct on the part of "Big Brother." Privacy is new in American life and in constitutional law. But so is the idea that the government has a right and a duty to regulate those areas of life which had been almost completely controlled by the churches for many centuries. Until very recently, state laws reflected the consensus of the churches on such topics as marriage, divorce, adultery, abortion, and homosexuality. American law was almost the embodiment of what most religious groups taught about those issues. The country was not a theocracy, nor did churches want to make it into one. But the symbiosis between the government and religious bodies on issues related to marriage and sex was pervasive.

That remarkable partnership still exists. Marriage is favored by American law in countless ways. Promiscuity is frowned upon. Prostitution is legally forbidden everywhere except in one county in Nevada.

But if the concept of privacy is employed and generally accepted,

will the present protective treatment given to certain ideals fundamental to the Judeo-Christian tradition be eroded or eliminated? The
question has not been adequately explored because few if any commentators are prepared to suggest that privacy is a two-edged sword.
Many critics of judicial activism lament that the United States Supreme Court has developed the concept of privacy and expanded it to
justify abortion. But there is no anti-privacy lobby as there is an anti-
abortion lobby. Privacy as a right derived from the Constitution was
born in the *Griswold* case in 1965. In a 7–2 decision, the Supreme
Court set aside a Connecticut law that forbade the sale and even the
use of contraceptives. The heavily Catholic Connecticut legislature
had refused to repeal the law which was enacted by an overwhelmingly Protestant legislature in 1869. Catholics in the 1960s in
Connecticut enjoyed taunting Protestants by retaining a law which
coincides with official Catholic teaching but which is now completely
foreign to Protestant thought.

The Supreme Court discovered the basis for its creation of a new
right of privacy in the Third, Fourth, Fifth, and Ninth Amendments
to the Constitution. The majority opinion reasoned that privacy is one
of the "emanations" of the guarantees in the Bill of Rights against
unreasonable searches and seizures and forced self-incrimination.
The dissent, while attracted to the idea of privacy, held that the
Supreme Court had no authorization to "invent" rights that are not in
the text of the Constitution.

The dissent of Justice Potter Stewart, joined by Justice Hugo Black,
made it clear that in Stewart's view the law in Connecticut was "un-
commonly silly," but that he could find "no such general right of
privacy in the Bill of Rights, in any part of the Constitution, or in any
cases before decided by this Court."

People welcomed the advent and the near-exaltation of privacy, and
few wondered if it would tend to erode and privatize some of the
fundamental moral values endemic to American life. The *Griswold*
decision clearly placed a shield of protection around the institution of
marriage. The opinion proclaimed that the intimacy of marriage
could not be invaded or even interfered with by the state. The
Griswold decision, in essence, said that if the churches, which had
always ruled on the contours of the marriage relationship, withdrew
their guidance, or if that guidance is not followed by spouses, the
government may not substitute its wishes for those of religious bodies.

The *Griswold* decision was and is enormously popular. One of the few persons to reject it was Judge Robert Bork; and his opposition to *Griswold* and its progeny was clearly one of the several reasons why the United States Senate refused to confirm him for a seat on the United States Supreme Court.

The *Griswold* decision said that the government may not interfere with any decision couples make as to whether they will or will not have children. That conclusion has won almost unanimous approval in American public opinion. Americans have always been opposed to actions by foreign countries which encourage or discourage the number of children couples decide to have. Americans, like most people, are horrified at China's present policy of limiting couples to one or at most two children.

But the privatization of marriage achieved in the *Griswold* decision has consequences. It means, in a sense, that marriage is no longer to be supervised by either the church or the state. It is assumed that the churches have no intention of re-Christianizing marriage by altering the basic civil law of America. And *Griswold* makes clear that marriage is a private arrangement which cannot be interfered with by the government. The *Griswold* decision did not, to be sure, hold that the state cannot set the minimum age before which no one can marry, or that it cannot require tests for syphilis prior to marriage, or that it cannot forbid incest or polygamy. But the protective zone of privacy was built around almost all aspects of matrimonial intimacy.

It was only the very perceptive critics of *Griswold* who saw, in the court's acceptance of the idea of privacy, the consequences for laws regulating abortion and homosexuality. These critics realized that the immunity of persons from any restraint by the state in all that pertains to childbearing—the core of the *Griswold* ruling—makes it difficult if not impossible for the government to require women, wed or unwed, to go forward with a pregnancy which they do not wish to continue. In a sense therefore, the *Griswold* decision made *Roe v. Wade* in 1973 inevitable.

Roe v. Wade, which permitted women to have an abortion at least in the first trimester of their pregnancies, has shattered the consensus which the churches and synagogues of America had developed on many legal/moral issues in the United States. Some Catholics, many Christian fundamentalists and some from other denominations remain opposed to *Roe v. Wade* and are vigorously pro-life. Many Protestant and Jewish groups favor *Roe v. Wade*, although they do not favor abortion as a routine method of birth control.

In a book like this, which seeks to analyze and strengthen the moral convictions on which religious groups in America generally agree, it would be convenient if the abortion issue could be omitted. But that is not possible. Nor, on the other hand, is it possible to describe or even to develop a consensus on what the churches in a pluralistic society should hold and do about the 1.6 million abortions that occur each year in the United States.

Any writer on abortion and the law risks resentment and rejection from both the pro-life and the pro-choice factions. These groups have been at least publicly so polarized that it is not clear that any accommodation or coming together is possible. Such polarization has not occurred on other legal/moral issues in contemporary American life—with the possible exception of government financing for church-related schools of less than collegiate rank. Why have churches and Jewish organizations been able to work together on civil rights, immigration, refugees, opposition to excessive military force, and other complex topics, but have been adversaries on whether the Constitutional guarantees of privacy should extend to abortion?

That is a question that has made abortion the "most politically divisive domestic legal issue of our time," as Justice Harry Blackmun put it in his dissenting opinion on July 3, 1989 in *Webster v. Reproductive Health Services*.

Is the basic disagreement over the scope of privacy? Or over the nature of the fetus before viability or birth? Or over what some would feel is the duty to all human life, even unborn life? Or is the clash derived in part from the feeling of some that if abortion is to be legalized it should be enacted by elected legislators and not un-elected judges?

There is solid evidence that demonstrates that if the United States Supreme Court had not taken jurisdiction in *Roe v. Wade*, and had ratified the decision below—namely the nullification of the Texas law outlawing abortion—the states would have moved toward the repeal of laws forbidding abortion. In 1973, before the decision in *Roe v. Wade*, almost one-third of the states had relaxed or repealed their laws forbidding abortion. New York State had wiped out almost all laws restricting abortion.

If abortion had been allowed by the democratic processes at the state level, would the demise of abortion laws have been accepted like laws were accepted allowing divorce and permitting the sale of contraceptives?

Some states would probably not have repealed their anti-abortion laws, but it is not clear that they would have been enforced. Most states did not enforce their anti-abortion laws prior to *Roe v. Wade*.

Would the pro-life activists have organized as they did after *Roe v. Wade* in order to prevent the repeal of laws banning abortions? If *Roe v. Wade* were ever reversed and states were free to re-criminalize abortion, how many of them would do it? If it is possible to conduct a rational and civilized dialogue about abortion and the law in the world after *Roe v. Wade*, surely these questions and others must be raised. Those who believe as this writer does that, as the Second Vatican Council put it, abortion is virtually the same as infanticide, cannot insist that this conviction settles the question of the relationship of law and abortion in the United States.

The legalization of abortion is not, of course, an issue unique to the United States. All the nations of Europe except Ireland and possibly one or two others allow abortion under some circumstances. The Communist nations do not forbid it. Indeed each year there are over 50 million abortions that we know about in the world. Regardless of what some think ultimately about the morality of abortion, there would be a consensus that the law should work toward a society where women and families could be able by voluntary means to avoid situations in which the parties feel that an abortion is the least unsatisfactory option.

Is there a chance that in the warm ecumenical atmosphere which churches and synagogues have developed in America over the last two generations, there could develop a dialogue and discussion from which some detente about abortion would emerge? Or is the nation destined to undergo another generation or more of battles where the major pro-life forces are funded and fueled by Catholics, religious fundamentalists and some other sincere opponents of abortion? The anti-abortionists see themselves as the new abolitionists, and like them, seek to remain adamant, unyielding, and persistent. The pro-choice forces feel just as deeply that *Roe v. Wade* vindicates the privacy rights adumbrated in *Griswold* and that women and families should fight to prevent the state from reassuming the duty of directing women how to decide about having children.

Catholic leaders are aware that women, including those who are normally opposed to abortion, feel strongly that the government and the church have downgraded the rights of women. As never before in the history of the Catholic church, women feel a sense of resentment against a male hierarchy. That feeling shows no sign of softening. Could it become so fixed that it could result in the departure of millions of women from the church—similar to the defection of millions of workers in Europe in the nineteenth century when they did not feel that the church was supporting their rights as workers in the early decades of the Industrial Revolution?

Some pro-life Catholic leaders would say that they have to insist on the sanctity and the inviolability of all human life, including fetal life, regardless of what reaction this might produce. That position has merit. And those who hold it are sometimes so adamant that they will not hear even a shadow of an argument that derives from privacy or pluralism. In a sense it is an asset to have absolutists on an important moral issue. At the same time the churches in America must remember that they are in a unique position: in a newly secularized society they are trying to reestablish those fundamental moral norms on which America was built and without which, one can argue, America as a good and moral society will not perdure.

In every area where there is a serious moral problem in America, such as race relations or family stability, the churches have a right and a duty to set forth their views on the issue. The churches have done so, although they have not been as organized or unified as many would have wished. And in many instances, the churches lost. Their views have not stopped racism or divorce or an escalation in gambling. And when the churches lose the battle after using persuasion and prayer, they attempt to go political. They want to use ecclesiastical power and authority to coerce politicians or voters or both to adopt or retain a certain legal/moral position. Churches may feel obliged to be political as well as prophetic; but when the voice of ecclesiastical authority uses or seems to be using that authority for a political objective, the prophet loses a good deal of credibility and may even be engaging in something counterproductive to his objective.

Modern-day prophets—and especially those who ardently desire to stop abortion—will probably not stop at the edge of politics if they feel in conscience that the political order offers them no hope of achieving their objective. They can argue that the prophets in the Old Testament entered into the life of the leaders of their day and denounced them for their inequities.

But in the unique situation in the United States where the churches have historically, with the consent of the people, commanded such authority and power, they have to look at the entire spread of the nation's problems nationally and internationally and recognize that, if the future public policies of the nation are to be just in the broader sense, the churches have to dialogue and debate and decide with a wide variety of considerations in mind. The churches cannot allow one issue or one great moral question to so dominate their agenda that they are not listened to, or worse, do not speak to the other urgent moral questions confronting the nation.

Despite all of this, it is still morally offensive to almost everyone that every third fetus in America is not born but is aborted. There has to be a way to lessen that number. Contraceptives and persuasive education are obviously one way. But the pro-life movement is not satisfied with such a slow and uncertain method. Activists against abortion would agree with Thoreau, who said that "all progress depends on unreasonable men."

It is to the credit of the anti-abortionists that they are lobbying and demonstrating for a moral objective that cannot help them personally. Those who are working to keep abortion legal are also altruistic, but the argument could be made that they are struggling to maintain a right from which they and their families could benefit.

But the antagonism between the parties in the struggle about abortion is not likely to diminish, unless religious forces can mediate or arbitrate to bring about some kind of detente or moratorium. If the Supreme Court does not reverse *Roe v. Wade*, the pressure to change the personnel on the Supreme Court will continue, in order to bring about a reversal of that 1973 decision. If the Supreme Court weakens or overturns *Roe v. Wade*, the political fight is transferred to the states. In either event, the subject will continue to be a point of difference between the Republican and the Democratic parties. In 1980, the Republican platform was changed so that it now advocates the recriminalization of abortion, the defeat of the Equal Rights Amendment and the enactment of measures to favor tuition tax credits for church-related schools of less than collegiate rank. These three changes were made at the request of conservative Christian fundamentalists, and especially Reverend Jerry Falwell, the leader of the now-defunct Moral Majority.

If the pro-life position becomes a political burden at the national or state level, will the GOP abandon or modify its commitment? One can argue that the pro-life position of Ronald Reagan and his party helped him to be elected in 1980 and 1984. But it is also clear that the 54 percent of all Catholics who voted for Mr. Reagan in 1980 and the strong vote he received from fundamentalist Christians in the same year were prompted by several factors, such as the upward economic mobility of these groups and their desire for a strengthening in the moral stance of the government on issues like narcotics, pornography, and crime.

The future of abortion depends, to some extent, on the vagaries of political forces, but it will also be affected by the abiding and perhaps deepening feelings which Americans have for privacy. All of the public opinion polls show that a majority of Americans want some kind of options available for women who urgently desire an abortion. Most Americans say with a good deal of fervor that they do not want a society in which "abortion on demand" is available, but that they do want a government that makes it possible for women to secure an abortion for almost any reason which she and her physician deem justified. Americans also have feelings that poor women should not be denied medicaid funding for abortion just because they are poor. Some persons, on the other hand, seem to feel that their opposition to abortion has a responsible and balanced ring to it if they allow abortion but deny government funds to carry it out for the poor.

Some Catholic members of Congress have tended to adopt this compromise. Medicaid funding for abortion is about the only issue related to abortion on which the Congress gets to vote. Some Catholic pro-life groups would like to insist that Catholics in Congress must morally vote to ban medicaid funding for abortion. But the issue is not that simple. There are complex issues of fairness, due process, and constitutionality involved in many of the situations related to abortion on which Congress has to vote. Should Congress, for example, vote to prohibit the District of Columbia from spending its own tax funds on abortions for the poor? Should the Legal Services Corporation be precluded from representing a poor woman after medical malpractice has apparently brought her injury in a procedure involving abortion? Should the U.S. Bureau of Prisons be prohibited from funding abortion for its inmates?

Some persons who are strongly opposed to abortion sometimes have difficulty in voting for a member of Congress who votes in favor of Medicaid funding for abortion. This problem is more complicated because by and large many of the "pro-choice" Catholic members of

Congress support nuclear arms control, economic programs, and civil rights measures more than Catholics who are "pro-life." If one compares the ranking of members of Congress given by Network, a Catholic social justice lobby, with the ratings of pro-life groups, this disparity is very clear.

Some pro-life groups are blunt in criticizing and deriding Catholic members of Congress who vote in favor of funding for Medicaid abortions. In the December 1988 issue of *Crisis*, a conservative Catholic magazine, photos of some Senators and Representatives who vote pro-choice are displayed with the caption, "rogue's gallery." The integrity of these members is attacked and the declaration is made that Catholic organizations and the church should "put sharp difference between them and these pro-abortion Congressmen."

The U.S. Catholic bishops have made it clear on several occasions over the past few years that Catholics should judge public officials for whom they must vote on a totality of some 14 points related to social justice. The list contains issues such as nuclear arms control, world hunger, domestic justice, race relations and so forth. Abortion is only one of the 14. The Catholic bishops have urged repeatedly that Catholics not become "one issue" voters.

Cardinal Joseph Bernardin of Chicago, has consistently urged that Catholics view together the "seamless garment" of issues related to life—nuclear weapons, the death penalty, and abortion. The bishops are not underestimating the moral importance of the abortion issue, but are seeking to put it into perspective in a nation and a world where all types of immoral attitudes and reprehensible practices are doing great damage.

The Catholic bishops of the United States are not about to reverse themselves in their position since *Roe v. Wade* that the law should once again re-criminalize abortion. That position was deemed to be required by the church's long-held teaching that an abortion cannot be justified. It was felt that the taking of a life, despite the compelling appeal of the argument for privacy, cannot be condoned or allowed. At the same time, the bishops are very aware of the inappropriateness of the official church pressing too far and too vigorously into the political order with a specific legal solution to a problem on which Americans are deeply divided, and about which they feel passionately. This is particularly true since Catholic officials generally do not have the broad-based support of other religious groups on abortion that they do have on issues related to nuclear war, race relations, and economic justice.

In a statement in "The Pastoral Constitution on the Church and the Modern World," the Second Vatican Council, while not speaking directly about abortion, stated:

> Often enough, the Christian view of things will itself suggest some specific solution in certain circumstances. Yet it happens rather frequently, and legitimately so, that with equal sincerity some of the faithful will disagree with others on a given point. (paragraph 43)

The Catholic laity have no "specific solution" to the practice of abortion in America, but there appears to be no solid consensus among Catholics that a re-criminalization of abortion is the way to stop the taking of the lives of 1.6 million fetuses each year. Catholics believe by and large in the teaching of the church concerning the sanctity and inviolability of every unborn child but they are not agreed that this conviction necessarily suggests that the removal of a nonviable fetus at the request of a woman should be a crime—for the physician or for the woman. But Catholics, like almost everyone else, yearn for some flexible legal arrangement that will inhibit the promiscuous use of abortion but allow it when those involved deem it the least harmful resolution of a painful situation.

The admonition of Vatican II, again in "The Church and the Modern World," is relevant: "They (Catholics) should always try to enlighten one another through honest discussion, preserving mutual charity and caring above all for the common good." (paragraph 43)

This prescription for charity and forbearance was echoed by the United States Catholic bishops in their statement after the *Webster* decision of July 3, 1989. That 5–4 ruling did not overturn *Roe v. Wade*, but it allows states more freedom to restrict and inhibit women who desire to have an abortion.

The Catholic bishops, after a reaffirmation of their opposition to abortion, had these words of caution for Catholics:

"Groups and individuals seeking new opportunities for protection of the unborn will best achieve their goal through mutual respect and cooperation. The movement and support of abortion on demand is united in its agenda; pro-life Americans must not give their adversaries an easy victory by launching attacks on each other over questions of political strategy."

Is the rise in the number of abortions one more reason to fear that marriage in America is decaying as an institution? The churches have reason to have that fear. After all, the begetting and the rearing of children was, during the first 2,000 years of Christianity, the principal if not the exclusive purpose of marriage. If a government rules that a woman may legally conceive a child out of wedlock and then abort the unwanted child, does this not shatter the idea of the sacredness and the integrity of marriage?

There are, of course, very rational arguments for the proposition that spouses can enrich their marriage and make it more stable by having the number of children they mutually desire, and at the times they deem best. There is general affirmation by Christians for this position, but the moral issues still remain as to the legitimacy of the reason that would justify an abortion. As abortion of a nonviable fetus becomes technically easier to accomplish, one has to ask if an abortion is morally acceptable because the spouses wanted a boy rather than a girl, or vice versa. Or does any kind of a personal interest or a preference justify the extinction of a fetus? Or would the presence of twins in the womb justify the abortion of one of them—if technical means were available to achieve such a result?

The growing acceptance of the moral values behind privacy suggests to Americans that the government and public officials should not be involved in the sincere decision-making of parents about the number and nature of their own children. Nothing more private and intimate can be imagined than the formation of a family.

But those opposed to abortion will insist that privacy stops when the right of an unborn child is involved. The Supreme Court has rejected that contention by stating the fact—not denied by a single Justice of the Supreme Court—that there is no decision in all of American jurisprudence that holds that an unborn fetus is entitled to be regarded as a "person," as that term is used in the Fourteenth Amendment. The Missouri legislature met that objective and enacted as a preamble to a law on abortion, the declaration that "the life of each human being begins at conception," and that "unborn children have protectable interests in life, health and well being." The act then mandates that state laws be interpreted to provide unborn children with "all of the rights, privileges and immunities available to other persons, citizens and residents of this state."

In the 1989 *Webster* decision, the U.S. Supreme Court sustained that preamble, by a 5–4 vote, on the ground that it was not intended to be an operative part of the statute in question. But if Congress enacted the "human life statute," stating in essence what the Missouri preamble declared, would that new federal law mean that federal judges and the Supreme Court would have to grant to non-viable fetuses the same rights that are now conferred on all persons after their birth?

The adoption of such a federal statute would, of course, directly collide with the notion sustained by the Supreme Court since the *Griswold* decision in 1967 that individuals, and especially married couples, have a right derived from constitutionally protected privacy to control the way in which they decide to have or not to have children.

There is also the issue of the religious origin of the concept strongly held by Catholics and many others that a fetus from the moment of conception is entitled to all the respect and rights of a human being. Would the acceptance of that principle be a violation of the establishment clause of the First Amendment? Justice John Paul Stevens, alone, among members of the Supreme Court, adheres to that idea. In the *Webster* decision Stevens stated that there is an unquestionably "theological basis" for the argument that life begins at conception but that "our jurisprudence . . . has consistently required a secular basis for valid legislation."

Justice Stevens continued by stating that he was persuaded that the "absence of any secular purpose for the legislature's declarations that life begins at conception and that conception occurs at fertilization makes the relevant portion of the preamble invalid under the establishment clause of the First Amendment."

It seems clearer all the time that if the states or Congress are to enact laws that reinforce traditional concepts of morality, they will be required to proffer a compelling justification rooted in the secular interests of the state rather than in the idea that the state should be enforcing the moral concepts of the churches or of the majority of the citizenry.

In 1981 the United States Supreme Court sustained a California law making it a crime for a man to have sex with a woman under the age of 18. The defense of the man was that the government must make it a crime for both parties in such an act, since to penalize the man and not the woman is a violation of the equal protection clause of the Fourteenth Amendment. The Court rejected the argument and sustained the conviction. The dissent, however, reasoned that if the state wants to deter fornication with its risk of pregnancy it should punish both persons involved, since this would be a greater deterrent than punishing only the man. All of the Justices appeared to assume that the state could criminalize fornication in order to prevent the nonmarital children who could result. No one seems to be recommending that the state enact and enforce laws against teenage intercourse, although if such laws were enforced the number of abortions would decline substantially. Again, the idea of privacy somehow mutes the discussion, since no one wants to be urging their policeman to intervene in the most intimate aspects of life.

The future relationship of abortion and the law in America is not clearly predictable. Several scenarios are possible. The Supreme Court could continue to refuse to reverse *Roe v. Wade* and the nation would settle down to accepting abortion as it accepted the legalization of divorce, adultery, and some forms of homosexuality between consenting adults. On the other hand, the Supreme Court could ease the restrictions in *Roe v. Wade* and some of the states would make abortion more difficult. But law enforcement officials might be very reluctant to enforce new restrictions on abortion—as they were in the days before *Roe v. Wade.*

The development of new scientific knowledge about conception and contraception might have a dramatic impact on the whole problem. If a woman knew conveniently and compellingly those few days a month on which she could conceive, she would be much more likely to prevent an unwanted pregnancy.

What is, however, very clear is that feminists in America are not likely to yield in their militant demand for the availability and accessibility of abortion for all women. Feminists believe sincerely and strongly that mandatory motherhood, as they sometimes phrase it, violates the dignity of women and the mandate of the U.S. Constitution.

How many of these feminists will feel that the churches—especially the Catholic church—are engaging in a war against women's rights if the churches pursue a campaign to make abortion unavailable? That obviously is a painful question for church- related groups opposed to abortion. Catholic officials probably find it particularly difficult since many Catholic women already have difficulty in understanding or accepting the exclusion of women from the priesthood and hence from essential decision-making positions in the church. American Catholic feminists, moreover, are still disappointed that the U.S. Catholic bishops did not endorse the Equal Rights Amendment—the greatest aspiration of women in America in this century.

The 1990s will pose difficult questions for Catholic officials as to how vigorous they should be in seeking legal and criminal sanctions against abortion. There is resentment and disapproval by many Catholics of the pervasiveness of the issue of abortion in the concerns of the Catholic press and the Catholic hierarchy. Many Catholics moreover, have fears that the isolation of Catholic officials on the abortion issue may adversely effect their influence on ecumenical relations with other churches and their relationship with secular groups devoted to civil rights and economic justice. There is also the grim reality that reliable statistics reveal that apparently the number of Catholic women obtaining abortions is not significantly different from the number of non-Catholics doing the same thing.

Those who see the true horror of abortion and realize that it is virtually the same as infanticide will hope that sometime in the future the nation and the world will realize that the legalization of abortion was a dreadful deviation from the majestic traditional role of law in the United States. When that moment of recognition comes the world will be grateful to those who kept alive the noble ideal that the life of an unborn child must be respected as a precious gift from God.

CHAPTER 5

Religion and Education in America

E ver since the creation of mandatory elementary education for all children, around the year 1850, pluralistic democracies in the West have sought to incorporate into the public schools instruction in the basic elements of religion. To Christians more than a century ago, it was unthinkable that the state would insist that children go to a government-controlled school for thirty hours a week during their formative years, and not have a good deal of information about religion communicated in that school. Indeed, from roughly 1850 to 1960 in the United States the government which directed the schools was a government made up overwhelmingly of believing Protestants; they saw no contradiction between their life in a pluralistic democracy and a requirement that all public schools reflect the Protestant ethos. Consequently, the daily reading of the Bible and the recitation of prayers were accepted as desirable and legitimate.

Other nations that were divided religiously by the Reformation likewise felt strongly that public schools should have religion as an important component of their curriculum. In England, Holland, Belgium, Canada, and Australia schools taught religion and Protestants, Catholics, and Jews, dissatisfied with the secular Protestant orientation of these state-conducted schools, established their own denominational institutions. After intense and immense political struggles, all of these Protestant-oriented countries eventually gave some form of subsidies to non-public schools. That arrangement emerged in 1910 in England when the Church of England demanded support for its sectarian schools—a demand that triggered comparable support for Catholic and Jewish institutions. Similar developments occurred in the Netherlands, Belgium, Canada, and Australia.

History may judge that the persistent denial in the United States of all aid to church-related schools of less than collegiate rank, and the prohibition of all devotional or religious exercises in the public schools, may have impeded—even destroyed—a possibility of the churches having a significant influence over the development of public morality in the United States. Many, of course, would deny that thesis completely and insist that the churches in America, by not being involved in the teaching of religion in the public schools or being tied up in the operation of state-financed church-related schools, have preserved their independence from the government and hence have remained free to rebuke the government in prophetic ways.

Whatever the ultimate judgment of history may be, generations from now, the mission of the churches in America has been sharply and severely narrowed by the always mixed, but persistent mandate of the United States Supreme Court, since 1947, that no financial aid go to any religiously affiliated grade or high school, and that simultaneously the government may not sponsor or promote or even allow religious instruction or religious exercises on the premises of a public school.

Contemporary observers of the place of religion in the public life of America are so near to the Supreme Court decisions of the last forty years separating religion and government that they cannot appreciate the full significance of the forced divorce of religion from the public school. The separation of religion from any form of government sponsorship has privatized religion in ways which are foreign to the place religion had in America from 1650 to 1950. Citizens today as never before have to look upon religion as apart from the government; if religion is not actually alien to the government in some ways, it is clearly not a partner, or associate, or ally. The religious convictions of parents and students are deemed to be of a private nature—not to be cultivated or even recognized by the government.

All fair-minded observers will recognize that there is a powerful case for the proposition that the secular state should not monopolize education. The state may proclaim neutrality as to any and all ideologies, but governments, like every other collective entity, seek their own survival as their own primordial objective. As a result the government in its schools inculcates patriotism (which can degenerate into nationalism), war-like attitudes to all potential aggressors, and indifference or even hostility to anyone in the group who is not an unquestioning cheerleader for the government.

The government in America has not monopolized higher education as it has dominated all schools of less than collegiate rank. The churches in America initiated higher education with the establishment of Harvard College in 1636. The Methodists established 110 colleges; Presbyterians, Baptists, Adventists, and other denominations launched colleges which were vigorously religious and denominational. Many, perhaps most, of these institutions are today virtually secular. Catholics still have about 300 colleges, all which are closely identified with the organized church and all of which are Catholic in their curriculum.

It is not entirely clear why the churches, aside from the Catholics, Orthodox Jews, some Lutherans, and a few others, acquiesced in the emergence of the public or common school. That institution, which employed the McGuffey reader with its pan-Protestant orientation, recited prayers and read the Bible. But it is still anomalous that denominations which were so zealous and generous in creating religiously affiliated colleges were so accepting of an institution which, despite the traces of piety that were permitted until the Supreme Court decisions in the 1960s banning them, could not be described as units which sought to interpret secular learning in the light of the Gospel. It must also be noted that the public schools, contrary to Christian teaching, locked out black children, leaving them to segregated or inferior schools where schools existed at all.

Was it the smugness of Protestants, who felt that the United States was a Protestant nation, that allowed Protestants to turn the schools over to the government? That did not happen in any other nation. Germany incorporated the teaching of religion, both Catholic and Lutheran, into the curriculum of its public schools. Italy and Spain insisted on Catholic doctrine being taught, while in Scandinavia religion in some form was a part of the program of the state schools.

These are immense questions that have to be asked and answered before one can reach some type of a balanced judgment as to whether the churches in America never understood their mission, or whether they abandoned it. Clearly the churches have never accepted the role as private organizations assigned to them by the Supreme Court in its interpretation of the establishment clause of the First Amendment.

It seems fair to say that the Protestant churches in America have been ambivalent and divided over their proper role in shaping the domestic and foreign policies of the country. The Catholic church as a minority organization felt so embattled for decades that it struggled not to form a public morality, but to combat prejudice against Catholicism. The Catholic church established an amazing array of Catholic-financed schools in order to protect its own identity in a pan-Protestant culture.

Much of that has changed today, now that all Christians are faced with a state that precludes the presence of religion in the public schools, although it generously encourages churches by granting tax exemption, banning work on Sunday, and extending some privileges to Sabbatarians, conscientious objectors, and religious dissidents.

The present position of the churches in America can be understood only in the light of how the United States Supreme Court has defined that role. But first it is important to point out the anomalous fact that in the development of American democracy it was neither elected legislators nor the voters who determined the place of religion, but unelected federal judges. For over forty years the Supreme Court has assumed and asserted that no religious majority or minority can formulate what the local or national government should do about the role or place of religion. The responsibility for decisions about the place of religion has been taken over by the nation's highest court. That court has banned any approval or subsidy by any government to any religious group. The fear is real, and possibly growing, that the Supreme Court has inadvertently established secularism—or a public indifference to religion—in place of the pro-religion attitude which characterized America from the days of the colonies to the end of World War II. Again, there are strong arguments and influential experts that point in the opposite direction and maintain that religions have been strengthened, not weakened, by the wall which the Supreme Court has decreed must exist between the government and religion.

There may well be substantial truth in that position, but the fact remains that the churches of America must now carry out their mission without access to the nation's children during their "business hours," when they are in school. The story behind this exclusion began in 1947, when the United States Supreme Court ruled, 5–4 in *Everson v. Board of Education*, that the establishment clause of the First Amendment forbids any public subsidy of institutions which aid one religion or aid all religions. Although the Supreme Court in *Everson* allowed reimbursement for the bus rides of the children going to church-related schools in a township in New Jersey, both the majority and the minority made it clear that any additional subsidy beyond bus rides would be banned. The court did allow state governments to loan secular textbooks in the *Allen* decision in 1968. But virtually every other form of financing has been struck down. A long series of decisions declaring unconstitutional several forms of aid culminated in the decision in 1985 in *Aguilar v. Felton* in which the Court, 5–4, declared unconstitutional a federal plan initiated in 1965 under the Elementary and Secondary Education Act, by which a limited number of students in need of remedial training secured such help on the premises of the Catholic schools which they attended. The Elementary and Secondary Education Act was the result of a long series of compromises reached by the Congress when it enacted the Anti-Poverty program as a part of the Great Society initiated by President Johnson. After this carefully crafted consensus was struck down by the Supreme Court in 1985, Catholic educators and parents have been wondering—not without a trace of bitterness—whether they are consigned forever to carrying alone the enormous financial burden of keeping their children in schools that are acceptable to them as Christians.

The logic of the *Everson* decision had prompt and dramatic consequences in 1948 when the Supreme Court, by an 8–1 vote in *McCollum v. Board of Education*, banned a program by which parents and religious groups collaborated with public school officials in a released-time religious education program on the school premises. The classes were voluntary. They were conducted by qualified religious ministers. Only children whose parents sought permission in writing could attend. Nonetheless, the Supreme Court, emboldened by its first venture into the religious clauses of the First Amendment in the *Everson* decision, expanded its new jurisprudence of a church-state relationship to ban all religious instruction on the school premises.

The thriving national organization that coordinated released-time religious education for up to 2 million youngsters was shocked and saddened. Largely Protestant in origin and orientation, it sought to remedy the vacuum concerning religion in the public schools by integrating voluntary instruction in denominational teaching into the curriculum of the public school.

The extensive uproar or protest over the *McCollum* decision was possibly the most vociferous challenge to any church-state decision in modern history. The charge was made that the Supreme Court had deconsecrated the nation and secularized the public schools. The sponsors of released-time religious education shifted their activities to sites off the school premises and waited for their opponents to challenge even this compromised version of integrating religion with the curriculum of the public school. The challenge came quickly, and the proponents of religion as a part of the public school program prevailed. In 1952 in *Zorach v. Clauson*, the Supreme Court, 6–3, seemingly backed away from the harshness of the result and the rhetoric of *McCollum* and allowed public school officials, parents, students, and church groups to collaborate in using the organizational machinery of the public school to channel students to classes in religious instruction off the school premises. The language of the majority in *Zorach* is irenic, conciliatory, and almost apologetic about what the Supreme Court had said in *McCollum*. In the four years between *McCollum* and *Zorach*, the court and the country learned about the enormous implications of what the Supreme Court had done—intentionally or otherwise—in its *McCollum* pronouncement. For the first time in American history, the Supreme Court had unleashed an onslaught against organized religion telling all of those involved that they were unconstitutionally misappropriating the use of public school classrooms for their sectarian purposes.

The *Zorach* approach is almost unbelievably different. In statements that read like a church-sponsored pronouncement about piety and patriotism, the Supreme Court intoned in the words of Justice William Douglas that "we are a religious people whose institutions presuppose a Supreme Being." The majority opinion continued by stating that "when the state encourages religious instruction or cooperates with religious authorities by adjusting the schedule of public events to sectarian needs, it follows the best of our traditions." Justice Douglas recognized in his opinion that the government should respect the "religious nature of our people," and accommodate "the public service to their spiritual needs." Justice Douglas did reaffirm the *McCollum* decision and stated categorically that the government "may not finance religious groups nor undertake religious instruction nor blend secular and sectarian education." But at the same time, the government need not be "hostile to religion" and should not "throw its weight against efforts to widen the effective scope of religious influence."

Justice Douglas admitted the importance of modifying the *Mc-Collum* decision when he wrote that "the nullification of this law would have wide and profound effects."

The majority view, in its thoughtful and appreciative tone with respect to religion, is almost unique in the Supreme Court's rulings about church-state matters over the past two generations.

The dissents of Justices Hugo Black, Felix Frankfurter and Robert Jackson are sharp and direct. Justice Black asserts that the collaboration between public schools and organizations involved in sectarian instruction is a device to manipulate the compulsory education laws in order to "help religious sects get pupils."

Justice Jackson virtually conceded that the Supreme Court was reacting to public opinion adverse to the *McCollum* decision when he stated that "today's judgment will be more interesting to students of psychology and of the judicial processes than to students of constitutional law."

The world after *Zorach* ushered in a period of calm and constructive action. Church officials and parents felt that perhaps a way could be worked out to blend the sacred and the secular in the public school setting. It is however significant that although *Zorach* has never been reversed, the program of religious education which it sanctioned had never flourished as a national movement. The sponsors of released-time religious education claimed after *Zorach* that this movement, with its imprimatur from the Supreme Court, would find sponsors and students in most of the school districts of America. That has not happened. Catholics have not been enthusiastic about the program, although they have collaborated. Jewish groups have generally not participated, and prefer their extremely well-organized after-school programs where Jewish young people learn Hebrew and the Bible. And Protestants seem divided or lukewarm about the need to integrate instruction and religion with the three R's. When, therefore, critics of the Supreme court charge that the rulings of that tribunal have secularized the public school, one has to look at the undeniable fact that the churches have not taken full advantage of all the liberties given to them in the *Zorach* mandate. Once again, the issue is whether the churches have backed away from extending their mission into the public domain or whether they have been impeded or restrained from doing so by the government.

If the *Zorach* decision created a certain detente between religionists and secularists, that era of good feeling was shattered in 1962 when the Supreme Court, in *Engel v. Vitale,* ruled out the use of a prayer written by the Regents of the State of New York and prescribed for daily recitation in the public schools of that state. The prayer was simple: "Almighty God, we acknowledge our dependence upon Thee, and we beg thy blessings upon us, our parents, our teachers, and our country." But the Supreme Court was clear that prayers composed by politicians were as objectionable as prayers written by the priests and the prophets.

The case against state-composed prayers was quickly followed by a ban on the recitation of the Lord's Prayer and the reading of the Bible in public schools. In *Abington School District v. Schempp* in 1963, the Supreme Court disallowed forms of piety which had been practiced since the very beginning of the public school in the middle of the nineteenth century. The effect was perceived to be negative and even hostile to religion, even though the author of the *Schempp* decision, Justice Tom Clark, a devout Baptist, went out of his way to stress that the Court was not outlawing objective treatment about religion in the public schools.

At least psychologically and symbolically, the *Schempp* decision prompted Christians to give up hope that the public schools could assist the churches in their task of transmitting Christian values into the public order. The *Schempp* ruling signaled the beginning of the movement of fundamentalist Christians to establish their own schools. In the late 1980s, Reverend Jerry Falwell boasted that religious fundamentalists were establishing three more Christian schools each day— 1,000 per year. Fundamentalists of all kinds now operate up to 20,000 Christian schools, largely in the South and Southwest. The dissatisfaction of the fundamentalists with the public school is derived not only from the absence of devotional practices, but from the perceived lack of moral and spiritual values—at least theistic values—in the public schools.

In 1980, the fundamentalists persuaded the Republican party to insert into its platform a plank favoring tuition tax credits for parents of children attending church-related schools. That pledge clearly attracted voters to the GOP in 1980 and afterwards. But little movement for the enactment of such tuition tax credits has ever developed in the Congress.

The Supreme Court has been consistent and aggressive in following up on its *Schempp* decision. In 1985, in *Wallace v. Jaffree*, the Supreme Court banned even silent prayers, reasoning that the measure it struck down was an attempt by the legislature of Alabama to evade the *Schempp* ruling.

It can be seen that the Supreme Court has been consistent in fleshing out its interpretation of the establishment clause. For over forty years it has prohibited virtually all help to religiously-affiliated day schools while simultaneously preventing the introduction of religious training or practices into the public schools.

Whatever resentment churches might have had about the exclusion of religious practices from the public schools tended to diminish in the 1980s. The aggressive campaign by fundamentalist Christians and by the Moral Majority to "restore God to the public school" prompted many mainline Protestants to suggest that such practices were after all marginal and largely symbolic. Any reliance or dependence which the churches might have had on such token acknowledgement of religion was, it was argued, misplaced since the presence or absence of religious practices which were almost inconsequential in themselves cannot be a measure of how the public schools support or slight religion.

But anxieties about the acknowledgement of the place and importance of religion in the orientation of the public school continued to be widely shared in the United States. Religious flare-ups about the recitation of a prayer before an interscholastic football game or the saying of a prayer at a high school commencement illustrate the deep-seated feelings of many people who want God and religion to be openly acknowledged as a common unifying bond among Americans.

The persistent angst about religion in the public schools—all but a neurosis or an obsession—resulted in the enactment by the U.S. Congress of the Equal Access Act (EAA) in 1984. The Equal Access Act, largely traceable to the activities of fundamentalist Christians, allows student-initiated groups in high schools, not grade schools, to conduct prayer or Bible reading sessions in periods which are available for other non-curriculum related clubs. The enthusiasm of the Reagan administration and the fear that members of Congress always have of appearing to be negative toward religion helped to enact the Equal Access Act by a vote of 337 to 77 in the House and 88 to 11 in the Senate.

Congress justified its support of the Equal Access Act by analogizing the rights of students in high school to the religious freedom of college students, who in the Supreme Court's *Widmar v. Vincent* decision in 1981, were granted the same freedom to the use of public facilities at the University of Missouri at Kansas City as were all other secular co-curricular activities. The Supreme Court ruled that if a university conducts an open forum, in the name of maintaining the separation of church and state it may not limit that privilege to secular activities.

The Equal Access Act is quite restrictive. No meeting may be permitted unless it is student-initiated, not sponsored by the school nor supervised by a teacher. The meeting of students must be conducted in non-instructional time before or after actual classroom teaching begins. There is no sanction if a school refuses to allow such student meetings, since the Equal Access Act specifically forbids the withdrawal of any federal funds for noncompliance with the EAA.

There is little empirical information as to how the Equal Access Act is working out at the grass-roots level. The mainline Protestant and Catholic churches do not seem to be very involved. In Texas, a young man named Galen Clark began a prayer group with six students but it soon escalated to groups between sixty and 150. Clark arranged that his group would distribute religious pamphlets "urging students to dedicate their lives to Jesus." A federal judge in *Clark v. Dallas Independent School District* agreed with school officials who refused to recognize the prayer group.

The U.S. Circuit Court of Appeals for the Eighth Circuit, however, reached the opposite conclusion in *Mergens v. Westside Community Schools*, a decision later affirmed by the Supreme Court. The case involved the efforts of 16-year-old Bridget Mergens to form a religious club of nine students in a public high school in Omaha. The students analogized this group to the chess, computer, or photography clubs, but school officials insisted that all of those clubs were an integral part of the school curriculum and were under the direct control of the school because they had a faculty sponsor. The Equal Access Act does not permit a faculty member to participate, although an outsider, including a clergyman, can speak to the prayer group "occasionally."

The federal district court in Nebraska agreed with the school officials but the Eighth Circuit reversed that decision, ruling that the broad deference of the lower court to the authority and discretion of the school officials would make the Equal Access Act meaningless.

The appeals court ruled that a public secondary school cannot discriminate against a group of students on the basis of the content of the speech of that group. In May, 1990, the Supreme Court affirmed the decision of the Eight Circuit, ruling that Westside School District had created a "limited open forum," requiring that the school permit the student prayer group to meet.

In a case out of Washington State the Ninth Circuit Court of Appeals reached a different result. The appeals court agreed with the trial judge that the Equal Access Act was not intended to restrict the discretion of school officials as to what is or is not "related to the curriculum." The EAA is triggered only if the school authorizes a "limited open forum." That forum comes into existence, EAA stipulates, when the school allows "one or more non-curriculum student groups" to meet on the school premises during "non-instructional time." Can a high school principal decree that the school simply does not have any "non-curriculum student groups" and hence disallow all student-initiated attempts to form a prayer or Bible study group? That remains one of the crucial questions in the unfolding of the law related to the Equal Access Act, even in the wake of *Mergens*.

The thrust of the Equal Access Act is of course different from—even hostile to—the approach taken over the past forty years by the Supreme Court toward religion in the public schools. Indeed, the Equal Access Act was designed to circumvent that approach—at least in part. Consequently, even though the Supreme Court, in deference to Congress and to the aspirations of high school students to pray together, has allowed the Equal Access Act to operate, it is unlikely that very much will be changed with respect to the overall orientation or ethos of the public school. The evangelical fundamentalists will stimulate and even direct students to organize prayer groups in high schools. But these students will not be players in the educational life of the schools; they will be, by definition and by the terms of the law itself, outsiders. The name of the law—Equal Access Act— implies more than it delivers. The law at most requires that school officials not forbid the use of a meeting room to students who want to gather for a religious activity outside of the regular academic program. The students who desire to meet for religious services have no statutory right to the use of the bulletin board or the loud-speaker system to announce the time or purpose of their meetings. Indeed, the law as enacted by Congress seeks to comply with the decisions of the Supreme Court restricting the practice of religion in the public schools. The Equal Access Act seeks only to elevate for high school students those limited rights granted in *Widmar v. Vincent* for college students.

The Equal Access Act signed by President Reagan on August 11, 1984, was the direct result of pressure on the Congress by the religious fundamentalists who at the time were, it can be argued, at the height of their political power. The aspirations behind the law reflect the frustrations of church authorities, parents, and some public officials at the separation of religion from the public school. The solution to the problem that emerged in the Equal Access Act may seem puny, inconsequential, or downright unconstitutional. But, many will argue, it offers some kind of a resolution to a problem caused, not by elected legislators, but by unelected judges.

But the Equal Access Act, however well-intended, may actually deepen the isolation of religion from the activities of the public school. It seems unlikely that the mainline churches will utilize the entree to the public school made available by the Equal Access Act. It seems highly improbable that a Catholic priest, for example, would accept the invitation of a student group to offer mass in a school prior to the beginning of classes on a holy day of obligation such as December 8, the Feast of the Immaculate Conception. Nor is it likely that a Jewish rabbi would join a group of Jewish students in a public school in order to lead them in religious exercises. Nor does it seem predictable that mainline Protestant clergymen will be anxious to join a student group which claims its right to pray on the school premises but outside of the framework of any official, or educational, or co-curricular activities authorized by the public schools. On the other hand, it may be that if the Equal Access Act is broadened or modified by the Congress, religious groups desperate for some opportunity to speak to students in a setting established by the students, and not by the school or the church, will seek to utilize the Equal Access Act for the benefit of the churches. Such a development would be more likely in areas of the country where the fundamentalists are numerous and powerful in a political sense.

But whether the Equal Access Act flourishes or fades away, the problems caused by the pervasive silence about religion in the public schools remains. Devoted and dedicated public school teachers will continue to try to inculcate moral and spiritual values. But those values, perhaps more and more, will be secular, non-controversial, and clearly, non-theistic. Students will be directed not to cheat, lie, or employ violence. But the messages which students get about sex outside of marriage, divorce, prayer, homosexuality, and a host of other issues will be muted or mixed. Those issues and related topics are deemed by public school officials to belong to the churches, or to parents, or to both. As a result, the public schools are seen by the students to be evading and avoiding any firm teaching on some—perhaps most—of the difficult moral questions of the day. One could argue that students are thereby directed to their churches and synagogues for guidelines on all of the hard moral issues which the public schools avoid. But this only deepens the idea that religion is private and that the government does not take a position, or even care about, a good solution to the most difficult questions of public and private morality.

It is not clear how or whether there can be a rethinking of the place of religion in the public schools that will turn out differently than the juridically mandated no-aid-to-religion solution which has prevailed since 1947. Again many observers, including devout believers, will argue that the separation of church and state is good for the church and for the state. Roger Williams took that position when he established the colony of Rhode Island after being driven out of Massachusetts. Roger Williams wanted a separation of church and state because he feared that the state would compromise and even corrupt the churches. Thomas Jefferson, on the other hand, advocated the separation of church and state because he believed that the churches would coerce the state to carry out the objectives of the church.

But nice aphorisms like those of Williams and Jefferson do not offer solutions to those who are convinced that the modern dominantly secular school system is unconsciously and inadvertently undercutting the mission of the churches in America. Seventh-Day Adventists believe that; as a result they finance Adventist schools from kindergarten through college for all of the children of their denomination. Adventists believe so strongly in the wisdom and necessity of the separation of church and state that they will not take even fringe benefits such as bus rides for the students attending Adventist institutions. Orthodox Jews have for generations sacrificed generously to create schools for children. Several conservative Jewish groups now have fully-accredited schools and some Reform Jews have established full-time schools for youngsters whose parents are Reform Jews. For over a century the official Catholic teaching has been that all Catholic parents should send their children to a Catholic school. In the 1950s, about one-half of all Catholic children were in Catholic grade and high schools. That number has declined, but in 1989 some 3 million children attended thousands of Catholic grade and high schools.

Fundamentalist Christians are the most recent group to embrace the conviction that the churches must offer an education to the young which combines the secular with the sacred. With financial sacrifices comparable to those of Adventists, Catholics, Orthodox Jews, Lutherans, and others, fundamentalist Christians have inaugurated a series of schools which can only be regarded as remarkable.

The argument has been made for decades that it is unfair for America to require parents who are conscientiously opposed to the public school to finance the education of their children in alternative schools. The argument has not been successful in any state or locality. And, as noted above, when the Congress agreed with the idea in a sharply modified way in the Elementary and Secondary Education Act of 1965, the Supreme Court invalidated all federal funds, however small, for assisting students in Catholic schools.

Parents who send their children to Catholic schools are divided on how to react to the persistent and perhaps permanent refusal of the government to assist them financially. The strain on their economic assets is intense and is increasing. Some of those parents attended Catholic schools in their youth and cherish what they learned there. They are strenuously determined to have their children share in the wisdom and sanctification which they received while attending Catholic schools. But they are also fearful that their children may be deprived of some academic benefits available in the public schools. They are also apprehensive that their children's chances of being accepted at elite colleges will not necessarily be enhanced by attendance at a Catholic high school, unless that school is itself one of the elite Catholic high schools which many want to attend, not necessarily for its religious orientation, but because it is recognized as a very superior school.

There is therefore some uncertainty in the Catholic community about the effects on young people of attending a Catholic school. Whatever valid studies exist confirm the view that those who attend a Catholic school for eight or twelve years are much more likely to think and act as Christians. That finding, which many would feel to be expected, has been explicitly validated in sociological studies.

It seems fair and almost self-evident to state that the ambiguity and indecisiveness of the church with respect to some of the central legal/moral issues of the day, derive in part from the fact that the churches have not had the opportunity of educating young people about the depths and implications of the great moral problems of the day. More than 90 percent of all young people in America—some 50 million—attend public schools. They are saturated with information about languages, mathematics, and science, but hear little about what their country is doing or should be doing about the daunting moral problems of the age. Those questions are presumably transmitted by the schools to the politicians or to the churches for resolution. The clear inference to be drawn by students is that the nation's public morality is a matter of dispute and that there are few, if any, inherited or traditional positions on public moral issues which the school communicates or even mentions. Almost inevitably, students conclude that since the politicians and the churches do not seem to be in agreement on the great moral questions, then the nation has to somehow muddle through. Again the concept that religion is a private and a personal matter is overwhelmingly conveyed to students in public schools.

It would be satisfying indeed if I or others had a solution for those awful problems that arise because of the exclusion of religion from the public school. But, in all probability, even if there were a consensus that something must be done, there is no one overarching resolution which would induce an agreement between the relevant parties.

But on at least one issue there would be agreement; the fact that the public schools of America should impart a good deal of information about the world's religions. The ignorance of Americans about the teaching of Islam became very vivid when Iran imprisoned fifty-two Americans for over one year. The abysmal lack of knowledge about the Muslim religion was also evident during the ten-year Iran-Iraq war. Americans, moreover, comprehend very little concerning the reasons why elements in the Muslim world desire to stop what they perceive to be the Westernization or the corruption of the Muslim world. America's role as a world power, assumed somewhat involuntarily at the end of World War II, will not decrease substantially even if the United States declines as a world economic power. It is therefore fitting, indeed imperative, that Americans understand the role which non-Christian religions continue to have in world history. The lack of knowledge in the United States of Buddhism, or of Chinese or Vietnamese history certainly contributed to the ill-starred intervention of the United States in the war between North and South Vietnam.

Clearly, objective teaching about the history and meaning of Judaism, Hinduism and African religions would be appropriate in America's public schools. And such instruction would clearly lead to the necessity of communicating facts about how Christianity supplements or supplants those religions.

Why is there apparently no strong movement toward adding objective instruction in the public schools about the history of world religions? Educators are wary about introducing any course related to religion, since it is likely to become controversial. The churches are hesitant to advocate instruction about other religions when the students are receiving no information about Christianity. And everyone associated with education and the government hesitates to inaugurate a course which is exclusively concerned with religion.

As a result, there is an impasse surrounding the introduction of anything related to religion in the public schools. The Supreme Court has forbidden Bible reading and prayers—and even a moment of silent meditation. The Congress has furnished the Equal Access Act, but this is a measure filled with ambiguities and is of very limited availability. And many, though not all, of the churches have acquiesced in the mandates of the Supreme Court which from 1947 to 1989 consistently and (in the Supreme Court's judgment) coherently outlawed any support or endorsement by the government of religion in the public schools.

Does the absence of any religious content in the public school impede religious bodies in the United States in their work to redefine the nation's public morality? It has to. Or at least it is a downward drag. The absence of religion in the public schools proclaims that the government has no affiliation with the teachings of any religion, and that it does not need to have those teachings communicated in any public institution. Government officials would probably reject this characterization of their position. They would proclaim that government is friendly to religion, that government depends on the values of religion and that, in the words of the *Zorach* decision, "this is a nation whose institutions presuppose a Supreme Being."

What can believers do to make the government, and especially the public schools, more responsive to that deep-down tradition in American life that moral agencies in American society, and not the government itself, make up the nation's public morality?

There are dozens of things that could be done. But the church is certainly under a handicap since it has little, if any, access to the public schools of the nation where, for millions of future citizens, the understanding of what America stands for is being developed.

CHAPTER 6

Religionists in America and Hunger in the World

The sight of human suffering, especially when it is preventable, is an agony for any human being. Because of the deepest instincts of human nature, every person has a sense of solidarity with every other person. That sense is deepened and made more central and crucial for a Christian because every believer in Christ sees the Redeemer Himself in the sufferings of any person. Christ made it clear in almost countless ways that when his followers deal with any other human being, they deal with Christ Himself. The story of the Good Samaritan is the essence of the love of all persons preached by Christ.

There has always been a strand of the Good Samaritan in the domestic and foreign policies followed by the United States. The concept of a war against poverty was in the minds of the original settlers in Boston and Plymouth Rock; they inherited the idea as an amalgam of Calvinist theology, the emphasis of the Old and the New Testament on helping the weak and the poor, and the notion that America is the promised land where there is and should be milk and honey for everyone.

But the idea that America should reach out to the dispossessed and the unfortunate has been followed only fitfully in the history of the United States. Like individuals, nations enter periods when their ideals become obscured and their moral aspirations clouded. Just as individuals sporadically embrace and follow both the best and the worst of their aspirations, so nations lunge from good to bad in unpredictable ways.

But at the core of America there is an aspiration, up to this moment not repudiated, which provides that America is different and better than any nation in the history of the world. America, the deep-seated ideal continuously tells us, has an obligation to be its brother's keeper. America is somehow the light unto all nations, the redeemer of mankind, the country which will at last deliver the earth from tyranny and repression.

Upon analysis, the dream, which is cloudy and vaguely religious, does not yield any logical and legal corollaries. But the idea of America's goodness and its moral mission to the world is more than a myth. It is not entirely the creation of prophets, poets, and politicians. America *is* different from other nations. It has streaks of virtue and goodness which some other nations do not possess. It has traditions which are not found in the histories of other nations. All of these characteristics are derived ultimately from the Christian and Jewish teachings which have always been at the heart of the idea and ideals of America. And even as those teachings become obscured in the national psyche, their essence somehow remains a part of the social and political assumptions of the nation.

The latent, seldom proclaimed but never repudiated feeling that America has a destiny to "do good" in the world offers enormous potential for a cause such as the alleviation of world hunger. But it can also lead to delusions, self-righteousness, and a sense of national arrogance. During the two generations of the cold war, Americans have boasted that they are the "saviors" of the "free world" and that America is the light of the world and the protector of dozens of nations and millions of people who otherwise would be conquered by the Communists. The deep-seated feeling of Americans that they are destined by God and by man to redeem the human race was a major source of the paranoia, the delusions, and the fantasies of the United States during those forty years, when some nations became free from colonialism. The United States, instead of helping them to a decent and democratic way of life, spent trillions of dollars on armies and nuclear weapons—all in the name of saving the "West" and these new nations from Communist aggression.

As the cold war fades away, America will be required to rethink what it has done in the world since it emerged as one of the superpowers at the end of World War II. Rethinking of fundamental priorities is always as difficult for nations as it is for individuals. There is no certainty that the United States will ever confront or confess error as to what it did to itself and to the world in the decades when the core of its foreign policy was the containment of Communism. But as the agony of the world's malnourished (800 million) and illiterate (1.3 billion) inhabitants becomes more undeniable and more urgent, the people of the United States, if not the politicians, will have to react to the appalling fact that the United States has failed to give leadership which recognizes and addresses their presence and their plight.

It has been clear for many years that, for the first time in the history of humanity, it is now possible to feed everyone in the world. Because of pestilence and plagues and other uncontrollable phenomena, in the past, the problem of famine was not solvable. Today, with the assistance of the United Nations Food and Agricultural Organization, the World Health Organization, and similar groups, the developed nations of the earth could, if only they really wanted to, ensure sufficient calories each day to the 5.2 billion persons in the world in 1991. The new miracles of agriculture and science will also, in all probability, be able to feed the universe when the population of the global village reaches a projected 8 billion people in the year 2025.

Through the years, America has attempted to extend its largess to the millions who are starving. In the 1950s, the U.S. Congress authorized the Food for Peace program. Conceived originally as a way to dispose of surplus agricultural crops, the Food for Peace program became a very worthwhile device to assist nations with an acute shortage of food. The United States contributed modestly, along with other nations, to UNICEF, collaborated with the United Nations Food and Agricultural Organization and the United Nations Development Bank. But all the initiatives by the United States have been sporadic, small, and done without any overall plan for the systematic reduction of hunger in the world.

Foreign aid was launched in the 1950s with a display of rhetoric about the moral and humanitarian mission of the United States in the world. For a time it appeared that the United States, which was the prime mover in the creation of the United Nations, might continue to extend its vast moral idealism to the creation of a world order where most people could feed their families. But foreign aid became unpopular in the Congress and in the country. Tales of corrupt dictators siphoning off the aid for their cronies and stories of U.S. aid being diverted to military purposes combined to persuade millions of Americans that aid to foreign countries was "money down a rat hole."

But the rhetoric and the dream of stopping starvation, a concept endemic to the American psyche, continued to surface. President Kennedy predicted in 1961 that within a decade the United States would go to the moon, and that within a generation no child on the earth would go to bed hungry. In 1974, President Gerald Ford and Secretary of State Henry Kissinger, morally compelled by Congressional demands to act, pledged to a meeting of the United Nations Food and Agricultural Organization in Rome that within ten years all of the children of the world would have an adequate diet.

Official rhetoric was less prominent in the 1980s but private organizations like Oxfam, Bread for the World, and UNICEF kept the dream alive. Pictures of starving children in Africa prompted Congress to give aid in sums which sounded generous but which, like almost all U.S. efforts through the years to relieve world hunger, were episodic, ad hoc, and non-systematic.

If Christian groups in America were made up of believers who agreed with St. John the Evangelist that no one can love God who neglects his neighbor's fundamental needs, would the Congress embrace a policy of working individually and through world agencies to end world hunger? The answer has to be yes. Indeed, of all the moral aspirations which America continues to embrace, the hope that the United States could cure world starvation is the most widely held. If there is any single moral objective which religious bodies in the United States could carry forward it is clearly the hope, endorsed by every religious and public interest group in America, that malnutrition at home and abroad be phased out.

There is no shortage (it should be noted) of churches and worshippers in America. In the 1980s, 344,000 churches and synagogues claimed 140 million adherents. Weekly attendance at religious exercises in the 1940s ranged between 30 and 32 percent of the members of a congregation. This number rose to about 50 percent in the late 1950s and leveled off at about 40 percent in the 1970s. In addition, some 30 million youngsters attended Sunday school or its equivalent.

With this intense religious dedication, why is the universally held aspiration of eliminating world hunger not being pursued? Are the churches too weak and ineffective in their presentations? Or are Americans so de-Christianized that they do not hear what all the religious groups in America are urging? After all, the young man in the gospel, told by Jesus to sell all of his wealth, walked away sad because he was rich.

Some will say, of course, that to speak of the needs in the world only in terms of eliminating hunger is an oversimplified and simplistic concept. They are correct, since the development of a nation means the introduction of all of the scientific, technological, medical, and agricultural information that has become available since the Industrial Revolution. But if believers in the moral values of the Judeo-Christian tradition concentrated on the necessity of providing bread to everyone—a duty that is so graphically taught in the Bible—the world would be changed in dramatic ways.

Some persons, when they are challenged to support a foreign policy that would lend or give more to the Third World, counter-attack by urging that the United States should take care of poverty at home before it shares its resources abroad. This approach is sometimes embraced by those who are to some extent disillusioned with foreign aid and frustrated as to how America's domestic problems can be solved. Indeed, those problems are acute. The number of poor people grew from 26 million in the late 1970s to 35 million in 1989. Federal appropriations for housing in the 1980s decreased from $27 billion to $8 billion—a drop that caused gruesome problems, including a shocking number of homeless persons in the richest country in the history of the world. Domestic poverty moreover, always impacts disproportionately on blacks and on children.

But however lamentable and unjustifiable poverty may be in the United States, the wretched conditions in parts of Asia, Africa, and Latin America cry out for a solution. And the wretchedness will almost certainly be worse in the year 2000. In that year, for the first time in human history, over half of humanity will be living in cities. Millions are migrating each year from rural areas into urban complexes looking for food, jobs, and schools for their children. Outside of every major city in Latin America, and elsewhere as well, there are vast shanty towns filled with misery, disease, and despair. Pope John Paul II has seen these vast cages for human beings and has protested in the strongest terms.

Hence, the question recurs: What can religious bodies in America do to alter the policies of their country so that the United States, along with the international community, can begin to provide bread for the world? The problem has become infinitely more complicated by the staggering new debts of nations in the Third World to lending entities in the developed countries and particularly in the United States. In

1989, Latin America had debts of over 400 billion dollars. Any attempt to pay even the interest on these immense debts skews the economies of nations like Brazil and Mexico. Worldwide, the problem is the same or worse. At the end of the 1980, the amount of money being transferred from the developing countries was larger than the amount developed nations sent to the underdeveloped countries! This is the exact reverse of what should be happening. Even if some variation of the plans prepared by Secretary of State James Baker and Secretary of the Treasury Nicholas Brady is adopted, the borrowing nations will be hobbled and even paralyzed by their obligation to repay loans which were given by U.S. banks, not to carry out some carefully crafted development plan, but for the financial convenience of American lending institutions, which had a vast surplus of money from the OPEC nations after those countries quintupled the price of oil in the 1970s.

A factor further complicating the problem of alleviating hunger in underdeveloped nations is the unbelievable amount of money spent by these nations on sophisticated military weapons. In the late 1980s, the total annual sum expended on weapons by the entire world was over \$950 billion. Although the United States and the USSR spent about two-thirds of that sum, the billions expended by small nations of Asia, Latin America, and Africa are astonishing. Clearly there are vast mercantile interests in the United States involved in the sale of tanks, military jets, and ammunition to nations that cannot afford such equipment—even if they needed it.

In view of all these interlocking factors, is it realistic to think that religious believers in the United States could, by persuasion and political pressure, bring into being a multi-faceted policy by the United States which would guarantee that families and children would receive each day at least that minimum number of calories which would prevent malnutrition and disease?

If there is a need to offer motives of self-interest before Americans will act politically to help foreigners, it can be persuasively argued that hungry hordes are a threat to the national security of America and of the developed nations. Even more realistically and pragmatically, there is the undeniable fact that if nations develop, they will be able to buy American consumer goods—at a time when the United States needs more foreign markets.

But self-interest alone is not adequate to impel the United States to alter its priorities and seek to abate hunger in the developing countries of the world. The fact is that some sacrifice is needed. The United States must make a decision that is idealistic and outgoing, as it did when it created the Peace Corps, the Food for Peace program, and foreign aid or AID.

Is America morally capable of reaching a decision, partly on moral grounds, that it should appropriate some billions of dollars so that 40,000 children worldwide will not die each day? Could some agency, or a series of domestic events, so move the American people that it would rescue the babies of the world as it rescued the banks after the scandals of the savings and loan institutions?

What kind of people live in the United States as America enters its third century? Has the idealism and the religious fervor characteristic of America for ten generations faded away? What kind of religion is communicated to the millions who worship every Sunday? What can America expect to see in the next century from the vast and astonishing array of churches in the land?

Is it possible that some new wave of religious devotion might arise which would persuade America that it must eliminate world hunger? As the cold war passes away, could the anti-communist energies of the churches be transformed to fighting hunger, disease, and illiteracy?

Although it is easy to criticize the churches for their lack of concern, or at least their lack of enthusiastic support, for efforts to phase out world hunger, it is possible that America would be even less involved in helping humanity if religious groups in this country had not been working diligently to make America a more moral nation. There have been clear religious motivations in many of the noble things America has done in its foreign policy since World War II. America's opposition to Communism has at least exalted the ideal of democracy and the sacredness of human rights. America has also been generous in receiving refugees and sending disaster relief when catastrophe occurs around the world.

But overall, America is the silent, and sometimes sullen giant. In 1989, the United States ranked only fifteenth out of seventeen nations that give foreign aid to the developing nations. The United States was, moreover, in arrears in its dues to the United Nations by some $500 million. Both the Reagan and the Bush administrations sought to cut back on what Congress appropriated for UNICEF. And, despite the desperate need for economic assistance, more than 50 percent of America's foreign aid was for military purposes.

Nations, like individuals, sometimes suddenly reform in certain respects; for unpredictable and unforeseen reasons. The United States has had moments of enlightenment when it changed its policies and entered a new era. It did this in 1964, when the Congress and the country adopted the Civil Rights Act and began a new era in American life. America responded to a perceived moral need in 1965, when it launched the war on poverty. And in 1970, America turned a corner on the environment, when it authorized the Environmental Protection Agency (EPA). In 1988, the Congress conceded that the federal government should not have detained 130,000 Japanese during World War II and authorized indemnification of $20,000 for each detainee. The 101st Congress enacted an unprecedented bill forbidding discrimination against millions of physically and mentally handicapped persons.

Why nations change and do the decent thing is almost as mysterious as why sinners repent and accept the grace of God. Some of the rhetoric about the place of civil religion in America seems to suggest that the American nation, like every human being, is under the direct guidance of God. Similar rhetoric about the role of God's providence implies or assumes that God is superintending the actions of the nation just as he does those of each person. God may in some remote way guide the destiny of nations, but he does it by inspiring and guiding the lives of men and women. Moral policies will not be adopted by a nation unless individual persons, leaders or followers, make such adoption possible.

One of the confounding facts in the problem of world hunger is that the United States government each year pays American farmers billions of dollars *not* to raise food. Contemporary U.S. farm policy began in the 1930s when the federal government, in order to stabilize the price of crops, paid farmers to set aside millions of acres of land from production. In the 1980s, despite the millions of acres that were not farmed, and for which farmers received billions of dollars, the United States raised gargantuan amounts of grain, corn, soy beans, and other crops.

If Kansas were keeping millions of acres out of production to benefit the farmers of Kansas while the farmers of Iowa were struggling against a drought and a pestilence, no one would tolerate the situation. But the United States is doing precisely that when it artificially props up the prices received by American farmers while allowing millions of families in the world to go without food.

Again, some will insist that the problem of global hunger is immense and that it cannot be solved by dismantling a series of farm policies which, despite their limitations, have produced a cornucopia of food products possibly never before seen in world history.

But at least the United States government could adopt a policy recommended by a presidential commission on world hunger in the administration of President Carter. That group recommended that the alleviation of hunger become the number one objective of U.S. foreign policy in third world nations. That was the thrust of the resolution on the Right to Food enacted by Congress in 1976. That resolution stated that it is the sense of Congress that the "need to combat hunger shall be a fundamental point of reference in the formulation and implementation of United States policy in all areas that bear on hunger."

Although the problem of hunger is complex, and in some ways intractable, it should be noted that two-thirds of those who are malnourished live in ten countries. In addition, several countries, such as China, have made enormous strides in the past thirty years in their efforts to furnish everyone with the basic necessities of nutrition. The problem is therefore solvable. The failure of humankind to arrive at a solution to the problem of hunger brings the deepest regret and guilt to everyone who sees the agony of parents watching their children die because the nourishment they need (abundant in the outside world) has not been brought to a particular community. The presence of malnutrition in almost 20 percent of the population of the world also tends to harden the attitudes and the consciences of those who live in affluence despite the misery of so many.

In the early 1970s, Reverend Arthur Simon, a Lutheran pastor, founded a Christian organization, Bread for the World, designed to lobby, work, and pray so that, quite literally, there would be bread for the world. As a member of the board of Bread for the World for several years, I saw firsthand the extraordinary impact which that group with some 60,000 members has had on American public policy. Bread for the World is completely ecumenical, political in the most sophisticated ways, and Christian in the fullest sense. If the vast numbers of Christians in America undertook to do the educating, the lobbying, and the praying which Bread for the World urges, the foreign policy of the United States would change in very significant ways. World hunger could be alleviated in twenty years or less.

How can the churches in America bring about such a result? No objective is more universal, less controversial, more admirable, and more achievable. The elimination of world hunger will not elicit the resistance brought on by the temperance movement to outlaw alcohol, or the pro-life movement to recriminalize abortion, or the movement to ban obscenity. Everyone desires the United States to undertake efforts immediately to make food available to everyone in the world.

Why then is the anguish of world hunger not being eased? Are the churches lax or lackadaisical in their efforts? Or do too many churches feel that they should preach the gospel but not get involved in anything that is even on the fringes of politics? Is the government insensitive to the problem of global hunger? Or is America really uncaring about world hunger despite all the piety from the churches and the posturing by the politicians?

America's inaction on global hunger seems to undercut every assertion by the United States that it is a nation based on a love of freedom and human dignity. How can the United States spend $300 billion per year on weapons designed to protect them from communism and refuse to spend a small fraction of that amount to save millions of children from death by starvation? Is American foreign policy the "theater of the absurd," in the phrase from Camus?

The earliest Christians in Roman times impressed the world to the point that people remarked, "see how they love one another." That designation would be earned again if Christians in America planned, lobbied for, and enacted a program which, in collaboration with all relevant international organizations, caused world hunger to go the way of leprosy, tuberculosis, and polio. Imagine the kudos for American Christians if fifty years from now historians could record that it was the Christians of America, working with all religious and public interest groups, who had developed and enacted a series of measures that made world hunger disappear.

Tenderness toward children is central to Judaism and Christianity. Christ dramatized the preciousness of a child and God's identification with children when he placed a child in the midst of his disciples and said that "anyone who welcomes one child like this for my sake is welcoming me" (Matthew 18:5). Do Americans, who love to insist that their country follows the Judeo-Christian tradition, really care for children? In 1989, nearly half of all black children in America lived in poverty; 68.3 percent of black children in households headed by women lived below the poverty line. Even more grim is the fact that Hispanic children in America who live in homes headed by women were slightly worse off than black youngsters in similar circumstances.

More appalling still is the fact that 40,000 children die needlessly each day. That is 15 million per year.

With a minimum of effort, the United States could prevent that slaughter of the innocents. Why are Americans who boast so publicly of their record for humanitarianism unable or unwilling to stop the preventable death each hour of the day of some 2,000 children?

CHAPTER 7

Alcohol, Tobacco, and Drugs

From the beginning of the American Republic, religious groups have been deeply involved in the enactment of legislation that curbs the use and sale of alcohol. Many of the strict and severe regulations controlling liquor have survived at every level of society. But the great experiment of Prohibition of all alcohol is now an all-but-forgotten instance of the misuse of ecclesiastical power to outlaw what one group of churches in America deemed to be sinful. It seems incredible today that two-thirds of both Houses of Congress and three-fourths of the states adopted the Eighteenth Amendment to the United States Constitution forbidding the sale or use of alcohol. The repeal of the Eighteenth Amendment by the adoption of the Twenty-first Amendment was a humiliating repudiation of the judgment and the jurisprudence of those Protestant denominations which used their ecclesiastical power to achieve a political objective.

One could argue with a good deal of evidence that the government should have continued to be strict in its control of "demon rum." In 1989, up to 18 million Americans were reported to be alcoholics or alcohol abusers. In 1986, alcohol was a contributing factor in 10 percent of work-related injuries and in 40 percent of traffic fatalities. Estimates of the numbers of deaths linked to the use of alcohol range from 50,000 to 200,000 per year. In 1983, according to the Justice Department's statistics, 54 percent of all jailed inmates convicted of serious crimes reported having used alcohol just prior to committing their offense.

But the temperance movement in the churches of America faded away after the Twenty-first Amendment, in effect, rejected the churches' approach to the problem of alcohol. There are still many barriers to the sale of alcohol such as heavy taxes, restricted hours for its sale, and some "dry" communities. But neither the churches nor the government have any substantial systematic campaign to stop the abuses against which the entire nation adopted the Volstead Act. Alcoholics Anonymous, the National Council on Alcoholism, and numerous similar groups educate about the dangers of alcohol, but the only new legal restriction on the use of alcohol was the raising of the minimum age for the purchase of liquor from 18 to 21.

Presumably the nation concluded, when it ratified the Twenty-first Amendment, that a total ban on a dangerous and addicting substance like alcohol cannot work because of the widespread craving for it, and because it is a substance which, unlike tobacco and narcotics, is not per se harmful. The re-legalization of alcohol came about because of a consensus at that time—and now—that the government cannot control the distribution of a substance when such attempted control leads to widespread violations of the law.

Curiously, the churches have never initiated a crusade against the use of tobacco as they did against alcohol. It was the medical profession, the American Cancer Society, and public health authorities that brought out the insidious and fatal consequences of nicotine. It is widely known that 360,000 persons die prematurely each year because of cancer or other diseases brought on or aggravated by smoking.

The war against the sale of tobacco has not featured any visible participation by religious organizations. Church groups in the Third World are now protesting vigorously against the massive advertising of cigarettes done by U.S. tobacco interests in Asia and elsewhere. The tobacco industry, seeing their sales in the United States decline drastically as the number of smokers has dropped to 52 million, is frenetically creating the addiction to nicotine in the lives of millions of people in the Philippines, China, Taiwan, and similar countries.

Efforts to discourage or tax such foreign sales have failed. Even the warning of the surgeon general on cigarette packages, required by federal law in the United States, need not be carried on the ads or the packages which are sold overseas.

It is heartrending to see in Third World nations some of the most sophisticated medical treatment for radiation and chemotherapy for those who have contracted cancer from smoking, while vast millions in these countries lack the fundamentals of primary health care. This is a situation which the United States Congress could control. At least it could require that U.S. tobacco companies, in their sales to the millions in the underdeveloped countries who do not now smoke, disclose the information which they are now required to reveal in the United States.

The World Health Organization considers tobacco the largest preventable cause of sickness in the world. Every thirteen seconds there is a death from tobacco-related diseases; some 2 million per year, nearly 5 percent of all deaths.

When one looks at the range of activities of American church bodies with respect to legal/moral problems in America, it is anomalous that the churches do little about the use of tobacco, from which 1,000 Americans die prematurely every day.

The tobacco industry spends some $2 billion in advertisements each year. The industry agreed to withdraw ads for tobacco from radio and television after a ruling by the Federal Communications Commission that if tobacco ads were allowed, the electronic media would be required, under the Fairness Doctrine, to allow public interest ads pointing out the dreadful medical consequences of smoking. When the sale of tobacco plummeted after these public interest ads were shown, the tobacco industry allowed Congress to ban ads for tobacco-related products on television and radio.

It seems clear that a program of basic education about the evils of tobacco would have a substantial and prompt effect. The influence of the tobacco industry, and the attraction of the media to the money they obtain from ads designed to attract the young to smoking continue to prohibit any serious curbing of ads for cigarettes. The notion that there is a First Amendment issue of free speech involved in the banning of ads for cigarettes is not really true, since the Congress could make tobacco a controlled substance as it has done with marijuana, cocaine, and heroin.

The Congress could also adopt a less drastic remedy and forbid all print ads for cigarettes. That is the recommendation of the American Medical Association and the surgeon general during the Reagan administration, C. Everett Koop, M.D. In 1988, Dr. Koop testified to the Congress that more Americans would die that year from smoking— 350,000—than were killed in all of World War II. The National Institute on Drug Abuse has reported that the nicotine in tobacco is "six to eight times more addicting than alcohol."

The tobacco industry recognizes that if it is to survive it will have to get young people to start to smoke; virtually no adults take up the cigarette habit. The advertising budget for cigarettes is directed at youth, women, and especially Hispanic women. The ads invariably associate smoking with youthful vigor, good health, and professional success.

Many, though not all, constitutional experts assert that the Congress could constitutionally forbid advertising for cigarettes. Congress can ban misleading or deceptive ads and, it can be argued, every ad for tobacco is deceptive, since every contact with tobacco is injurious.

What then is the best moral approach to the use and sale of narcotics? The 1980s saw an explosion of anger and action over the sale and use of illegal drugs. The policies adopted by the United States are riddled with ambiguities, contradictions, and hysteria. No one denies the seriousness of the problem. In 1989, for example, the costs of intensive hospital care for crack-addicted babies totalled $2.5 billion. Florida will spend in $700 million in three years for health care, social services, and special education to prepare for kindergarten 17,500 infants born in 1987 and exposed to cocaine.

But the problem of drugs is small in relation to that of alcohol and tobacco. In 1985, according to the National Council on Alcoholism, 3,562 people were known to have died from the use of all illegal drugs. An estimated 35 to 40 million Americans consume illegal drugs.

Police now make about 750,000 arrests per year for violations of the drug laws, or less than 2 percent of all users. The arrests have swamped court dockets. In 1986, drug law violations in Washington, D.C. accounted for 52 percent of all felony indictments, up from 13 percent in 1981. In 1986, drug offenses accounted for 135,000 (23 percent) of the 583,000 felony convictions in state courts. State and local agencies spent at least $2 billion in 1988 to incarcerate drug offenders.

Ironically, the greatest beneficiary of all of this law enforcement has been organized crime. More than half of all the revenues of organized crime are believed to derive from trafficking in illicit drugs; estimates range from $10 billion to $50 billion per year.

The consequences of the war on drugs are vast and dramatic. The number of persons in federal and state prisons has doubled in the past fifteen years. The total now is in the range of 700,000—the largest number in U.S. history, and a number that is larger absolutely and proportionately than in any other democracy in the world. The United States will, moreover, be spending billions for more jails; one-third to one-half of the inmates of these institutions will be there for the use or sale of narcotics. The volume of drug-related criminal cases has changed and distorted the way in which courts in America operate.

Attempts to interdict the importation of controlled substances confront almost insuperable difficulties. The profits are so excessive for the growers and the traffickers that they will take all kinds of risks. It is doubtful whether all the power of the Coast Guard, customs service officials, and even U.S. military forces can stop the drug lords from Colombia getting their product into the ghettos of American cities.

The idea of decriminalizing the use and sale of narcotics is almost unthinkable in the present atmosphere of hysteria and political frenzy. But Ethan A. Nadelmann, Professor of Politics and Public Affairs at Princeton University, made the case for legalization in *Science Magazine* in 1989. Logically, there are strong arguments that the present policies are counterproductive and are leading to more damaged and ruined lives than decriminalization would do.

But there is fear everywhere that if drugs were legalized they would and could become as popular as alcohol. Such fears are so widely held today that there is seemingly no likelihood that drugs will be decriminalized in the foreseeable future. The vast majority of Americans feel that cocaine, heroin, and other illicit substances are hazardous and should be banned and eliminated by the use of whatever criminal sanctions are necessary. The anti-drug mood of the country was intensified by the presidential campaign of 1988. And it is likely to last through the presidential campaign of 1992.

But there are signs that the ineffective and enormously expensive policies that are now being pursued may yield to a more realistic assessment of the problem and the possibilities. Complicating this picture is the fact that about 25 percent of all AIDS cases in the United States and Europe are thought to be contracted from illegal intravenous drug use. The governments of England, Australia, The Netherlands, and several other nations have attempted to stop the spread of AIDS by instituting free syringe-exchange programs. But governments in the United States have resisted initiatives of this kind on the grounds that it would encourage the use of illegal drugs.

Professor Nadelmann makes some persuasive arguments that the legalization of cocaine and heroin would not necessarily lead to a greater use. A heavy tax could be levied on their sale, warning labels could be required, sales could be restricted to certain places and times, and crackdowns on driving under the influence of drugs could be carried out.

But the chances of legalization seem slim indeed. Clearly, there is absolutely no political movement in that direction. Those advocating decriminalization always admit the uncertainty and the dangers in their proposal, but make them nonetheless, because the present situation is increasingly impossible to justify or even endure. If anything is to happen it will have to happen because of nongovernmental forces.

The Protestant churches, which once brought a constitutional amendment to ban alcohol to fruition, have said little if anything about what the law can do to remedy the abuses of tobacco and drugs. Legal restrictions on the sale of tobacco here and abroad could be imposed if there were a lobby to do so—a group organized like public interest groups devoted to the protection of the environment, the consumer, the elderly, and the handicapped. Action for Smoking Health (ASH) and similar groups do exactly that, but they have not yet succeeded.

There are scores of groups seeking to improve the law's handling of narcotics. Virtually every one of them wants better law enforcement. Any group designed to legalize drugs would surely be resisted and even scoffed at. But citizen lobbyists should at least point out the inconsistencies in America's policies on addictive substances. The United States helps American cigarette companies to open markets to sell tobacco to those nations which send drugs to the United States. More people will die in Thailand from the effects of American cigarettes than will die in America from heroin imported from Southeast Asia. The United States has become the primary purveyor in the world of disease and death by tobacco.

The absence of the churches from the struggle over narcotics— except perhaps to cheer on tougher law enforcement—is another sign and symbol of the privatization of religion in America. In this instance, the churches themselves, chastened and humbled by the repudiation of their policies on alcohol, are in effect stating by their silence that there is no one Christian position on the law's handling of narcotics. But it is sad and melancholy to see the nation's religious leaders, in essence, assent to a policy of stopping the importation and sale of drugs with sanctions and penalties as harsh as can be conceived. That policy has produced violence between competing drug dealers in the nation's ghettos and shoot-outs with the police.

America's agony over hard drugs may go on for years, even decades. The laws against drug dealers and drug users will get more and more draconian. The death penalty may actually be carried out for someone selling drugs. The political rhetoric against drugs will continue to escalate, making it impossible for any opening to new solutions to come from political leaders of any ideology.

The horror stories will multiply. The billions of dollars spent on the problem will mount. All the options will look increasingly unattractive. The thousands of drug dealers in jail will be replaced by thousands of others on the streets. It is possible that in due course, even the police and the prosecutors will give up.

Underlining all the vast discussion of the nation's attempts to control drugs is the inexorable conclusion: there has to be a better way. The religious bodies of America can and should be contributing to the development of that "better way." Whether they will or not is quite uncertain. The churches have no illusion that they can command the type of following which they secured for the adoption of the Eighteenth Amendment. After the demise of the Moral Majority, and the decline in the power of the religious right, church bodies in America are inclined to speak with humility and with appropriate deference to others in a religiously pluralistic society. Nonetheless, the churches, like countless Americans, tremble at the possibility that America could turn itself into a police state through its concern over drugs, mandatory testing, oaths not to take drugs required of students who receive financial aid, and similar measures.

In a fallen world, there will always be persons who will become addicted to substances like alcohol, tobacco, and drugs. The function of government is to minimize that number by education, by example, and by enforcement of the laws. The American government, perhaps more than other democracies, has always assumed the function of inculcating virtue into its citizens. Helping to prevent addiction to dangerous substances is surely one of the finest moral duties of government. It is a duty which supplements the task of all religious bodies, which should be unanimous in urging all persons to refrain from any excessive use of alcohol, nicotine, or drugs. In this area, there are few, if any, clashes between the aspirations of religion and government in America. There is a total blending of the objectives of church and state. The churches stumbled in their approach to alcohol, seeking to turn America into a theocracy on the one issue of alcohol. But the nation needs the religious zeal and the moral convictions that lobbied through the Eighteenth Amendment to be applied to the liberation from the addiction to liquor, nicotine, and narcotics that the citizens of America yearn for.

CHAPTER 8

Morality and Prisons

Several shattering events in the 1970s and 1980s caused Americans to panic over crime. The number of serious crimes did not rise rapidly or substantially, but for many observers the presence of gangsters, drug merchants, youth gangs, and even white-collar criminals seemed to be destroying American life. For millions, a response seemed to be imperative.

The response against crime was related to the reaction by countless persons in America—many from organized religion—who rose up against the relaxation of laws regarding pornography, homosexuality, and marijuana. The reaction against criminals has been immense. The federal government and many states abolished parole for prisoners and decreed stiff sentences for crimes against property.

By the end of 1989 there were 731,978 persons in federal and state prisons and 341,851 in local jails, for a total of 1,055,829. That number has increased enormously. In 1972 there were about 200,000 inmates in federal and state prisons, with less than 150,000 in local jails.

Billions of dollars for new prisons will create in the 1990s a vast array of institutions which are still euphemistically called "houses of correction."

There apparently exists in America the vague feeling that since the churches and the schools are not conveying the moral attitudes which will stop and deter crime, the government must crack down and seek to deter, punish, and correct those who will not respect the rights of others.

The awful truth, of course, is that there is uncertainty and ambiguity about what America is doing to its criminals. A mood of rage has arisen in the country—a mood which cannot be changed by reason, by statistics, or, up to the present moment, by the enormous financial burden on the taxpayer for incarceration at an annual cost of up to $30,000 per inmate per year.

The jurisprudential theory behind locking up more and more criminals is at best murky, and at worst false. The rate of recidivism for prisoners is very high. The institutions tend to debase and degrade rather than reform and rehabilitate. The legal and civil penalties on former prisoners are severe. In thirty-nine states a former felon can lose his right to vote, in twenty-seven the right to hold public office, and in thirty-six states a felony conviction provides a ground for divorce.

But the mythology continues—punish the malefactors and crime will decrease. The juggernaut rolls on. Pressure builds for legislators to write more draconian laws, for prosecutors to be tough, for juries to be severe and for judges to hand out sentences that are longer than ever before.

The punitive and revengeful mood in the nation about criminals is new. Perhaps Americans, consciously or otherwise, feel the nation's standards of personal honesty have declined and that the government must fill in for what private agencies like the family and the churches are not doing. Whatever the underlying reasons, the situation is new and ominous.

Here are some startling statistics about prisons in 1989:

1. During the last 8 years some $15 billion has been spent on the construction of new prisons in the United States.

2. Prisons in 38 states and the District of Columbia are under orders from federal and state courts to improve their facilities so that they will not be in violation of the Eighth Amendment's ban on "cruel and unusual punishment."

3. The unbelievable increase in the number of prisoners is made graphic in the attached chart from the American Correctional Association.

4. The United States incarcerates twice as many persons as Canada, four times as many as West Germany. Only two industrialized countries lock up more people than the United States—the Soviet Union and South Africa.

Years	US population in millions	Number of prisoners	Prisoners per 100,000 population
1988	246	582,000	237
1987	244	546,000	224
1983	235	420,000	180
1980	277	321,000	142
1970	203	196,000	97
1960	179	213,000	119
1950	151	166,000	110
1940	132	174,000	132
1930	123	148,000	121
1925	106	93,000	88
1918	92	75,000	82
1900	76	57,000	75
1890	63	45,000	71
1870	40	33,000	83
1860	31	19,000	60
1850	23	7,000	30
1840	17	4,000	24

5. Up to 50% of all offenders in prison were involved in some drug-related crime.

6. Blacks now make up 61% of incarcerated juveniles, 42% of the nation's prisoners on death row, and 41% of those in local jails.

Clearly all religious bodies in America have not been a part of the recent sharp crackdown on persons convicted of crimes. The churches have been to some extent on the sidelines, furnishing chaplains for the prisons, but having no real role in the radical change in the ways legislators and judges treat criminals.

Religious periodicals point out the elements of racism in the situation as, for example, the fact that 46 percent of all inmates in federal prisons in 1985 were black. Religious voices also urge that those who commit crime in the suites should be punished like those who engage in crime in the streets.

But religious groups are as perplexed and troubled as everyone else at the amazing rise in the number of persons who are incarcerated. Few think that this is the wisest course to follow. But the national panic over drugs and crime has, in ways almost beyond reason, assumed a life of its own. Will the number of persons sent to jail double once again in the decade or two ahead? What will America do if the new army of former prisoners turns out to be a powerful and dangerous group of felons? Lock them up again? Or do something more drastic to them?

The unprecedented increase in prisoners is obviously linked to narcotics. The desire for cocaine and crack is intense and immense. It is clearly beyond the understanding of most people. Why, in the most affluent nation in human history, where education and leisure in manifold forms are available to so many, is there such a widespread craving for mind-altering and mood-changing drugs? Has a segment of society been so turned off by the materialism and the consumerism that they want to blank it out of their souls by seeking a tranquilizing substance that will make them "happy"?

All of this is baffling to almost every American over the age of thirty-five. Millions taking illegal and dangerous drugs, causing thousands to go to jail, constitutes an entirely new experience in the life of the nation. Has something fundamentally different occurred in American society that suggests a sea change in what is accepted as the basic morality of the nation? Or will the close connection between the widespread use and sale of narcotics and the doubling of the number going to jail be a phenomenon which will pass away?

No one knows. And everyone is deeply concerned. The presence of narcotics and all that that presence connotes for American society is clearly one of the most fundamental legal/moral issues in America today.

The politicians have tended to exploit the issue for their own purposes by urging young people not to take drugs; they have similarly railed against the drug merchants and have enacted enormously harsh laws against their very existence.

But few raise the essential questions of morality and religion—why is it wrong or immoral to take narcotics which make you "feel good"? Young people often assert that they take drugs for the same reasons that their parents drink alcohol. Many parents ridicule the analogy but the question remains: should the government be in the business of banning all or most mood changing substances? And if so, why?

Posing the question points up the profound vacuum which exists in public policy as to the employment of sound religious, moral, and psychological reasons for deterring citizens from conduct which is injurious to them but not necessarily harmful to the common good. Should there be crimes where there are no victims? Putting it differently, should sin be a crime? That is one of the most tormenting problems for the church and for the state in America today.

The basic issue comes to this: Does the government have a right to employ the values of religion in deciding on the appropriate punishment for persons who violate the law? And if the government does not have that right, then how can it punish people whose conduct may harm themselves but does no injury to others?

This issue contains several sub-issues not all of which are clear in the minds of Americans or in the assumptions underlying American law. It may be that some Americans are afraid to explore the question because they might discover that the emperor (the government) has no clothes. If the government is silently operating on the notion of personal sin rather than the idea of the public good, the government will have fewer and fewer resources as the churches change or weaken their notions of sin. As a result, the government's power to punish its citizens will become confined to those acts which clearly affect the right or the privacy of other persons unwilling to participate in the conduct.

Many religious persons shrink from the idea of a government that acts as a police officer only when there is conduct which openly violates the rights of the third party. Christians in America have a tradition of expecting the government to inculcate virtue into the lives of its citizens. The government in America is not value-free. But the question has to be asked; whose values does the government have a right to adopt?

The question of which moral values the government can or should follow lies at the root of many of the great problems that now face the Congress and the country. It is acutely present in the problem of the appropriate sanction for individuals who commit crimes which derive from, or at least are aggravated by, the dreadfully deprived lives of the violators. When unemployed high school dropouts who come from fragmented homes engage in robbery or assault does it do anyone any good to lock up these persons in cells for twenty years? The cost of such a practice can be astronomical, but more importantly, it can dehumanize, even brutalize both the prisoners and the prison guards.

But the contemporary climate of opinion in America concerning crime will not abide any approach that looks like "coddling." The attitude of hostility and revenge toward law-breakers is pervasive, regardless of any and all mitigating circumstances.

It may appear to be naive to suggest that the churches have a duty to try to alter the hard-line positions against criminals which now dominate the American way of thinking. But it has to be recognized that the national mood which kept one million Americans in prison in 1989 cannot be rationalized or justified by any coherent set of moral or political principles. That phenomenon is one of the results of the ambivalence and confusion which characterize America's approach at this moment to several basic legal/moral problems.

The facts about America's fixation with incarcerating persons are nothing short of gruesome. The National Council on Crime and Delinquency (NCCD) reports that a century ago the number of persons incarcerated on any given day was about 120 per 100,000. Today it is about 300 per 100,000—almost a threefold increase. In addition to the number confined at the end of 1989, there were 2.5 million adults and juveniles on probation or parole.

The vast increase in prisoners has occurred at a time when the crime rate has been fairly constant. The crime rate, despite the vast increase in the number of persons confined to jail, went up in 1988 by 1.8 percent. That figure reversed a declining trend that began in 1981, according to the Bureau of Justice Statistics of the U.S. Justice Department. The total number of crimes in 1988 according to the Justice Department was 35.9 million.

The doubling in the number of prisoners is not attributable primarily to an increase in the number of persons sentenced, but to longer sentences for those who are convicted. The longer sentences and the withdrawal of parole means that states like California will again double their prison population by 1995. Thus California, which already has the largest number of inmates in the country, will have an adult prison population in 1995 of 110,000.

In recent years the proportion of black and Hispanic people admitted to prisons has doubled. The NCCD stated in 1987 that "more than half of all black males will be arrested and imprisoned before they reach their thirtieth birthday." Hispanics are incarcerated at a rate three times higher than whites.

Although it is often assumed that most prisoners have engaged in violence, the fact is that only 30 percent of those now sent to prison have been convicted of violence—a rate which has actually declined since 1926.

A book published in 1988 entitled *After Conviction*, by Richard Goldfarb and Linda Singer, reported that the consensus among prison officials is that only 10 to 15 percent of all inmates really need to be incarcerated to protect the public from physical injury.

The average rate of return to prison after three years, the time when most ex-convicts are likely to return, has regularly been about 30 to 35 percent.

Do prisons achieve the result the politicians and the public hope for? The Rand Corporation, in a 1986 study, compared groups of felons sent to jail with carefully matched groups granted probation and found that those sentenced to prison had significantly higher rates of rearrest after release than those on probation.

The only certain way to cut down on overcrowded prisons is to shorten the sentences. The length of time which convicts serve has increased significantly in the recent past; the number of years chosen by the legislators have been the arbitrary result of public opinion perceived to be calling for tougher sentences. If the sentences are not reduced, prison populations will continue to rise indefinitely into the twenty-first century.

The extraordinarily large use of prisons in the last decade is the product of vindictiveness, rage at crime in the streets, and the supposition or the myth that deterrence will result from harsher penalties.

If moral arguments will not change the desire of many Americans to incarcerate wrongdoers, the staggering financial costs may induce the country to reconsider its new belief in prisons.

The National Council on Crime and Delinquency in 1987 estimated that the construction of each new bed in a prison costs $268,000. Assuming a constant $25,000 yearly operating cost per inmate with a 2 percent inflation rate annually, taxpayers will spend over one million dollars for each prisoner they incarcerate over a thirty-year period. The exploding costs of prison construction and maintenance will almost certainly compromise the funding of educational, medical, and other essential public services.

Clearly, the only solution for the problem of prison overcrowding is the shortening of sentences. The key question in this area has really never been examined: How much time in prison is enough to carry out the purposes of the system which presumably wants to punish, to deter, and to reform. The awful truth is that research on this crucial and central question is most inadequate.

A large number of religious denominations have issued statements on criminal justice in recent years. In 1970 the World Council of Churches, after a conference on penal policies with delegates from fourteen countries, issued a report critical of prison practices. In the United States, the Lutheran Church in America, the Episcopal Church of America, and some religious orders have made studies critical of American criminal justice.

One of the most comprehensive statements made on prisons was the declaration, "The Reform of Correctional Institutions," issued in November, 1973, by the United States Catholic Conference. In a 7,000-word document the 300 Catholic bishops of the United States argued that rehabilitation, not punishment, should be the primary concern of correctional institutions. In a strong and even radical statement, the bishops criticized large institutions and, in urging individualized treatment, openly went against the trend which was then beginning by stating that "bigger, better, more modern buildings are not the answer."

The bishops were blunt in their approach: "There is general agreement among qualified commentators that the correctional institutions of our land have, in most cases, failed in the matter of rehabilitation." The U.S. Catholic Conference buttressed its statement by twenty-two specific recommendations directed at the government and at the laity.

The Catholic bishops were prescient in their statement in 1973, and hit hard at the principal misuses of the prison system which were then beginning.

In 1978, in an even stronger statement entitled "Community and Crisis," the Catholic bishops indicted America's jails in these words: "Our present prison system does not reflect Christian values. Numerous studies document the fact that prisons are dehumanizing and depersonalizing . . . Prison life . . . provides the opportunity for an education in crime rather than for rehabilitation."

It is hard to imagine a more sweeping condemnation of the present penal system in America than is contained in the Catholic bishops' statements in 1973 and 1978. In a stinging rejection of America's vengeance-based retributive justice system, the hierarchy reminded every American that "in efforts to reduce and prevent crime, believers have to strive to exemplify the attitudes of Christ our Lord, who loved his enemies, who forgave those who persecuted and executed him, and who taught that love and forgiveness are the only forces that can overcome evil and hatred."

A wide range of religious organizations have issued statements on prisoners similar to the pronouncements of the U.S. Catholic bishops. There is a broad consensus that prisons are not working, that there is a spirit of revenge operating in the land, and that the United States has no coherent moral policy in the way it treats those who are convicted of crime.

There are some painful questions to be asked about the dreadful scene of over one million people deprived of their liberty in ways condemned by most of organized religion. Are the state and the citizenry so vindictive and vengeful that they simply do not hear the voice of religious groups in America? Or are the blindnesses caused by materialism and selfishness so deep that the people follow the government rather than the church when the government reinforces all of the feelings of distaste and disgust which people have for those who annoy and anger them?

The United States has certainly committed its share of "sins" in its public policies. But in a certain sense its failure to help to feed the hungry of the world and its over-reactive hostility to Communism were sins of omission. But when America locks up over one million of its own citizens, detains them for longer periods than ever before in American history and then releases them, humiliated and degraded, into a world for which they have not been trained or prepared, one has to say that these are sins of commission.

The churches are obviously deeply concerned about the disorders in the policies which the United States has adopted in the recent past with regard to persons convicted of a crime. But if churches are unable to modify or mitigate the harshness of America's new attitudes toward lawbreakers, at least the churches could help in organizing groups which would visit and comfort people in prison. There is nothing more central to the gospel. Christ said (Matthew 25:36): "I was ill and you comforted me, in prison and you came to visit me. Then the just will ask him: Lord, when did we visit you when you were ill or in prison? The king will answer them: I assure you, as often as you did it for one of my least brothers, you did it for me."

There is violence in America—perhaps worse in some ways than in some other countries. It is more prevalent among the least educated, the poorest housed, and those who are unemployed, or under-employed. The dreadful penalty of being deprived of one's liberty descends on members of this group far more than on those who have more advantages. That of course is one more reason why religious groups should be deeply involved in the lives and futures of those individuals who are charged with crimes.

Imagine what the impact would be in America and throughout the world if groups of believers in America regularly visited thousands of prisoners, helped them obtain an education, and informally "adopted" them after their release. This sign of Christian charity and compassion would restore the sense of dignity in many criminals, edify countless observers, and demonstrate that even if religious groups in America cannot control public policy as to the way guilty defendants should be treated, at least believers in America can reach out personally and institutionally to the last, the lowest, and the least in America.

If it is true, as Dostoyevski said, that you can judge the quality of civilization in a country by the state of its prisons, the United States is in deep trouble.

CHAPTER 9

America's Addiction to Guns

Is there some penchant for violence in the American psyche? The level of homicides each year (usually committed with handguns) exceeds that of any nation in the world. The fact that at least 60 million persons possess guns gives some indication of the potential for further violence. Despite continued pressure from religious and public interest groups there seems to be little likelihood that the number of handguns or the murders in which they are used will be substantially curbed.

Unlike neighboring Canada, the United States is unable or unwilling to place restraints on guns in the possession of adults. The National Rifle Association, a powerful group with 3 million members and a very substantial budget, is the principal tangible reason why proposals for federal gun control have always been defeated or gutted. But there is a larger reason—the belief apparently held by millions of Americans that one can shoot to kill an intruder in one's home, even if it is clear that he wants to steal property and not destroy lives. Law enforcement officials are not allowed in American law to shoot to kill persons suspected of property crimes, even if otherwise they would escape. But somehow millions of Americans think that they are morally permitted to protect their home even if they kill someone in the process.

The origins and the depth of America's love affair with guns has been explored in a copious literature. But no satisfactory psychological or theological explanation has ever been reached. Other nations like Japan, England, in fact most nations of the world, stand aghast at the death by guns in America—a problem unknown in any other country.

Did this streak of violence begin with the slaughter of the Indians? Or is it the residue of the decades during which Americans settled the "wild west" and organized a system of self-appointed vigilantes to keep law and order? Or is it the result of countless movies which crudely portray the victory of the "good guys" over the "bad guys" by guns, violence, and terrorism?

Until rather recently some of those questions could be categorized as academic, since violence in America was deemed to be concentrated in a very small part of the population, largely isolated from mainstream America.

Time magazine, in its issue of July 17, 1989, features the photos of 464 Americans who were killed by handguns in the week of May 1–7, 1989. Twenty-six pages of pictures and profiles of almost 500 persons killed in one week should have devastated America. But the carnage continues. *Time* concluded its story with this question: "How can America think of itself as a civilized society when day after day the bodies pile up amid the primitive crackle of gunfire across the land?"

Guns take more American lives in two years than did the entire Vietnam War. Only automobile accidents (with 48,700 deaths per year) surpass shootings as the leading cause of injury-induced fatalities. Gunshot deaths have roughly doubled since 1938.

In a February, 1989, Cable News Network-*Time* magazine poll, 84 percent of Americans were of the opinion that gun violence is becoming a bigger problem. A majority felt that the National Rifle Association had "too much influence" in keeping gun control laws from being passed. But in the same poll 84 percent of the public endorsed the view that "people have a right to own a gun." And only 20 percent agreed with the idea that a law should be enacted which would prevent any person from having a gun. But in every poll over the last several years, strong majorities have expressed a desire for tougher gun control and mandatory registration for all firearms.

By any norm, the United States engages in more violence by guns than any other nation. The statistics are incredible:

1. Since 1974 an estimated 50 million handguns have entered the private sector. If this rate continues there will be more than 100 million handguns in the possession of Americans in the year 2000.

2. Assuming that homicide rates remain at approximately their current rates, a child born in Atlanta will have one chance in 25 of

being murdered, in Washington, D.C., one chance in 36, and in New York City, one chance in 60.

During the Reagan administration the possibility of gun control experienced bleak years. After the attempted assassination of President Reagan, a short time after the assault with a gun on Pope John Paul II, there was some hope that the two world leaders might work to bring about laws that would curb the sale of guns. But President Reagan, a lifelong member of the National Rifle Association, remained unconvinced that laws curbing guns would be useful.

Five presidential commissions have reinforced the majority view of the public. In 1965, the Commission on Law Enforcement and the Administration of Justice, appointed by President Johnson, recommended that states should enact laws prohibiting certain categories of persons such as drug addicts, mental incompetents, persons with a history of mental disturbance, and persons convicted of certain offenses from buying, owning, or possessing firearms. This Commission also recommended that each state should require the registration of all handguns, rifles, and shotguns; and that if after five years, some states still had not enacted such laws, Congress should be required to pass a federal firearms registration act that would be operative in those states.

The Commission, which was chaired by Mr. Nicholas Katzenbach, also recommended that each state require a person to obtain a permit before he could either possess or carry a handgun. And the Commission recommended a continuing effort to find less deadly weapons to replace the handgun, so that the victims of guns would be merely incapacitated and not murdered.

The Presidential Commission on Civil Disorders, created by President Johnson in 1967 and chaired by Otto Kerner, made recommendations like those of the Katzenbach study. The Kerner Commission, in a report which has been widely cited, firmly stated that federal legislation on handguns is essential, and that both local and state governments should enact laws controlling the storage of firearms and ammunition in order to diminish the possibilities of theft.

In 1968, the National Commission on the Causes and Prevention of Violence, chaired by Dr. Milton Eisenhower, concluded that the only way to reduce gun violence in America is to diminish sharply the number of handguns in civilian hands. The Eisenhower Commission called for the establishment of minimum standards for state firearm control systems, and a national standard for handgun licensing. The report also recommended a federally financed program to purchase handguns from private citizens and to grant amnesty to persons turning over handguns which were illegally possessed.

Another commission on the reform of federal criminal laws, chaired by former California Governor Edmund G. Brown, recommended that Congress ban the production and possession of, and trafficking in, handguns, with exceptions only for military and law-enforcement officials. The Brown Commission recommended the registration of all firearms.

The National Advisory Commission on Criminal Justice Standards and Goals, chaired by Russell W. Peterson, recommended that all existing laws relating to handguns be strenuously enforced. It further recommended that states undertake publicity campaigns to educate the public fully about laws regulating the private possession of handguns. The Peterson Commission, unlike its predecessors, urged an extended prison term with a maximum sentence of 25 years for committing a felony in the possession of a handgun.

The fact that virtually none of the recommendations of these five presidential commissions were enacted, indicates the depth and the vehemence with which Americans desire to retain their guns; and that there is some force that believes in the possession of guns which does not bow to public opinion, nor to the rational and well-thought-out conclusions and recommendations of prestigious presidential commissions.

Guns have always held a prominent role in American life. A survey made in Jamestown in the year 1624, reveals that there was a firearm for each colonist. But unlike Switzerland (where the Constitution requires that able-bodied men keep weapons in their homes), America almost inevitably turns to violence when firearms are present. Indeed, the impact of the gun is enormous. The gun has appeared to be a necessary element of masculinity in traditional American life. For many reasons, the gun is somehow linked to manhood.

No substantial legislative activity with regard to firearms occurred at the state level until around 1900. No proposals at the federal level were offered until after World War I. In 1927, Congress enacted a law prohibiting the mailing of concealable firearms to private individuals. In 1927, the first national crime commission recommended more stringent uniform state laws. The first serious discussion of a proposed federal role in firearms regulation came in the early 1930s, when the national fear of gangsters, personified by John Dillinger, prompted federal proposals to ban the submachine gun.

The National Firearms Act of 1934, followed by the Federal Firearms Act of 1938, constituted the first and only significant attempts to impose federal controls on the commerce and possession of a broad spectrum of firearms. The actual thrust of the bills was not, however, a severe restriction on the availability of guns, since the federal law of 1938 was shepherded through the Congress by the National Rifle Association!

The objective of the 1938 legislation was to create an independent federal policy banning the receipt of firearms by a group of people deemed to be the criminal class of society. The legislation was, however, inadequate and deficient in many respects, and was further crippled by a tradition of little or lax enforcement by the Internal Revenue Service.

It is generally thought that the assassination of President Kennedy on November 22, 1963, was the catalyst for the gun control legislation that finally passed the Congress in 1968. But a closer inspection of events around that time suggests that it was possibly the increase in inexpensive imported firearms, largely military surplus, that helped to bring about the 1968 act which was restrictive of imported firearms.

It seems very clear that the assassination of Dr. Martin Luther King and the murder of Robert Kennedy were the tragic events which prompted Congress to enact the Gun Control Act of 1968. Nonetheless, the domestic violence of the mid-1960s had significant impact on the provisions of the Gun Control Act of 1968. It seems relatively clear that increasing turmoil and fear, especially in urban areas, created an increased demand for firearms as instruments of self-defense. Handgun sales, for example, averaged 600,000 a year during the first four years of the 1960s. By 1968, the market had risen to the astonishing number of 2.4 million.

President Johnson signed the Gun Control Act on October 22, 1968. This measure, while well-intended, was structured in such a way that it has had only a very small impact on the control of firearms. In 1968, Congress was also seeking to respond to a perceived threat to public safety that resulted from the importation of low-priced so-called Saturday-night specials. The evidence offered to Congress was overwhelming that these guns were cheap and plentiful, were of low quality and unsafe, and were frequently used in violent crimes. Unfortunately, the law enacted by the Congress was so filled with loopholes that the importation of the Saturday-night special was not really forbidden. All that the firearms producers in America had to do in order to keep dealing these guns was import the parts and assemble them within the continental United States.

The administration of the Gun Control Act of 1968 was as weak as the enforcement of its 1938 predecessor had been.

It is very uncertain whether any new federal legislation restricting handguns can be passed, or even considered seriously, by the Congress within the foreseeable future. This is anomalous in view of strict legislation and tight enforcement in other nations. In West Germany, for example, a buyer must prove a specific need before he can purchase a weapon. He must also prove experience or training in the use of firearms and take an examination in the presence of a police officer and a licensed civilian. In Japan, the prospective buyer must get permission to own the weapon from the public safety commission in his own province; this is granted only after a strict background check. In Spain, where the controls are even more strict, the licenses must be renewed each year.

In France, virtually any reason is accepted for granting a license to carry a gun, but there is an elaborate background check on every applicant. In Italy, there are severe controls on those who are licensed to own a gun. In Great Britain, the few licenses that are granted are generally limited to farmers, for use on their own property, or to persons with membership in gun clubs. It is significant to note that London, with a population of 7 million, had 179 homicides in a recent year, compared to 1,557 in Los Angeles and 1,733 in New York. In Japan, a nation of 115 million people, only 171 crimes involving use of a gun were committed in 1979.

The United States is the only major country without effective national handgun-control laws. Virtually all other nations on earth have stringent laws regulating the possession and use of firearms. Twenty-nine European nations require either a license to carry a firearm or registration of the ownership upon the sale of each firearm.

It seems unbelievable that the Congress has been unable or unwilling to devise a remedy for the slaughter of some 20,000 persons each year, 50 percent of them killed by handguns, with most of the remaining 50 percent killed by rifles or knives. But the fact is that there appears to be no likelihood, at this time, of any movement in the Congress on gun control.

Logically, legally, and constitutionally, the enemies of gun control legislation appear to be bereft of solid arguments. Clearly, the Second Amendment to the Constitution does not furnish them with any credible reason to prevent legislation that could curb handguns. The Second Amendment states that "a well regulated militia, being necessary to the security of a free state, the right of the people to keep and bear arms, shall not be infringed." Five decisions of the United States Supreme Court and every decision of a federal court concerning this issue have ruled that the Second Amendment is not really relevant and that a government can, under its police power, constitutionally enact firearms control laws. Provisions similar to the Second Amendment that appear in the constitutions of thirty-seven states have never been construed to prevent the regulation of firearms.

Those who urge that guns are necessary for the self-protection of their owners also have a case that is hard to sustain. All of the numerous studies that have analyzed the self-protection value of firearms agree that any self-protective benefits offered by handguns are far outweighed by the liabilities they create for the owner, the family, and the community.

Some opponents of gun control legislation suggest that easy access to handguns is necessary to protect the poor and the blacks. The fact is that blacks and the poor suffer more than any other groups from handguns. Over the last ten years the African American community has suffered an average of 5,000 handgun murders a year. Polls show that the black community is even higher in its support for restrictions on handguns than the nation as a whole. The Congressional Black Caucus, and every one of its members individually, support tough restrictions on handguns. Likewise, every civil rights organization, including the Leadership Conference on Civil Rights (representing 170 organizations), supports the objectives of strict handgun control or even the outright ban on their manufacture, sale, and private possession.

An organization to combat the National Rifle Association, called Handgun Control, Inc., was established in 1974. This organization describes itself as a David before Goliath. The National Rifle Association, a century old, has a built-in constituency of gun owners, gun dealers, and gun clubs. Handgun Control, Inc., established by Pete Shields, a former DuPont executive, after his 23-year-old son was killed by a handgun, struggles valiantly, not to add new legislation against handguns, but to maintain on the books the essence of the 1968 Gun Control Act.

Hopes that handguns can be controlled arise regularly, but always seem to fade away. When a deranged person killed five children and wounded twenty-nine in Stockton, California, in 1989, there was a flicker of hope that at last there might be some sensible legislation. But the House of Representatives refused to reconsider its vote of September, 1988, (228–182), by which it killed the Brady Amendment. This amendment, named after former presidential press secretary Jim Brady, who was hurt when President Reagan was fired at, would have mandated a seven-day waiting period for gun purchases.

A further complicating element in the struggle to control guns derives from the fact that the National Rifle Association now has the fifth largest political action committee in the country, and consequently can give thousands of dollars to members of Congress who help the NRA to kill all gun control legislation.

There is a certain weariness among the proponents of gun control in the United States.

The church groups have been clear and consistent in their opposition to the continued slaughter and to the use of handguns.

The United States Catholic Conference echoed what all religious groups in the country have been saying. In 1978, the U.S. Catholic Conference said it all with these words:

"Since such a significant number of violent offenses are committed with handguns and within families, we believe that handguns need to be effectively controlled and eventually eliminated from our society. . . ."

CHAPTER 10

The Death Penalty

M any religious believers feel that the contemporary opposition of church-related groups to capital punishment is an indication of a development in religious doctrine that is salutary, and indeed inspiring. Many churches have not been opposed to the death penalty until recently. But now virtually every nation in the West—all of those countries that claim they follow the Judeo-Christian tradition—have abolished the death penalty, except the United States.

The retention of the death penalty in thirty-seven states and its use in several, is surely an anomaly in a country which prides itself on being a moral, and indeed a religious society. The Catholic countries of Europe and Latin America have phased out the death penalty. France has sent the guillotine to the museum, and all of the nations of Europe are in the process of outlawing the resumption of the death penalty by entering into a multilateral treaty.

The United Nations General Assembly has twice, in 1971 and 1977, urged the abolition of the death penalty. The whole thrust of international law and practice is now in favor of phasing out the death penalty. Amnesty International, which has made the abolition of the death penalty one of its top priorities, has the hope that by the year 2000, capital punishment will be virtually eliminated in the world.

Why then does the United States have over 2,300 men and a few women on death row? England and Canada, whose law and constitutional practice most resemble those of the United States, abolished the death penalty by a decision of the Parliament and, contrary to the recommendations of conservative governments, have recently refused to revive it.

If the United States Supreme Court had decreed that the death penalty violated the ban on "cruel and unusual punishment" in the Eighth Amendment to the Bill of Rights—as it declined to do in 1976—capital punishment in America might well be a dead issue today. Such a decree would have been consistent with the emerging practice of the world, with the sentiments of mainline churches in America, and with the feeling of the people of America at that time as revealed by public opinion polls.

But the 5–4 decision in *Gregg v. Georgia* in 1976, to the effect that the states may execute criminals if certain safeguards are observed, seems to have changed the course of history in the United States on the question of the death penalty. Somehow the explosion of antipathy toward criminals, combined with the tendency in America to over-interpret decrees of the Supreme Court, produced a wave of decisions in favor of the death penalty never before seen in American history.

No one knows how many of the 2,300 persons on death row will eventually be executed, whether hundreds will be added to their number, and what the situation will look like in the year 2000. The whole picture is unexpected, anomalous, and frightening. Could the collective desire for revenge suddenly become so intense that hundreds could be executed in one year? Many observers say that such a scenario is unlikely since the legal, moral, constitutional, and procedural reasons for delay are so powerful. Nonetheless, the number of persons waiting to be electrocuted, hanged, injected, shot, or gassed to death (the five ways used in the United States to execute persons) could double, and even triple in the next decade.

The religious, moral, and constitutional arguments against the death penalty have been recorded and repeated in scores of books, legal briefs, religious periodicals, and pulpits. In 1974, the U.S. Catholic bishops declared their opposition to capital punishment because of a commitment to the value and dignity of human life. In 1978, in "Community and Crime," the Catholic bishops reiterated their opposition, stating that a "return to the use of the death penalty can only lead to the further erosion of respect for life in our society."

Without categorically denying some validity to the argument in favor of the death penalty, the bishops asserted that "past history . . . shows that the death penalty has been discriminatory with respect to the minorities, the indigent, and the socially impoverished." In addition the bishops, citing an extensive array of scientific, academic, and professional articles, asserted that "recent data from corrections resources definitely question the effectiveness of the death penalty as a deterrent to crime."

In a clear repudiation of the death penalty on theological grounds, the bishops stated:

> The critical question for the Christian is how we can best foster respect for life, preserve the dignity of the human person, and manifest the redemptive message of Christ. We do not believe that more deaths is the response to the questions. We therefore have to seek methods of dealing with violent crimes which are more consistent with the Gospel's vision of the respect for life and Christ's message of God's healing love. In the sight of God, correction of the offender has to take preference over punishment, for the Lord came to save and not to condemn.

In November 1980, the Catholic bishops of the United States, by a vote of 145 to 31, with fourteen abstentions, resolved that the death penalty be abolished as a "manifestation of our belief in the unique worth and dignity of each person from the moment of conception, a creature made in the image and likeness of God."

The unanimity among religious bodies in the United States on the death penalty is striking. In a booklet entitled "Capital Punishment: What the Religious Communities Say," issued by the National Council of Churches, the declarations against the death penalty by twenty-two religious denominations are recorded. Baptists, Lutherans, Episcopalians, Disciples of Christ, Mennonites, Presbyterians, Methodists, and Catholics agreed with the American Jewish Committee that capital punishment is wrong.

The amazing convergence of opinion on the death penalty among America's religious organizations is probably stronger, deeper, and broader than the consensus on any other topic in the religious community in America. Churches are united in condemning racism, war, sexism, and poverty. They are divided on abortion and aid to church-related schools and other issues. But with the exception of the nation's 10 to 15 million fundamentalist Christians, the religious organizations of America are opposed to the death penalty. Ironically, on one of the few issues on which the churches are solidly unanimous, the country is opposed to them. Politicians who are usually prepared to believe or pretend that they believe in the positions of the churches are by and large in favor of the death penalty. President George Bush, who is a practicing Episcopalian, is defying the position of that church and most American churches in his recommendation that Congress enact a death penalty.

It is, however, not certain that the statements of the churches disapproving the death penalty are agreed to by those in the pews. In 1989, about 70 percent of all Americans favored the death penalty; an astonishing percentage compared to the 42 percent that approved of capital punishment according to a Gallup poll in 1966. There is little evidence that the pronouncements of church leaders have changed the attitude of the majority of believers on this explosively emotional issue.

But Catholic leaders have been stressing what they call the seamless web of life—the principle of the inviolability of all human life which forbids its destruction by abortion, the death penalty, or nuclear war. The principle is clear and coherent and is being communicated in a more and more comprehensive way in the Catholic press and in Catholic communities throughout the country.

Clearly, the religious leaders in America have a unique opportunity of altering public opinion on the death penalty in the United States. Very few persons are entirely comfortable with the present posture of the death penalty issue in America. The elements of revenge and racism that permeate the situation are clear. And the fact that the United States is so completely out of step with the rest of the world is troubling.

Strong action by the churches on the question of the death penalty could be decisive. The issue is emotional, but it is more manageable than racism, abortion, or prisons because the numbers are much smaller. From 1930 through 1983, there were 3,870 recorded executions in the United States. Since the end of the moratorium imposed by the United States Supreme Court on the death penalty (1967–1977), the number of persons executed is less than 150.

But the task of the churches will be difficult. In November, 1982, in Massachusetts, a state more than 60 percent Catholic, the voters elected to reinstate capital punishment even though the four Catholic bishops of the Bay State spoke out strongly against the death penalty. Vetoes by Governor Michael Dukakis, and a ruling by the Supreme Judicial Court of Massachusetts prevented the restoration of the electric chair in Massachusetts.

In mid-January 1983, Pope John Paul II became the first pontiff in history to urge the abolition of the death penalty. Speaking to the diplomatic corps of the Holy See, the Pope called on the world's governments to grant clemency or to pardon prisoners sentenced to death.

Between 1975 and 1984, about 204,000 persons were murdered in the United States. During that period 2,384 defendants were convicted of murder and sentenced to die.

The rate of reversal in cases involving the death penalty is unusually high. Between 1967 and 1980, death sentences were reversed in 1,899 of the 2,042 cases appealed; a reversal rate of about 80 percent. In noncapital cases, the reversal rate in federal criminal cases was only 6.5 percent. Thus, some of the worst offenders escaped the ultimate penalty because of legal grounds unrelated to their blameworthiness.

Racism and geography also play a controlling role in who is executed. That was the principal reason why the United States Supreme Court, in its 1972 decision *Furman v. Georgia*, set aside all death sentences then in effect on some 600 persons across the country. In a 5–4 ruling, the Court held that the Constitution did not permit the execution of a capriciously selected handful out of those convicted of capital crimes. Justice Potter Stewart compared the country's capital sentencing methods to being struck by lightning.

Justice William Douglas said it well when he observed that the Court would not permit any law which stated:

> That anyone making more than $50,000 would be exempt from the death penalty . . . nor a law that in terms said that blacks, those that never went beyond the fifth grade in school, those who made less than $3,000 a year, or those who were unpopular or unstable would be the only people executed. A law which in the overall view reaches that result in practice has no more sanctity than a law which in terms provides the same.

But the tide in favor of the death penalty in 1972 prompted the states that allowed capital punishment to modify their statutes to comply with the directives of the *Furman* decision. In *Gregg v. Georgia*, in 1976, the Supreme Court, again in a 5–4 vote, sustained the new statutes and began the buildup of the unprecedented number of 2,300 persons on death row.

In an article in *The New Republic* for December 12, 1983, David Bruck, a South Carolina lawyer, pointed out that after the *Gregg* decision in 1976, the "lottery of capital punishment is rigged by race."

An article by Dean Jack Greenberg, then Professor of Law at Columbia University, in the *Harvard Law Review* in 1986, corroborates Mr. Bruck's finding that racism and freakishness still dominate every aspect of the procedures followed in carrying out the death penalty.

The death-penalty abolitionists felt that a case demonstrating the racism inherent in the way in which sentences of death come about would be persuasive to the high courts. An elaborate empirical study done by Professor David Baldus of the University of Iowa Law School demonstrated that black defendants convicted of murdering white persons are substantially more likely to go to death row than are whites. Baldus found that killers of black victims are punished by death less than one-tenth as often as are killers of white victims.

In the *McClesky* decision in 1987, the Supreme Court rejected the argument that the racial discrimination implicit in the nation's carrying out of the death penalty is itself an argument to abolish it. The study done by Professor Baldus and others revealed that prosecutors in Georgia where the Warren McClesky case originated, sought the death penalty in 70 percent of the cases involving black defendants and white victims, but asked for the same penalty in only 19 percent of the cases involving white defendants and black victims. McClesky, a black who killed a white, made the claim that discrimination against him on the basis of race was clear. He noted that of the 376 people executed in Georgia from 1930 to the present day, 304 were black.

Some slim hope that a majority of the Supreme Court might conclude that the death penalty violates the ban on "cruel and unusual punishment" in the Eighth Amendment to the U.S. Constitution was born in the decision in 1988 that William Wayne Thompson could not be executed for a murder he committed because at that time he was only fifteen. The 5–3 decision (Justice Kennedy did not participate) reversed the Supreme Court of Oklahoma and held that Thompson could not be executed for the crime because "under the evolving standards of decency that mark the progress of a maturing society" no state may execute a person who committed a crime when he was younger than sixteen. The Supreme Court concluded that there is a consensus in America that the normal fifteen-year-old is "not prepared to assume the full responsibilities of an adult."

Justice John Paul Stevens, writing for the majority, admitted that the Justices had no statute or preexisting interpretation of the "cruel and unusual" clause to guide them. He openly admitted that the Supreme

Court approved a rule followed in eighteen states that expressly mandates that the defendant in a capital punishment case must have attained the age of sixteen at the time of the offense. Justice Stevens revealed that the majority of the Supreme Court relied on their conviction that "the imposition of the death penalty on a fifteen-year-old offender is now generally abhorrent to the consciences of the community."

Abolitionists will continue to build their case on Justice Stevens's admission that the Court does seek to discover what is "generally abhorrent to the conscience" of a community.

But Justice Antonin Scalia, joined by Chief Justice William Rehnquist and Justice Byron White, rejected what they apparently felt was the judicial activism of the majority, and in dissent found the young age of William Thompson insufficient to reverse the conviction of the jury.

But the hope raised by the *Thompson* decision was not realized in 1989 when the Supreme Court rejected the argument that persons who committed an offense when they were under eighteen cannot be executed. The Court allowed the *Thompson* result to stand, but held that it is not "cruel and unusual punishment" to execute a person who committed an offense at an age when he was too young to vote.

This result of the Supreme Court goes against the ban on the execution of persons for crimes committed when they were minors contained in the United Nations Convention on Civil and Political Rights—a treaty binding as customary international law. The U.N. recently adopted the International Convention on the Rights of the Child, which also prohibits the execution of persons for crimes committed when they were minors. Although the U.S. is expected to ratify the Children's Convention, the application of the death penalty to minors will require that the American acceptance be with reservation as to that point. An execution of a person who committed a crime when under the age of eighteen could not have taken place in South Africa, China, Libya, Iraq, the Soviet Union, and many other nations.

There is something morally inappropriate in executing a person who at the age of seventeen or younger committed a capital offense. The nation is still shocked at the 1944 electrocution in South Carolina of George G. Stinney, Jr., a black youth of fourteen, for the murder of two white girls, eleven and eight.

Hope that the Supreme Court might stop the execution of mentally retarded persons arose when the Supreme Court agreed to hear the case of Johnny Paul Penry, a man convicted of murder in Texas who had an IQ between 50 and 63, or a mental age of a seven-year-old and the social maturity of a child between the ages of eight and ten.

Penry's crime was indeed horrendous. While delivering a refrigerator to a home in Texas, Penry, then 22, beat, raped, and killed a 21-year-old housewife. At trial it became clear that Penry could not read or write and had never finished the first grade. He had been in and out of a number of state institutions and had been beaten and abused as a child.

At Penry's trial, three psychiatrists differed as to whether he was insane; all agreed that he had mental limitations. But the jury rejected Penry's defense and found him guilty of capital murder.

Eleven organizations filed a brief in favor of Penry's position. James W. Ellis, a law professor and the president of the American Association on Mental Retardation made this argument:

> Of all the convicted murderers in this country, fewer than 2% are ever sentenced to death, and only a fraction of these are actually executed. The Supreme Court has held that the only constitutional basis for selecting those who can be executed . . . is the level of their personal responsibility for their crime. No person with mental retardation is in that top one or two percent in his level of understanding, and foresight, and responsibility.

The NAACP, one of the groups supporting Penry, noted that of the 105 murderers executed since the death penalty was reinstated in 1976, at least six had been diagnosed as mentally retarded. But the hope of the NAACP and many others to obtain a ruling that Penry could not be executed was not fulfilled.

The Supreme Court, 5–4, decreed in 1989 that mental retardation by itself is insufficient to trigger the Eighth Amendment's ban on cruel and unusual punishment. Justice Sandra Day O'Connor concluded for the majority that "there is insufficient evidence of a national consensus against executing mentally retarded people convicted of capital offenses for us to conclude that it is categorically prohibited by the Eighth Amendment."

In strong dissents by Justice William Brennan, joined by Justice Marshall, and Justice John Paul Stevens, joined by Justice Harry Blackmun, the minority concluded that the execution of a mentally retarded person is unconstitutional.

Although the decision of the Supreme Court allows, in effect, an eight-year-old to be executed, the Court did recognize that there are moral considerations to be taken into account when the Supreme Court has to construe the meaning in contemporary society of the prohibition against any "cruel and unusual punishment." Justice Scalia conceded that the convictions of Americans and of humanity concerning the execution of mentally retarded individuals are relevant to the decision-making process of the Supreme Court.

There is something repugnant about the execution of a person who is too retarded to finish grade school. The legislature of Georgia recognized this and enacted a law in 1987 that bans the execution of the mentally retarded. A survey conducted by Amnesty International in Florida shows that 71 percent of the respondents oppose the execution of the mentally retarded.

Centuries ago, Anglo-American law decreed that an insane person should not be punished if it is established that he cannot comprehend the nature of the criminal act with which he is charged. The Supreme Court would have to agree with that conclusion, since it is the statutory law of most states.

There would seem to be little hope that in the foreseeable future, the Supreme Court will reverse itself and find a bar to the death penalty in the cruel and unusual punishment clause of the Bill of Rights. Similarly there is little hope that the thirty-seven states where capital punishment is legal will alter that position. Indeed, in New York state the struggle is to retain its law that precludes the death penalty. New York State has not had an execution in twenty-seven years. Two Catholic Democratic governors, Hugh Carey and Mario Cuomo have kept it that way by the use of the veto. Cardinal John O'Connor of the Archdiocese of New York has opposed the death penalty, pointing out that an "overwhelming number of persons executed by the state are minorities," and that "every time we deliberately take a human life . . . we desensitize ourselves to the sacredness, the wonder, the beauty of all human life." Other voices were equally eloquent. Joseph Lowery, president of the Southern Christian Leadership Conference, denounced the death penalty, lamented that 80 percent of all executions carried out in the United States occur in the "Bible Belt" and begged New York legislators not to duplicate the "aberrations" being carried out in Texas, Louisiana, Florida, and Georgia.

Catholic leaders in New York reminded the faithful that the "seamless garment" approach to the sanctity of all human life should induce Catholics to oppose capital punishment, killing by nuclear war, and abortion.

There is a remarkable consensus against the death penalty held by the widest range of organizations in America. Virtually all of the churches stand together with the American Civil Liberties Union, the NAACP, Amnesty International, and Americans for Democratic Action. This coalition on the death penalty is almost unique. These groups are not together on other legal/moral issues such as abortion, affirmative action, aid to church-related schools, or on issues related to the cold war. But all of these groups, covering an astonishing range of American ideology, are united in advocating the total abolition of the death penalty.

Why then do these forces appear to be so ineffective, even powerless? Who makes up the public morality of America? Why have 70 percent of the American people refused to accept the passionately felt convictions of so many of America's moral leaders on the death penalty? Why, moreover, is a strong majority of the American people rejecting the clear and strong consensus of other nations that the death penalty is cruel, counterproductive, and inhumane?

There is no clear answer to that question. But one can speculate. Perhaps the American people have come to believe that violence and killing are permissible when the objective is important to America. For forty years the American people have agreed to accept the idea that the United States has the right to threaten immense and irreparable nuclear damage and death to the people, not the governments, in Communist nations if these countries invade Western Europe. For many years, the majority of Americans have expressed the conviction that the termination of the life of a fetus whose birth would be inconvenient can be justified. Americans have also believed in the possession and use of handguns against individuals who threaten to take away their property.

Is it possible that the moral reasoning employed by Americans on these issues has induced them, consciously or otherwise, to feel that the death penalty is moral for persons who kill another human being?

We do not know. But America stands alone in the world in its belief in the death penalty. The facts go against what Americans want to believe. There is no believable evidence that the death penalty deters. In 1975, the year before Canada abolished the death penalty its homicide rate was 3.09 per one hundred thousand. In 1986, the rate was down to 2.19, the lowest in fifteen years. In 1987, Amnesty International issued a 300-page book supporting the case against the death penalty. It noted that detailed research "has produced no evidence that (the death penalty) deters crime more effectively than other punishment." In fact Florida, where executions were resumed in 1980, experienced, in the following years, the highest murder rates in the nation's recent history. In Georgia where executions were resumed in 1983 the homicide rate increased 20 percent in 1984, a year in which the national homicide rate fell by 5 percent.

In 1989, retired Supreme Court Justice Lewis Powell confided his view that if he were a state legislator he would vote against the death sentence, "since it has not so far deterred murder and creates so many collateral problems."

One can ask if the presence or absence of the death penalty is after all one of the great moral questions in America. As of November 1, 1989, only 118 persons had been executed since the Supreme Court permitted the resumption of capital punishment in 1976. But many will argue that the fact that the state takes a life constitutes, symbolically and psychologically, a lessening of the value of human life, even its debasement. It teaches that even the sanctity and inviolability of all human life must yield to the claim of the government that it has to take life in order to protect it.

If no moral argument can persuade the state legislators of America to limit or eliminate the death penalty, the possibility of error might be persuasive. On January 15, 1988, a dramatic event occurred when two men who four years earlier had come within sixteen hours of being executed were set free. After eight years on Florida's death row, the men were freed after it became clear that they had been wrongfully convicted by a jury from which the prosecution illegally withheld crucial evidence.

The American Bar Association and several of America's top law firms worked diligently on behalf of many of the 2,300 persons on death row. Careful legal work seeking post-conviction remedies now results in the mitigation of their sentences for one-third to one-half of those on death row.

How will the United States work its way out of the multiple problems caused by 2,300 persons on death row, with 300 more being added each year? Perhaps the country will come to believe in the ideas contained in an opinion filed on April 29, 1985, by Justice William Brennan and Justice Thurgood Marshall. Dissenting from a denial of review in a death penalty case, Justice Brennan argued with astonishing persuasion that an electrocution is "nothing less than the technological equivalent of burning people at the stake." Justice Brennan assumed that the Supreme Court would disallow death by "disemboweling, while alive drawing or quartering . . . burning alive at the stake, crucifixion, and breaking at a wheel." Religious organizations and human rights groups all around the world would agree with Justice Brennan, and have looked upon his retirement from the Court in 1990 with trepidation. Without his voice and his vote, the chances of the Supreme Court putting a stop to the executions in the immediate future have become more remote. Little is known about the views of David H. Souter, the federal appellate judge appointed by President Bush to replace Brennan in late 1990.

It may be that the voices of the death-penalty abolitionists will eventually be heard, much as the advocates of the abolition of slavery were finally listened to in the last century. It may be that prosecutors and the officials who manage the administration of justice will recognize the injustices and the racism in the way America conducts the business of condemning people to die. These individuals may quietly decide not to ask juries to prescribe the death penalty. Or the nation might witness the international trend away from the death penalty and decide to terminate America's unique role as the one major democracy left in the world that still employs capital punishment. People in America are not happy to be compared with South Africa, Iran, the USSR, and China.

Perhaps the nation—even in the near future?—will agree with the late Nobel Peace laureate Andrei Sakharov, who summed up what the vast majority of religious groups in America have concluded about the death penalty:

> I regard the death penalty as a savage and immoral institution that undermines the moral and legal foundations of a society. I reject the notion that the death penalty has any essential deterrent effect on potential offenders. I am convinced that the contrary is true — that savagery begets only savagery.

CHAPTER 11

Should Gambling Be Curbed?

For almost two centuries America virtually banned gambling, lotteries, and almost every form of games of chance. It was a part of Puritan morality. Calvinist theology suggested that God favors those who get rich, but the riches have to come by hard work or at least through the ingenuity of a capitalist who invests wisely.

Churches, especially Protestant churches, liked the ban on gambling. In one of the last protests against gambling before it suddenly became a business on which Americans spend an estimated $278 billion dollars per year, the *Christian Century*, a non-dominational Protestant weekly, lashed out at lotteries, which "demean the human spirit because they exploit greed." In a signed editorial on December 11, 1974, James M. Wall, now the editor of the *Christian Century*, lamented the fact that over a period of a decade thirteen states had legalized gambling. The editorial regretted that Congress was in the process of relaxing federal restrictions against gambling at the state level. Mr. Wall wrote:

> The liberal view that the individual should have the right to pursue his or her own private vice—so long as it does not harm others—has gradually replaced the old Protestant moral stance that fought Demon Rum and the gambling den with the fervor of Old Testament prophets.

The editorial expressed sadness that the adoption of this "laissez-faire moral position by Protestant leaders leaves us with a situation where states are engaged in the business of exploiting human weakness—and there is no other way to describe gambling—as a means of raising state revenue."

Mr. Wall is very certain of his position that "the view of humanity found in the Christian faith clearly indicates that gambling is an exploitation of greed which builds upon the human need to find fulfillment in tangible resources."

The editorial concludes with some strong sentiments about the reasons why state-authorized lotteries are wrong:

> Lotteries demean the human spirit because they exploit greed. Far from being a throwback to old time pietism, opposition to lotteries is in keeping with the post-Watergate morality, which insists that the role of government is to develop the strengths, and not play upon the weaknesses, of the individual citizens.

Assuming that the position of the *Christian Century* in 1974 represented more or less the pan-Protestant approach to gambling, the country has moved far away from that position. As of January 1, 1990, lotteries were operating in 32 states and the District of Columbia. Four states were added to that list—Idaho, Indiana, Kentucky, and Minnesota, whose voters approved lotteries in referendums in November, 1988. The lotteries took in $17 billion in 1988, up 230 percent from 1983.

Last year 48 cents of every dollar bet on state lotteries went for prizes, while another 15 percent covered the cost of promotion, sales, and administration. The 37 percent of the $17 billion received by the states in 1988 is an amount viewed by state legislators as a free lunch.

As the lotteries proliferated, so did the jackpots. The $115.5 million drawing in April 1989 in Pennsylvania prompted bettors to come to Pennsylvania from all over the country to buy tickets.

It seems possible that in the near future all or most of the fifty states will be operating and aggressively advancing government-sponsored lotteries.

All of this is a far cry from the decades from roughly 1850 to 1960, during which the federal and state governments affirmatively discouraged and disallowed gambling. Up to 1850, some of the states ventured into lotteries but on a small scale. Historian John S. Ezell tells the story of early America's flirtation with gambling in his 1960 book *Fortune's Merry Wheel* (Harvard University Press). Between 1790 and 1860 twenty-four of the thirty-eight states sponsored lotteries to finance the construction of roads and canals. Some 200 churches received some funds raised by those lotteries.

In 1833 the lotteries' susceptibility to fraud and their victimization of the poor became so evident that the states began to drop them.

Louisiana was the last state to do so. In the late 1800s the U.S. Congress added the force of federal law to the universal ban on lotteries.

The churches—and particularly the Quakers—constituted a principal moral and political force in the abolition of gambling. John Woolman, a pioneering Quaker opponent of slavery, declared bluntly that "the spirit of lotteries is a spirit of selfishness which tends to confusion and darkness of understanding."

Professor Ezell concluded in his classic study that lotteries "cost more than they brought in if their total impact on society is reckoned." He concluded that the experience of 160 years indicates that "the most careful supervision cannot eradicate the inevitable abuses in a system particularly susceptible to fraud" (page 281).

The contemporary explosion in state-approved gambling began in 1964 when New Hampshire, one of the few states with no personal or corporate income taxes, initiated a program to raise revenue from gambling. Some religious organizations protested, but in general the churches in America have abandoned or have become silent about their long policy of opposition to gambling. The apparent success of the New Hampshire lottery prompted other states to take the easy way of legalizing gambling rather than raising taxes. The majority of states made gambling attractive by stipulating that its fruits would go to education or to the needs of the elderly.

It is amazing how little hard information we have about the actual impact gambling has on the psyche or the morals of the American people. A study authorized by the U.S. Department of Justice in 1972, conducted by sociologists Wen L. Li and Gerald W. Smith, entitled "A Survey of Gambling in the United States" shows that gambling attracts people from every social stratum, although the wagers placed by low-income people have a more decisive impact on their lives and families since they have significantly fewer resources to share. The Li-Smith study also showed that only one of three adult Americans spent money on gambling in any form, private or public, legal or illegal.

It seems certain that more people bet at this time than in 1972. In a poll conducted by the *New York Times* and CBS News, published in the *New York Times* on May 29, 1989, 25 percent of all men and 21 percent of all women revealed that they bought a lottery ticket each week. Twenty-two percent of all Protestants and 29 percent of all Catholics participated weekly in lotteries in those states where they were legal. Noted also was the fact that 71 percent of all Protestants and 89 percent of all Catholics approve of lotteries. Even for those who stated that their religion was "very important," the figures are not substantially different; 63 percent of Protestants in that category and 85 percent of Catholics still approve of lotteries.

The figures in the four-part series on lotteries that began in the *New York Times* on May 28, 1989, are staggering. $161.9 billion was bet in casinos in 1988. Pari-mutuel bets totalled $17.6 billion, with lotteries netting $17.1 billion. Bingo trailed at $4.1 billion. All of this means that about $1,000 dollars was bet for every man, woman, and child in the country in 1988.

Amid the betting frenzy in America it is hard for anyone to deny the hypocrisy in which the government is involved. While banning private lotteries, the governments use every device of modern marketing to promote the sales of lottery tickets. If the government is morally correct in forbidding citizens to bet in nonpublic lotteries, it is difficult to justify its super-aggressive tactics in huckstering the state's own games of chance. The states are blatantly seeking to have it both ways. It seems clear, moreover, that the hyping of legal gambling is increasing several forms of illegal gambling. Will the next step be for the governments to allow private corporations to enter competitively into the same business in which the majority of state governments raised $17 billion in 1988? Can the government contain the mania which it has created in order to avoid the travail of raising taxes?

The emergence of gambling out of the shadows of immorality and crime is nowhere more apparent than in Las Vegas, Nevada. In 1988, 17.2 million visitors—a 50 percent increase over 1982—traded $3.1 billion with the casinos for the chance of getting rich.

Although the gaudiness and tawdriness of Las Vegas are repugnant, one has to ask whether the frenzy of Las Vegas and Atlantic City will spread to other communities. The lure of instant and immense wealth is so attractive that private corporations, governmental entities, and even the federal government may enter the business of gambling.

There has been no serious proposal for a federal lottery, although nations as diverse as Ireland and Israel operate them. If the states can gross $17 billion in one year, imagine what the federal government with its vast capacity to educate and to indoctrinate could raise!

State-conducted lotteries began in the 1960s on the theory that some people are going to gamble anyway and the government might as well get the money instead of the mob. Now the state governments are in the process of creating new classes of gamblers, luring the young and the old, the rich and the poor by tricks that are demeaning and degrading even when engaged in by private organizations.

How many gambling addicts are being created? One estimate says 5 million Americans have serious problems with uncontrolled attraction to gambling. The four-part article by James Barron in the *New York Times* in 1989 reports that psychiatrists are seeing more patients with gambling-related problems. Lawyers say that gambling is behind many bankruptcies and divorces, while law enforcement officials see more gamblers turning to crime in order to pacify the bookmaker and the loan shark.

According to several specialists in the field of addiction, the number of compulsive gamblers has increased. Gamblers Anonymous has more entrants than ever before.

In 1984 the U.S. Senate conducted hearings on gambling. The focus was not on the morality of lotteries, but rather on possible links between organized crime and legal or illegal gambling.

Despite the surge in gambling, church organizations have been almost silent about the subject. The conservative periodical *Christianity Today* still talks about the evils of gambling and the necessity of curbing it. But the *Christian Century* has not published a major article on the topic since a thoughtful piece by Paul M. Minus, Jr., on March 21, 1973. Professor Minus of the Methodist Theology School in Delaware, Ohio set forth the classic religious case against gambling. In a vigorous summary of all the theological and moral arguments against gambling, he pleaded with the churches to adopt some form of resistance. Professor Minus concluded:

> Though it is not the business of government directly to teach morals its policies and programs inevitably promote some values and discourage others. A government lottery undermines values by which healthy communities are bound together. It feeds upon and nourishes greed. It encourages the individual to become so preoccupied with his own gain that he ignores the fact that his gain is the direct result of others' loss. And a lottery fosters citizens' excessive dependence upon chance rather than the development of their God-given skills and talents for their own and their communities' advancement.

Professor Minus concludes with this exhortation: "Here is an important issue for the churches. They must seek to prevent state lotteries from being given a welcome place in American life."

The only recent occasion when the churches collectively opposed the extension of gambling occurred in 1988 when the Catholic bishops of Minnesota joined the highest ecclesiastical officials of the Lutheran, Presbyterian, and Baptist churches of Minnesota in opposing gambling. They were joined by virtually every Christian group in Minnesota. Their statement urged the citizens of Minnesota to vote against a proposal to permit a state lottery. The ecumenical statement of October 3, 1988, conceded that the Minnesota legislature passed a bill allowing a referendum on legalizing gambling because Minnesota risked losing millions of dollars to surrounding lottery states and Canadian provinces if it did not establish a lottery. The church leaders also recognized that the lottery appeared to offer an attractive way to raise state revenues.

But the statement of the religious leaders insisted that the revenue available from a state-run lottery would be modest and would be attained "only through active and aggressive government promotion of legalized gambling." The small amount of revenue collectible from gambling will moreover come from the "most vulnerable members of society . . . the poor." The religious officials expressed agreement with a 1975 study entitled "Gambling in America," which asserted that "legal gambling is a regressive form of taxation."

The Minnesota religious leaders put their case this way:

> The appeal of a state lottery is due largely to the fact that it offers a chance of instant wealth. Those most in need are very vulnerable to the suasion of advertising. Any public policy which directly appeals to and depends on the vulnerabilities of a class of citizens in order to raise money has to be called into question.

The statement, made up of only fifteen paragraphs, was low-key and pragmatic, with no reference to any theological or Christian argument. In tone and content the Minnesota rejection of legalized gambling was very different from the denunciation of lotteries which were commonplace in religious literature for a century prior to the 1960s.

The voters of Minnesota rejected the advice of their religious leaders and in November 1988 voted to legalize a lottery.

Even in the Bible Belt plebiscites which would legalize gambling are receiving an affirmative response from the voters, despite the public opposition of Protestant officials.

Has church opposition to gambling collapsed? Could it—or should it—be revived?

Catholics are on the fringes of this debate. In recent times, Cardinal Joseph Bernardin of Chicago and Cardinal John O'Connor of New York have wondered aloud whether bingo and raffles were appropriate ways for churches to raise money. It seems unlikely that Catholic leaders nationally will follow the lead of the Catholic bishops of Minnesota in opposing legalized gambling, even when there is unanimous Protestant support. But the surge of gambling may create such problems of addiction and government hypocrisy that religious leaders may reenter the field.

It is difficult, even impossible, to justify on any rational basis what thirty-four state governments—perhaps eventually all fifty—are doing when they organize schemes to appeal to the avarice and the greed of their own citizens. A policy that allowed gambling under supervision would make much more sense than a government-initiated scheme where the government does the collecting and the advertising in an area where delusions and addictions are common and predictable.

Governments should try to limit and treat compulsive behavior. That clearly is the policy of the government in its approach to liquor, drugs, and tobacco. Its success in those areas is open to question, but at least the government does not openly and aggressively promote liquor, narcotics, and tobacco—as it does gambling. Only four states provide any form of treatment programs for compulsive gamblers.

Will the number of those addicted to gambling increase sharply as legalized public and private lotteries increase in number and aggressiveness? Probably. But of more importance is the question whether the surge of gambling and the government-induced frenzy to bet regularly will erode the character of the American people. When the government finances billboards, TV ads, and a massive propaganda campaign catering to the cravings of its citizens to find fulfillment in wealth and leisure, the government can hardly be said to be building upon the nobler moral elements in the lives of its own people. Governments, says a fine and firm American tradition, are commissioned to enhance the public well-being and not to exploit the weaknesses of their own citizens. The ad campaigns of many of the states belie the claims that the sole emphasis of the lotteries is fun, not the prospect of winning. In the televised ad campaign for the local lottery in Washington, DC, the emphases are "quick cash," "hit the jackpot," "it's money," "D.C. Lottery helped me do things I wasn't able to do before!" The lottery in the national capital is marketed as an instant cash cow, not a whimsical way to have fun and help the city government.

Will the next struggle over the desirability of legalized gambling occur when or if the federal government desires to tap into the windfall now being reaped by the states? It seems almost inevitable that the federal government, plagued by a national debt of $2.6 trillion and an annual deficit of up to $200 billion will yearn for the monetary fruits of gambling forbidden by federal law for over 100 years.

The anti-gambling tradition and teachings of most Protestant churches in America have apparently gone into eclipse in the United States. The churches may have exaggerated the perils of gambling in some of their rhetoric. They may have been too strict and stern in their demand that the American people abstain totally from gambling. But those who view the explosion of legalized gambling that has occurred in the last two decades must wish that the churches had persevered in their opposition, or that they had been listened to by the citizens and the states.

The advent of widespread gambling is a phenomenon that has come to America almost unnoticed. It has been odorless, tasteless, and invisible. No one really knows how pernicious or how permanent it might be. But no one is rejoicing that Americans have discovered the joy of gambling. While few if any observers want to abolish or recriminalize gambling, there is everywhere a feeling that state governments, in their lust for more money for useful purposes, have inadvertently demeaned and degraded their own people in order to balance their budgets.

Some may feel that this judgment is overly severe, since the vast majorities of bettors do it in a spirit of fun and frivolity and do not have their character harmed. There is merit in this approach; but one has to wonder, nonetheless, whether the Protestant churches that kept legalized gambling off the law books of America for a century did not preserve the American people from countless temptations to forget the work ethic and dream of becoming rich, not by industry, but by chance.

Is there some way to cut back on gambling, aside from the moral argument? The *London Economist* on July 1, 1989 deplored the advancement of greed by gambling in America. The *Economist* points out that there is deception inherent in the entire system. Applying free-market principles to the lottery, the *Economist* suggests that if consumers could receive accurate and full information about the odds against winning and the share of each ticket's value paid out in prizes, they would, according to sound economic principles, not invest. But the instinct to gamble, to get something for nothing, is so much a part of human nature that it is doubtful whether the prescription of the *Economist* would work.

When one confronts all of the legal/moral problems in America, it is hard to get angry over legalized gambling. It seems like a small problem compared to racism, militarism, and violence, a vice less personally harmful than tobacco, drugs, and alcohol. But the character of a human being can be destroyed by small defects indulged in over a period of time. Could the strength of a nation be weakened when millions of its citizens, at the invitation of their government, each day spend some of their money in the hope that tomorrow they will be millionaires?

CHAPTER 12

Can Nuclear Bombs Ever Be Justified?

C hurches in America have always been judgmental of the society in which they live. It has been a tradition, even a moral duty, for churches to react to almost every major policy adopted by the government. From the beginning of the nation, both the body politic and the churches have agreed that in America more than in any other nation the citizens want to create a society guided by those principles which are justifiable by the Judeo-Christian ethos or approach.

The role of the church as prophet has been understandably evoked more by the question of war than by any other issue. Although nations in the past have killed their enemies in the name of religion, it is still an awesome thing when a country decides to take the life of even one human being in the name of some moral, economic, or political objective deemed to be important or essential to the nation.

There is little record of religious objection to the Revolutionary War against England. The thirteen colonies, made up almost entirely of some 3.5 million devout Protestants, concluded, apparently without any overwhelming debate about the morality of war, that it was morally permissible to fight the mighty power of England in order to seek relief from the grievances set forth in the Declaration of Independence. There were, in fact, moral and religious justifications offered by both lay and clerical leaders in the days of the revolution.

It seems clear that the attitude of America's churches toward war was conditioned by the fact that the United States was born as the result of a bloody war and that all of the moral and spiritual goods brought to Americans and to the world by the creation of the United States would not have arrived if the colonists had not taken up arms.

The attitude of America's religious bodies to war was also conditioned by the war between the states. Church authorities in both the South and the North sought generally to justify, on moral grounds, what the citizens of their region of the country were doing on the battlefield.

There is some evidence of church dissent from the nation's involvement in World War I. The Quakers protested and obtained a qualified privilege for conscientious objectors to gain permission to do alternative service rather than be conscripted into the military. But the mainline churches, in general, supported the war efforts designed to ensure democracy to all the nations of Europe.

Ecclesiastical support for the government in World War II was overwhelming. Then and today, moral theologians share a consensus that World War II was a "good" war, a crusade to end Nazism and Japanese tyranny. Serious questions about the morality of obliteration bombing were raised; in a thoughtful and prophetic article on this topic in *Theological Studies*, by Father John C. Ford, S.J., some of the basic legal/moral issues of war were set forth in a striking manner. But during and after World War II, the churches assumed and sometimes asserted that the United States served humanity and did not violate its own moral mission or Judeo-Christian morality in advancing its war in Europe and in the Pacific.

Serious questions were raised by religious and secular groups about the assault on Hiroshima by a nuclear device, in which 140,000 civilians were killed. The bombing of Nagasaki a few days later raised even more questions. In the years after World War II, moral scruples developed over the fact that the United States developed the nuclear bomb and was the first and only nation to use it. But the criticism of churches was muted because, the argument was, the use of the nuclear weapon accelerated the end of the war and spared the nation the casualties that would have been necessary if the United States had been required to launch a land invasion against Japan. There was also the question of how or whether the destruction of Hiroshima and Nagasaki were different from the saturation bombings of Dresden, Tokyo, and other cities.

But regret and remorse over Hiroshima grew as the nuclear era continued. More and more voices were added to the growing chorus that they were ashamed at the fact that their country developed the nuclear bomb, used it, and subsequently created some 30,000 nuclear weapons in a triad that included weapons on the ground, in the air, and in the sea.

But the churches were unusually silent in the 1950s and the 1960s as the cold war emerged and the superpowers flaunted their massive military might to each other and to the world. Churches appointed commissions on disarmament, supported efforts by the United Nations against war, and preached peace and love. But the collective forces of religion did not come together in one unified voice against the militarization of America.

That state of things more or less came to an end as the Vietnam War unfolded. The National Council of Churches and the mainline Protestant bodies began to oppose the war a year or so after it escalated. The Catholic bishops were slow to come out against the war in Southeast Asia, and did so in an ambiguous statement only in 1968. But the overwhelming opposition of the majority of religious bodies to the continuation of the war in Vietnam was clearly one of the several reasons why the Congress de-funded that conflict in 1973.

But the agonizing reappraisal of war and militarization by the churches of America did not occur until the 1980s. That reassessment of war by religious groups in America reminds one of the way individuals come to recognize and realize the sins they have committed in the past. The road to repentance is filled with unanticipated, surprising, and frightening events. The horror of one's sins and the scandals they cause suddenly becomes a daily reality. Even if one feels excused and pardoned by God or man or both, the heinousness of the sin perdures. This painful process is described vividly in the Psalms, the Prophets, the Gospels, and the thirteen Epistles of St. Paul.

In the early 1980s, religious bodies were seized by grief and guilt over their silence, their acquiescence, and even their abdication of responsibility concerning the arming of America. It is not clear what precisely aroused the churches to reexamine their position at the beginning of the 1980s, but one principal reason was clearly the 1980 election which brought Ronald Reagan to the White House. He indulged in rhetoric about the "evil empire" in the Soviet Union. He pledged to "rearm" America and to double the military budget which stood at $150 billion in 1980. Millions of people were frightened. The peace movement was reinvigorated, and proposed the nuclear freeze. The Democrats denied that there was any military threat to the United States or that the United States was strategically weak. But the Democrats, who in 1980 had lost control of the Senate, were not in a position to countermand the desires of the new commander-in-chief with respect to the military.

For a wide variety of reasons, the three hundred Catholic bishops of America decided in 1981 to consult extensively, to deliberate prayerfully, and to issue a pastoral on the application of traditional Catholic moral theology to America's military position. The decision of the U.S. Catholic Conference reflected the fact that the majority of the bishops had been consecrated after Vatican II (1962–65), and wanted to use their prestige and their pulpits to implement what that ecumenical council said about war and peace. The new activities of the bishops also reflected the pressure within the American church of a vigorous group called Pax Christi, of which forty members were bishops. The unprecedented initiative of the Catholic bishops also signalled the attainment of intellectual and spiritual maturity on the part of America's Catholics. Up until 1981, Catholics had tended to feel that they were aliens of a sort, residing in a nation dominated by a pan-Protestant majority. They felt prepared in 1981, however, to speak out with or without the support of non-Catholic groups.

But the most important reason for the bishops' assumption of leadership in 1981 was the feeling everywhere that the United States was morally adrift in its foreign policy, and that it was thundering and threatening to employ military measures that could or would be immoral, ineffective, and counterproductive.

The first draft of the pastoral eventually entitled *The Challenge of Peace: God's Promise and Our Response* reiterated what Vatican II had said in its 3,500 words on war. A nation may go to war only after all other means have been exhausted, only for the gravest reasons, and only when it is clear that the goal to be achieved clearly outweighs the harm that will be produced. Vatican II reiterated the tradition of the just war theory, which goes back to St. Augustine. But Vatican II is not very sophisticated or nuanced on how the definition of a just war can be appropriately applied to a modern war. Vatican II is also less than satisfactory in its treatment of the question whether a nation may possess nuclear weapons, not to use them (since all use of nuclear weapons is morally forbidden), but only to deter aggression from an opponent. The 2,300 bishops at Vatican II asserted vaguely that the coexistence in terror brought about by the possession of nuclear weapons brings about "peace of a sort." But it did not forthrightly resolve the contention of those who insist that no one can threaten to do an act which he or she may not morally carry out.

The bishops of America did not feel that they were authorized to go beyond what Vatican II had said about the possession of nuclear weapons. But the U.S. Catholic Conference did state categorically in its third and final draft that the use of nuclear weapons is immoral under virtually every circumstance. The use of a nuclear weapon in a surgical strike for tactical reasons against a military target was not totally precluded, but was vigorously frowned upon.

The bishops' pastoral issued on May 3, 1983, was undoubtedly a denunciation of many of the policies followed by America since the beginning of the nuclear era. The document probably represents the most sweeping indictment of America's approach to war by any religious organization in all American history. But the *Challenge of Peace* does accept the moral legitimacy of some use of force in international affairs. The document thus assumes that there is some continuity in the use of the just war theory before and after the beginning of the nuclear age.

Consequently, the bishops, in effect, reject the position of those who say that only permissible moral position in the nuclear age is the rejection of deterrence. In a volume edited by Walter Stein, entitled *Nuclear Weapons and the Christian Conscience* (1961), a group of Catholic philosophers argued that any use of nuclear weapons would clearly violate the principle of proportionality and hence would be inconsistent with the firm holding of Catholic tradition regarding immunity from attack for noncombatants. Anthony Kenny reaffirmed that position in his volume *The Logic of Deterrence* (1985).

The bishops' statement does not explicitly reject this position but it does not agree with the position that since nuclear deterrence requires the intention to do what one threatens to accomplish the strategy is immoral. Nonetheless the pastoral is strong and clear.

The pastoral letter rules out absolutely any directly intended attack on civilian centers. It follows Vatican II in condemning such strikes; it disallows them even if U.S. cities have been hit first. The pastoral favors a position that the NATO nations should take a pledge of "no first use." The bishops recognized that such a policy was contrary to existing U.S.-NATO policy and expressed a willingness to support some increased spending on conventional forces in Europe.

The bishops take a less absolute position on "limited nuclear war," but they express a radical skepticism about its usefulness and clearly place the burden of proof on those who would justify such strikes.

The judgment on deterrence is what the bishops call "strictly conditioned moral acceptance." Deterrence is acceptable only if there are steps being taken to move away from the fragile and paradoxical basis of a nuclear deterrent as the reason for peace. The strictly conditioned justification of the deterrence rests, the bishops assert, on its role of "preventing the use of nuclear weapons or other actions which could lead directly to a nuclear exchange." Deterrence is acceptable in other words only as a means, a method to prevent nuclear war.

The bishops opposed a quest for strategic superiority and any blurring of the decisive differences between nuclear and conventional weapons. They favored immediate, bilateral, and verifiable agreements to halt all underground testing of new nuclear weapons and the bishops strongly called for negotiations aimed at deep cuts in the arsenals of the superpowers.

While the pastoral received widespread acclaim and won more applause than any church-generated document in generations, it also encountered criticism. Many were disappointed that the pastoral failed to rule out absolutely all use of nuclear weapons; the argument was made that there is no credible evidence to show that a limited use of nuclear weapons is possible. Many also criticized the pastoral for its alleged failure to abide by the moral logic of the arguments it employed.

The bishops wrote their pastoral at a time when the basic concept of deterrence was as never before coming into question. For three decades, the concept of deterrence was at the heart of the strategy that evolved from the idea of "massive retaliation" to the concept of "mutual assured destruction" (MAD), then to more euphemistic articulations of the same idea. History will judge whether the bishops should have been even more skeptical of the effectiveness and morality of the concept of deterrence than they were. Clearly the bishops felt that if they rejected deterrence outright they could be dismissed as nuclear pacifists whose participation in the ongoing dialogue with strategists and arms controllers would not be relevant or helpful.

Father J. Bryan Hehir, one of the architects of the pastoral, sums up the present state of things in an essay in *Ethics in the Nuclear Age* (1989) in these words:

> The future of this critique of deterrence is difficult to estimate. It is clearly easier to criticize deterrence than it is to replace it . . . The strategic literature and the speeches of statespersons as well as the fears and doubts of a newly engaged public all seem dissatisfied with a notion that there is nothing beyond deterrence.

The vast literature about nuclear strategy is filled with pronouncements that deterrence has "worked." But the assumption always has been that the Soviets, absent the threat of annihilation, would invade Western Europe and take over dozens of countries around the world. That assumption, of course, is very difficult to justify. But in the name of that assumption, conditions have grown up in the world which are absolutely incredible. Not all of these aberrations are directly traceable to the threat of nuclear annihilation but they are related to it:

1. The explosive yield of the 57,000 nuclear weapons stockpiled today amounts to 18,000 megatons. This is the equivalent of 3.5 tons of TNT for every man, woman, and child on earth. Only 11 megatons of explosive power were used in the three major wars of this century which killed 44 million people.
2. In current dollars, military expenditures of the world reached $944 billion in 1987; the total in 1988 was over $1,000 billion.
3. In the last thirty years the political obsession with military force consumed $17 trillion of the world's resources.

These facts, taken from the 1989 thirteenth annual report entitled *World Military and Social Expenditures,* by Ruth Lager Sivard, demonstrate the madness that sets in when the superpowers follow a policy of threatening massive death and destruction in the name of preserving freedom or prosperity.

Although there was unprecedented support from religious bodies for the pastoral on peace by the Catholic bishops, the endorsements did not come from every sector of the religious world. Some fundamentalists, with their unrelenting opposition to communism, found it difficult to praise the document, which at least theoretically was easier on the Communists than on existing policy. The National Council of Churches which represents all mainline Protestants, endorsed the pastoral. Virtually all Jewish groups expressed support for the conclusions and the reasoning of the pastoral of the Catholic bishops. That support meant that for the first time in the history of the nuclear era, virtually all religious bodies in America were united in solid opposition to some of the key components of U.S. foreign policy. It was clear that religious organizations in America were morally opposed to the U.S. strategy of threatening its antagonists with extinction if those antagonists did serious political or economic harm to the principal objectives of the United States in the world. The fact that the bishops did not categorically forbid the possession of nuclear weapons, but allowed their continued possession pending negotiations to phase them out made it possible for persons and groups who were not nuclear pacifists to subscribe to the pastoral of the U.S. Catholic Conference.

But the Methodist bishops of America candidly and courageously spoke up in opposition to the conditional acceptance of the possession of nuclear weapons allowed by the Catholic bishops. In their statement, "In Defense of Creation," the Methodist bishops rejected both the just war theory and the pacifist tradition. They confessed that the churches' response to primal nuclear issues over the past few decades has been "fitful and feeble." But the bishops welcomed the phenomenon of the 1980s and expressed their delight that ecclesiastical bodies are now "freshly engaged in the nuclear debate."

The Methodist bishops stated that "war is incompatible with the teachings and examples of Christ. We therefore reject war as an instrument of national foreign policy and insist that the first moral duty of all nations is to resolve by peaceful means every dispute that arises between or among them."

The declaration of the Methodist bishops has been criticized as being coherent neither with the Just War tradition nor the pacifist approach in Christian tradition. The Methodist bishops are unwilling to accept as moral the possession of nuclear weapons, since their use or the threat of their use cannot be condoned. As a result, they reject the Catholic bishops' position that deterrence and consequently possession of nuclear weapons may be a short-term necessity.

Despite the differences between the positions of the Catholic and the Methodist bishops on the question of how rapidly the United States must cease to rely on deterrence, the areas of agreement among all of the faith communities in America are extensive. They believe that:

1. Nuclear weapons may never be used.
2. There can be sin in nationalism when it reaches the idolatry which is sometimes involved in the trust which nations give to military power and weapons systems.
3. All believers must prefer nonviolent means to seek justice and resolve conflict.
4. There is a violation of justice in the use of scarce human resources for an arms race that inevitably robs the poor.

There is growing dissent inside the Catholic church with respect to the bishops' statement. Father Francis X. Meehan, a moral theologian, wrote in the anthology, *The Catholic Bishops and Nuclear War* (edited by Judith A. Dwyer), that "the church is moving and, I believe, must move to such a realistic evaluation of modern war that for all practical purposes it will become a church of nonviolence . . . Thus the just war principles themselves . . . may help us to move to the necessity of a total rejection of war, and thus to a moral posture of nonviolence."

A powerful, if somewhat one-sided, critique of the Catholic bishops' pastoral is set forth in a 1986 book, *Nuclear Deterrence, Morality and Realism,* written by John Finnis, Joseph Boyle, Jr., and Germaine Grisez. These authors hold that deterrence is immoral since it threatens to intentionally take the lives of innocent persons. Consequently, immediate unilateral disarmament is required. They admit that "the menace of Soviet power is horrible." Nonetheless, the threat to kill the innocent is also so "horrible" that all are required to cease all support and approval of "the nuclear deterrence system."

Shortly after the release of the Catholic bishops' pastoral, President Reagan announced preparations for the Strategic Defense Initiative, or "Star Wars." The concept is, of course, grounded on the repugnance which so many have for a policy of deterrence which requires the threat and ultimately, if necessary, the use of nuclear weapons. The SDI would be a sort of Maginot Line which no enemy nuclear weapon could penetrate.

The SDI has been rejected as impractical by the Union of Concerned Scientists, by a wide variety of peace and professional groups, and by the U.S. Catholic bishops. Even if SDI were technologically possible—which is open to the gravest doubts—it would still rely on deterrence, since the United States would retain all the means necessary to retaliate against its enemy in the event that the SDI did not operate, or malfunctioned.

As Eastern Europe fragments and the cold war fades away, more and more people in America and around the world will look back in puzzlement and pain at the years from Hiroshima to the emergence of Gorbachev. What kinds of nationalistic pride or hubris possessed America in those years? Did America consciously or otherwise set out on a course inconsistent with all that a virtuous, God-fearing, pan-Protestant nation aspired to before World War II? Is it possible to return to the America that followed the moral traditions of its forefathers and sought to produce a society that believed in the old-fashioned virtues associated with piety and prayer? Or, in all candor, have the materialism and the obsession with possessions so corrupted America that, absent a conversion of heart, Americans cannot be expected to hear, much less listen to, their religious leaders?

Have Americans become so involved in the lives of their elected leaders that they do not care what religious leaders say or think?

It is a difficult time for religious persons of all kinds. These individuals are more sophisticated than ever before in American history about their moral duty of providing enlightenment to the political and social leaders of America. But the leaders and their followers are, for several reasons, deaf to the plea of the nation's religious authorities. People have little respect for authority, whether civil or ecclesiastical. Indeed, ecclesiastical authority has never been held in less esteem in the history of America than it is now. The concept has almost been lost. It is therefore easier now than ever before for Members of Congress to reject or simply not notice the statements and the pastorals of religious leaders.

But religious forces in America must also be faulted for their long silence about nuclear war. Where were they in the 1940s, the 1950s, and the 1960s when the United States invented, manufactured, used, and stored thousands of nuclear weapons? The Catholic bishops were not very visible in the field of arms control until Cardinal John Krol testified in 1969 in favor of the ratification of SALT II.

And how vigorously are the churches working now to get their ideas accepted?

The question keeps recurring: will the United States ever be able to return to its days of innocence when it did not possess nuclear weapons—instruments qualitatively different from any and all conventional weapons? Presidents and politicians are unlikely to urge a recommendation for the abolition of nuclear weapons; they would be afraid of being accused of being naive, unpatriotic, and unrealistic. Even if the Communists abandoned all of their nuclear weapons pursuant to treaties or by unilateral action, the United States would cling to the weapons which it came to love after Hiroshima and after the Cuban missile crisis.

It seems clear that the issue of the use and the possession of nuclear weapons is the most serious problem confronting theologians in America. Problems related to racism, violence, gambling, and moral decay are urgent. But what the United States does about nuclear weapons affects the fate of the earth. For four decades, the center-piece of America's foreign policy has been its steadfast determination to employ nuclear weapons to deter, and if need be, to decimate its enemies. Neither the United States nor any other nation has ever before had the resources to make such a threat to any foreign nation. That threat goes on day after day despite all the revolutionary changes in the USSR and in Eastern Europe.

Religious bodies in the United States have joined in the most re-markable development to condemn one of the essential elements in America's foreign policy. The confrontation is direct, head-on, and almost incapable of being compromised. Churches today, like many churches in the years prior to the abolition of slavery, are demanding that the Congress and the White House negotiate away the possession of nuclear weapons. The churches insist—after a clear and compre-hensive presentation of their case—that the United States may not morally continue to threaten the death of millions of innocent people. Of all the admonitions which American theologians and believers are pressing on their government, the demand for a cessation of nuclear threats is clearly the most important and the most urgent.

Catholics are increasingly impatient because, as the tenth anniver-sary of the publication of the first draft of the pastoral nears, there has been little perceptible alteration of the military posture of the nation. Some small progress was made with the acceptance of the phasing out of intermediate range nuclear missiles. But the United States has refused to accept the recommendations on which the Catholic bishops and most of the religious communities in America have concurred.

Have the religious groups failed to speak out with sufficient clarity and persuasiveness? Or do the people and the politicians feel that in the name of protecting America's sovereignty, the United States can use nuclear weapons and cause the havoc of Hiroshima multiplied many times over?

It has long been assumed in America that the churches have a right and a duty to speak up and to help to formulate the basic moral ideals to be pursued by the government. The churches have no right to dictate or to dominate. But if the government is in basic disagreement with the vast consensus of the religious communities in America, that should at least call for a reexamination of the premises which led to a polarization of the government and the religious communities.

Will there be such a reexamination? The movement for a nuclear freeze in the early and mid-1980s intended to bring that about. The objective of that movement was to freeze everything and to examine where the nation was. The idea was approved in the House but failed in the Senate. Can there be an updated version of the freeze?—an excellent idea for consideration in the era after the USSR and the United States have entered into a period of conciliation never before witnessed in the history of the cold war.

The policies which the United States follows in the 1990s will be crucial to the kind of existence millions of people will have all over the globe. If the United States fails to heed the amazing opportunities which are now available, it could be that the cold war will be recommenced, by Mr. Gorbachev or Soviet leaders after him, who will become convinced that the United States has imperialistic designs which it intends to carry out by military means.

It may be, therefore, that the work of theologians and of other religious entities in the United States must be combined and intensified even though the starkness of the confrontation between the superpowers has been eased.

Historians and humankind around the year 2050 will be making judgments about the wisdom and the courage of religious and humanitarian groups in the United States during and after the cold war. They will conclude that the forces of religion were silent, or at least not effectively heard in the years from Hiroshima to the early 1980s. Perhaps they will be able to record that the religious organizations of America, strengthened by the careful analysis they entered into in the 1980s, helped to fashion the agenda that in the 1990s transformed the United States into a nation that refused to use or possess nuclear weapons because such conduct would be immoral.

CHAPTER 13

American Christians and the Future of Israel

History may record that Jews who resided in the United States in the twentieth century had available more opportunities and enjoyed more freedom than did comparable groups at any other period in the history of the Western world.

Christian churches in America can probably take some credit for this, but it can also be argued that the freedom of Jews in America is more attributable to the fact that in the United States, the Constitution and the law prevented the churches—even if they wanted to—from denying religious freedom to the Jews and to other Christians or non-Christian minorities.

The tragic tale of how Christians persecuted Jews through the centuries is graphically related in the classic book, *The Anguish of the Jews*, by Father Edward Flannery. This study demonstrates how for a thousand years, the Christians either insisted on the baptism of the Jews or confined them to ghettos. The story of what Christians did to Jews is a tale which most Christians would like to forget, and which Jews feel that they must remember or perish.

Father Flannery's carefully researched book chronicles the horrors of the Holocaust and offers specific recommendations for the improvement of Christian-Jewish relations. One hopes that in America, and in Christendom, there will never again be pogroms, persecutions, or even discrimination aimed at the Jews. In 1965, the Second Vatican Council expressed, in *Nostra Aetate*, the regret of the Catholic Church for the unbelievably terrible things that were done to Jews in Europe prior to the Enlightenment, and again during the days of the Nazis.

Nostra Aetate is not satisfactory on all counts, but it is at least the first attempt of the Catholic Church to make amends for its past offenses and to urge Catholics to develop a new relationship with the Jewish community.

Protestants and Catholics in America in the 1900s sought in several ways to eliminate anti-Semitism. Christians in America were horrified when they learned of the Holocaust. More recently, many Christians were shocked and saddened to learn in David Wyman's book, *The Abandonment of the Jews*, that the United States could have or should have known about the Holocaust while it was happening, but American governmental officials were unable or unwilling at that time to take action.

It seems fair to say that the Christians of America have been experiencing a deepening sense of guilt concerning the dreadful things that happened to the world's sixteen million Jews in the centuries before the Holocaust, in which alone, six million Jews were slaughtered. But for many—perhaps most—Christians the story is so incredible that they refuse to listen or state simply that the repression of Jews was a part of ancient history and that it is unthinkable to fear that anything like that could ever happen in the modern era.

The Jews, understandably, wonder whether the Christians have in fact relinquished the attitudes which for nineteen centuries ghettoized the Jews and engaged in what Jules Isaac, in a striking book, called "The Teaching of Contempt."

The theology of contemporary Judaism has been transformed by the Holocaust and the creation of Israel. The theology of Judaism remains as it has been for centuries, but the core of contemporary Jewish conviction is centered on the Holocaust and the establishment of Israel in 1948. These twin events have permeated and dominated Jewish culture in the past forty years.

Have Christians in America absorbed the change that has brought such shock waves to the Jewish Community in America and around the world? Many Jews would feel that the answer to that question has to be "no"; in their view, American Christians have been insensitive to the deep concerns and the profound anxieties of American Jews. Christians in America have been less anti-Semitic than any generation in the history of the Christian era. But they still do not appreciate how central the Holocaust and the founding of Israel are to the six million Jews in the United States. American Jews may not confront Christians with their feelings about the Holocaust and Israel, but there is a deep sense that American Christians have not really been responsive to the twin crucial concerns of Jews, in America, and around the world.

The Jewish community cannot understand why the Holy See has not extended formal diplomatic recognition to Israel, as it has to over 100 nations. The official explanation of the Holy See is that it does not exchange ambassadors with nations until all border disputes and comparable issues have been resolved. That has in fact been the tradition of the Holy See, and is the technically correct reason why the Vatican has withheld diplomatic recognition from both Israel and Jordan. But for Jews who have countless reasons to distrust Christian officials and Christian countries, the explanation is not satisfactory or acceptable. The Holy See is perceived as an organization, afraid of losing Arab support in countries which have engaged in four wars since 1948 to protest the very presence of Israel.

The Jewish community is also disappointed, even stunned, at the perceived insensitivity of Catholics who created a Carmelite convent on the grounds of Auschwitz, even though they knew, or should have known, that this would be objectionable to the Jews of Europe and America who look upon Auschwitz as a uniquely sacred shrine for Jews, because so many million Jews perished there.

Jews likewise wonder about the depth of the commitment of Protestants in America to the existence and safety of Israel. In the months prior to the establishment of Israel in 1948, *The Christian Century*, a Protestant weekly, editorialized vigorously against the creation of a Jewish state. The hostility of many high-ranking Protestant officials to the recognition given to the State of Israel was one of the reasons why Reinhold Niebuhr founded the magazine, *Christianity and Crisis*. Although Protestant bodies have long since declared their allegiance to the State of Israel, their deep involvement in the activities of Christians in Arab lands gives rise to suspicions on the part of Jews as to which side Protestants would take if they had to choose between the survival or safety of Israel and the religious freedom of Christians in Arab lands.

All of the tensions and suspicions between Jews and Christians in America have been intensified by the fact that Israel receives some three billion dollars each year in military and economic aid from the United States. The support in the Congress in favor of this subsidy is overwhelming. But will that response alter if Christians in America raise more and more doubts about the soundness of Israel's national and international policies and practices? Will aid to Israel be less favorably looked upon if the United States becomes more dependent on Muslim countries for oil or other essentials? And will the traditional argument that Israel is a bastion of democracy against Communist influence be less persuasive if the Soviet Union continues its policy of not exporting aggression from Moscow?

For several reasons, therefore, America's supporters of Israel have reason to be concerned about what religious groups in America think about Israel. Churches in the United States clearly have a critical role to play in a continuation or a change in America's policy towards Israel. Indeed, of all the legal/moral issues which have to be renegotiated or rethought in America, one of the most important and most sensitive is that of the relationship of the United States toward Israel.

It seems fair to say that the United States is the best friend Israel has in the family of nations. The United States has shielded Israel from the slings and arrows of its unfriendly neighbors by casting vetoes in the U.N. Security Council. But the United States was not able to prevent seventy-two nations, voting in 1975 in the General Assembly, from vilifying Zionism as "a form of racism." Nor can the United States shield Israel from the anger and indignation of many nations at how Israel has related to the Intifada, or the uprising, of Palestinians in the West Bank and in Gaza.

It was the initiative of President Truman that was largely instrumental in the establishment of Israel. It is probably true that the generally overwhelming feeling of support for Israel in the United States derives in part from the guilt which American Christians feel about what Christians have done to the Jews for most of the nineteen centuries of the Christian era. When Israel was founded in 1948, American Christians were stunned at the Holocaust and chagrined that the United States took in so few Jews after World War II. Christians were also attracted to the religious dimensions of Zionism and welcomed the idea that the Jewish people, after twenty centuries of wandering in the deserts of the world, had a right to return to Jerusalem and the Holy Land. There has always been, moreover, a strand in Protestant theology in America which has been very attracted to the themes of the Old Testament and the idea of a chosen people.

Christians in America generally sided with the Israelis as they struggled in the wars of 1948, 1957, 1963, and 1967. In Israel's struggle against the score of surrounding nations, it was David against Goliath. It was a tiny nation of three million defeating a coalition of twenty-one nations with a population of some 150 million people. At the same time, Christians in America—especially since the occupation of the West Bank and Gaza—have urged a settlement of the differences between the contending parties in the Middle East. In this, the Christians have not been hostile to Israel or insensitive to its demands, since they have advocated what Abba Eban and the Labor Party have been strenuously urging since 1967; a compromise resolution of the problem in a way which will guarantee Israel safe and protectable borders and some sort of political entity for the Palestinians around Israel.

Christians welcomed the 1978 Camp David Accords between Israel and Egypt, negotiated by President Carter. The religious press hailed President Carter as a committed and courageous Christian for his diplomacy, and expressed the hope and prayer that the thirty-year-old hostility between Israel and the Arab world would be peacefully resolved.

Christians in America, in the 1980s, faulted the Reagan administration for not following up on the Camp David Accords. But, increasingly, Christians and others have wondered why the United States does not condition its very substantial aid to Israel on a pledge by Israel to seek peace with its neighbors in every obtainable way. At the same time, Christians are very aware of the continued dangers to Israel, and will continue to support that level of military assistance which is necessary for the protection of Israel.

In the decade and the century to come, the attitudes of Christian churches in America with respect to Israel will be crucial. What Christians think and do in the United States may very well determine whether Israel will prosper, or even survive. It is frightening to think that a nation like America, founded by devout Protestants, but now a pluralistic and secular country, will have such power with respect to the one Jewish nation ever established in twenty centuries. In the 1990s, the United States will have to decide whether it will continue to keep massive weapons on the land, in the air, and at sea to protect Israel. While it is true that Israel has extraordinary capability to protect itself, it is also true that the United States in the 1990s will have to help protect Israel from the effects of the massive sale of U.S. arms to the Arab nations, authorized by the United States in the 1980s. Incredible as it seems, the United States, the defender of Israel, sold sophisticated military aircraft capable of destroying Israel to hostile nations in that part of the world. Even as the Cold War continues to diminish, it may be that the United States will still have to keep extensive military installations in the Mediterranean and in the Middle East. If such an eventuality comes about, the churches of America will be severely tested as to the strength of their desire to protect and preserve Israel. That defense could run into billions of dollars; and money will be desperately needed at home as the United States begins to feel the terrible consequences of the tripling of its debt in the 1980s. The debt in 1990 requires $160 billion in interest—some 15 percent of every dollar collected by taxes in the United States.

There are reasons to be hopeful that in the next decade and century, theologians and Christian groups in America will be responsive to the needs of Israel. The cordial relationship between Christians and Jews that now exists in the United States is probably unrivaled in anything that has ever occurred in the history of the Christian centuries. Christian and Jewish groups have collaborated on a wide variety of issues related to social justice and international peace. There are differences, and serious ones. But American leaders of both Christianity and Judaism are apprehensive of a government operating on principles not derived from, or not at least consistent with, the Judeo-Christian tradition. Both groups fear the secularization of society, although they would define it in somewhat different ways.

Both bodies are in total agreement on the morality and the constitutionality of expanding the religious freedom of individuals. And both groups want to protect and enhance the safety and the sovereignty of Israel.

There are solid reasons to feel, therefore, that Christian leaders and followers in America will be prepared to extend to Israel whatever special measures may be necessary to preserve its integrity as a Jewish state. The overwhelming consensus in the Congress on behalf of aid to Israel replicates what the churches of this country feel. That consensus, to be sure, is made more certain by effective lobbying on behalf of Israel, but it is also built on a moral and theological understanding of a kind that is unique in American history and politics. All presidents from Truman to Bush, without exception, have echoed and reinforced the common view that began in 1948 that there is a very special relationship of trust and partnership between the United States and Israel. That conviction has official support from the churches of America—support that is particularly enthusiastic for fundamentalist Christians who see in Israel a fulfillment of promises made in the Bible.

There is, moreover, a growing understanding in the Christian community in America that Judaism has not been superseded by Christianity. Judaism is a religion founded by the God of Abraham, Isaac, and Jacob—the same God whose son is Jesus Christ. In addition, there is agreement that the attitudes toward Judaism on the part of Christians in the long centuries of anti-Semitism must be rejected and repudiated. Father Hans Kung put it well in his book called *The Church*: "Only one thing is of any use now: a radical metanoia, repentance and rethinking; we must start on a new road, no longer leading away from the Jews, but towards them . . . ."

Christians are also recognizing that just as racism is the problem of whites and not of blacks, anti-Semitism is the problem of Christians and not of Jews.

The irreconcilability of anti-Semitism with a Christian outlook was expressed graphically by the ardent French Catholic writer, Leon Bloy, in these words:

> Suppose that there were people round you continually speaking of your father and mother with the utmost contempt, who had nothing to offer them but insults and offensive sarcasms, how would you feel? Well, this is just what happens to our Lord Jesus Christ. We forget, or rather we do not wish to know, that our Lord made man is a Jew, nature's most perfect Jew, the Lion of Judah, that his mother is a Jewess, the flower of the Jewish race; that the apostles were Jews, as well as all the prophets; and finally that our whole sacred liturgy is drawn from Jewish books. In consequence how may one express the enormity of the outrage and blasphemy of vilifying the Jewish race?

Americans have in recent years learned a great deal about the nature of bias and prejudice. They are perhaps more conscious of the presence of racism, sexism, and ageism, than persons in most other countries. Christians in America, therefore, are likely to have some direct experience with the nature of anti-Semitism. They are becoming more aware of the truth of the comments of the Protestant theologian Reinhold Niebuhr, on the persistence and peculiarity of anti-Semitism. Niebuhr noted often that the hatred manifest in anti-Semitism is unique in all of human history because of its permanence and its geopolitical pervasiveness. All other prejudices remain by contrast localized and transitory.

American Christians are also aware that anti-Semitism has metastasized from European Christian countries to the Muslim world. Christians are aware that the virus of anti-Semitism could break out in the world in which some 800 million Muslims reside.

But there are also negative signs about possible future positions of American Christians towards Israel. Christians in the United States may be affirmatively against all forms of anti-Semitism, but their deep and widespread conviction does not necessarily translate into a desire to protect Zionism against its political enemies. The connection has not been made between Judaism and Zionism. Israel is a state formed by an ethnic group; it is not perceived as a religious state based on the indivisibility of Judaism and Zionism. Christians in America do not see, in other words, the inherent connection between Judaism and the land of Israel—an element which is essential to almost all forms of Zionism.

There is another and a more ominous reason to fear that the public policy of America might shift away from its steadfast commitment to Israel. That fear comes from the possibility of the de-Christianization of millions of people in America in the next few years. Some 90 million Americans have no formal affiliation with a religious body. That number may increase or decrease. But almost independently of the number of observing Christians, there appears to be a lessening in America of an adherence to Christian principles. Although the sin of anti-Semitism can arise in the hearts of believers as well as nonbelievers, the believers have at least the clear, consistent, and compelling teaching of all the Christian churches that anti-Semitism is a special sin against faith and against justice.

The paradox, therefore, is that the continuation of America's support for Zionism and for Israel may very well depend on the presence of committed Christians making policy for the United States. Some will object and suggest that all of history demonstrates that Christians in the past, however knowledgeable they may have been, acted in anti-Semitic ways. That is unfortunately true, but it is also true that Christians, who at least today are well-informed and committed to Christianity, have to consider anti-Semitic acts as fundamentally in opposition to every form of Christianity. The Catholic Church has said that, Popes have proclaimed it, and Vatican II spelled it out.

Christians who are loyal to the teachings of the Church cannot be anti-Semitic in thought, words, or deed. And Christians who understand the heinousness of what Christians have done to Jews through the centuries will have to say that Christians have a very special obligation to assist in the flowering of Zionism in the land of Israel.

Christians in America have a unique role to play in the next several years with regard to Israel. It is a role which is intermingled with theology, law, and policy. There will be challenges to the fundamental role of support and partnership which the United States has extended to Israel since 1948. Well-informed Christians will want to continue that role, although there will be deep disagreements about how, whether, and how far the United States should direct the national and international policies of the Knesset. But the Christian communities in the United States should continue their basic agreement that the United States should exercise leadership to assist the world's one Jewish state. That duty can be justified by America's own pragmatic interests. More importantly, it can be justified by everything that America has proclaimed for 200 years.

CHAPTER 14

Third World Debt: A New Form of Feudalism

The policies of the United States toward Latin America in the 1900s have not been one of America's shining glories. From the "annexation" of Panama to the chaos produced in Central America in the 1980s, the United States has engaged in carrying out policies which, deemed at their inception to be helpful to America's interests, have almost uniformly turned out to be unhelpful to America and disastrous to the nations of Latin America.

It is difficult to generalize about the reactions of American churches toward U.S. policy in Latin America prior to the 1980s. Central and South America are overwhelmingly Catholic; official Protestant involvement has tended to be limited to the interests of Protestant missionaries in the nations of Latin America. Catholic connections with Latin America have likewise tended to concentrate on the needs of the Catholic dioceses in Latin America.

Churches did cheer for President Kennedy's Alliance for Progress, and followed the initiatives of the Peace Corps in many of the nations of Latin America. But Latin America was not at the center of the efforts of those Christians in America who sought to influence and improve the moral objectives of America's foreign policy. Even when the nations of Latin America changed the focus of their attention from Spain and Portugal to the United States, and later to Japan, religious organizations in America tended to remain aloof from any plans to furnish a blueprint for economic and political emancipation of the continent.

The political instability of the nations of Latin America, the absence of democratic structures, and the domination of the military were features so alien to the American experience that they almost frightened American observers. In addition, there was a certain disdain by Protestants, academics, and liberals for the Catholic nature of Latin American countries.

Much of that has changed over the last generation. Today, church groups in the United States are deeply involved in making recommendations for changes and improvements in the Latin American scene. Congress and the White House have not been responsive to many of these recommendations. Indeed, in the 1980s, the policies of the federal government toward Latin America have almost defied most of the major recommendations of the principal church-related groups in the United States.

The attitudes of most North American Catholics and Protestants toward Latin America began to change as the consequences of the Second Vatican Council began to come clear. That meeting of the 2,300 Catholic bishops of the world energized and transformed the church everywhere—but particularly in Latin America. For the first time in history, the Catholic bishops stressed that the promotion of faith and the advancement of justice must go together. The millions of people who are deprived of basic social justice cannot be expected to believe and to persevere in faith. The church, furthermore, cannot fulfill its mission in carrying out the message of the Gospel unless it identifies itself with the poor and the powerless. This message, so commonplace in Catholic thinking today, was revolutionary when it was promulgated by Vatican II. It is not new, of course, in Catholic teaching. It was implicit in the Papal encyclicals on the social question, which began in 1891 with *Rerum Novarum* of Leo XIII. But the option for the poor, as stressed and spelled out by Vatican II, was to change completely the face of the church in Latin America.

In 1969, the bishops of Latin America gathered at Medellin, Colombia, to assess and apply the meaning of Vatican II. Their pronouncements at Medellin shocked the continent, because of the episcopal denunciations, both of communism and of capitalism. The continent was alarmed at the episcopal cry of anger and anguish against what the document called the "institutionalized violence" of the present economic system of Latin America. Although the bishops did not use the exact term, "liberation theology," that way of looking at Christianity and the modern world was in essence born or baptized at Medellin.

In 1979, the bishops again gathered, this time at Puebla, Mexico. The meeting was delayed after the sudden death of Pope John Paul I, in order to be able to bring Pope John Paul II to Mexico. The new pontiff vigorously reinforced the demands for justice made by the bishops. Indeed, the Pope, apparently shaken and saddened by the poverty and misery he saw in the shantytowns surrounding every Latin American city, vehemently pleaded for substantial changes in the economic systems of Latin America. The Pope's rhetoric sounded so anticapitalist that it seemed to endorse elements of socialism. Pope John Paul II has returned several times to Latin America, and has never backed away from the demands which the bishops made at Medellin and Puebla. If the Pope and the Holy See have raised questions about liberation theology, it is not to doubt its validity—which the Holy See affirmed as an "authentic form of spirituality"—but only to urge that liberation theology be severed from any Marxist analysis.

The reforms in the church in Latin America following Vatican II have been sweeping and unprecedented. A church perceived by many to be close to dictators, military rulers, the elite, and the wealthy is suddenly on the side of the poor and the powerless. Needless to say, some bishops, many industrialists, and not a few military authorities were gravely disturbed at these developments; many went so far as to say that the Communists were infiltrating the church in order to carry out their alleged long-held ambition of taking over Latin America—especially its southern cone in Argentina and Chile.

Conservative anticommunist groups in North America shared the apprehensions of those in South America who were troubled by the changes there. The misgivings of persons in the United States about the radical alteration in the Latin American scene came to a head when the Sandinistas toppled Somoza in Nicaragua in 1979. No one denied that Somoza presided over a corrupt and dictatorial regime. But the Sandinistas, anticommunists in America kept insisting, are Communist and not, as the Sandinistas themselves stated, Catholics carrying out the mandates of Vatican II, Medellin, and Puebla. The Carter administration had faith in the Sandinistas and helped to persuade the Congress to appropriate $75 million for the new government in Managua for specific projects related to the infrastructure of that country. This initiative of the Carter administration was very different from the traditional policies of prior administrations and the State Department, which had always feared the advent of communism to Latin America. President Carter's openness to the new government in Nicaragua was at odds with the policy the Nixon administration followed in 1973, when it helped anticommunists to depose the popularly-elected Dr. Salvador Allende, and installed General Augusto Pinochet as the president of Chile. It was also different from the policy pursued by the Eisenhower administration which, in 1954, overthrew the popularly-elected Arbenz government in Guatemala.

But the Reagan administration quickly turned the desire to rid the hemisphere of communists into a crusade against the Sandinistas. The CIA, the Pentagon, and the National Security Council helped to organize dissident anti-Sandinistas into a military force designed apparently (this was never made entirely clear) to dislodge the Sandinistas from the government in Managua. The Congress was persuaded to arm these Contras, and U.S. military officials gave them extensive guidance in Honduras and elsewhere. The Contras were in effect mercenaries and proxies to carry out the White House's determination to destroy the Sandinistas.

The zeal and the financial support manifested by the Reagan administration to decimate a foreign government, with which the United States had normal diplomatic relations, is unparalleled in modern American diplomacy. It received no support from any country of Latin America, and was rejected by Mexico, which presumably, as a neighbor of Nicaragua, would be adversely affected by having a Marxist nation on its border.

The Reagan policy led to the withdrawal of the United States from the jurisdiction of the World Court, when Nicaragua brought action there for the wrongful mining of the harbor of Managua by the United States. The policy also led to the imposition of economic sanctions against Nicaragua—again an action not joined in by any major ally of the United States.

Church-related groups in America were overwhelmingly opposed to a policy by which the Colossus of the North sought to change the government of a tiny nation of three million people in Central America. Religious groups, along with many public interest organizations, lobbied against aid to the Contras, and eventually prevailed in the Congress. The United States Catholic Conference, representing the 300 Catholic bishops of America, spoke out again and again against the policy of "renting" the Contras to displace a government which conducted an election which, if flawed, nonetheless did demonstrate wide support for the Sandinistas.

The Washington Office for Latin America (WOLA), a church-financed ecumenical group representing the interests of 11,000 Americans doing religious work in Latin America, was opposed at all times to the scheme of using the Contras to displace a government. While WOLA, as a nonprofit entity, took no official position on aid to the Contras, its constituent members made it clear that they thought the policy was madness. Dozens of religiously affiliated groups organized to raise financial assistance for Nicaragua, which was devastated by the economic sanctions imposed by the Reagan administration.

The anticommunist fervor which led the United States government in the 1980s to make war by surrogates against the Sandinistas led to an American involvement in El Salvador, which can only be described as bizarre and tragic. Shortly after the inauguration of President Reagan, his administration sent fifty-five U.S. military officers to El Salvador to help the incumbent government fight against a guerrilla insurgency. Again, the contention of the White House was that the Communists, with outside aid from Eastern Europe, wanted to establish a beachhead in El Salvador. The insurgency, of course, has been going on since at least 1931, when thousands of peasants organized to bring about land reform, but were put down when some 30,000 of them were slaughtered in La Matanza (The Massacre). The survivors of that battle regrouped and fought on. They were reinvigorated by Vatican II, Medellin and Puebla. The Carter administration sought to have the government of El Salvador accommodate the insurgents' demands for land reform. But, again, the Reagan administration saw the situation in an entirely different way. The White House, in 1981, planned to destroy the insurgency—perceived as a communist conspiracy—by military means. In the 1980s, the United States sent $3.5 billion to El Salvador; this was more aid than the entire continent received during that period. In 1989, the aid was at the rate of one million dollars a day. In 1990, despite the aid, the economy was in shambles, twenty percent of the five million citizens were refugees inside or outside the country, and a military-oriented government was still in charge.

Again, religious organizations in the United States have protested the massive intervention by America in the 1980s into the life of El Salvador. Catholics have been especially militant in the United States in their opposition to the East-West interpretation placed by the Reagan administration on events in El Salvador. Galvanized by the mission and the martyrdom of Archbishop Oscar Romero on March 24, 1980, Catholics and virtually all religious groups in the United States have pleaded and protested for a total change in America's diagnosis of what is transpiring in El Salvador.

Protests have continued against subsidies to a nation which authorized or allowed the wanton slaughter of four American churchwomen on December 2, 1979, and the murder of six Jesuits on November 16, 1989.

The Bush administration has continued the hostility to the Sandinistas and the illusion that a military solution is available for the civil war in El Salvador. Although the end of the cold war has changed the entire way in which Americans should be looking at the world, it may take some time before highly-placed authorities in the Pentagon, the State Department, and the Congress will alter or abandon their long-held position that the United States, by military means, can get rid of insurgencies whose demands relate to land reform and food for their children.

At no time in the 1980s was there any conscious attempt by the administration to weigh carefully what American religious groups felt about the situation in Latin America, where religious issues were clearly involved in very substantial ways. The pernicious over-simplification was always that the United States, by strengthening the military forces of the enemies of communism, could bring democracy and human rights to the desperately poor nations of Latin America.

During the 1980s, the Catholic bishops repeatedly and urgently denounced the military aid to El Salvador and lethal aid to the Contras. Protestants were almost as united and adamant in their rejection of a proposed military solution for the agonies of the 26 million people in the five nations of Central America, to which some American diplomats referred demeaningly as "our backyard."

It may be that the combined voices of religious organizations in America, the protest of the peace movement, and the unseemly idea of giving aid to the Contras brought assistance to this group to an end. But it is an example of how a foreign policy on a particular issue can be arrived at out of emotion, anticommunist hysteria, a disregard of the voices of religious organizations, and a defiance of the recommendations of the most competent scholars on Latin America in the United States.

No one says that the views of religious organizations should be given any special preference in the formulation of national or international policy. But they are entitled to a respectful hearing, since in America the basic morality of the country should not be invented or controlled by elected or appointed officials. The policies of the nation should be derived from the conscience and the moral consensus of its citizens. This consensus may well be formed in part by the teachings of religious groups. All of American tradition—and the history of America's major mistakes—suggests that the voices of the nation's religious groups should be listened to with special care and credence.

The massive foreign debt accumulated by the Third World in the 1980s constitutes one of the formidable problems facing the underdeveloped countries in which two-thirds of humanity reside. The total debt owed to lending institutions in the developed world in 1990 was $1.3 trillion. That debt tripled in the 1980s. The debt owed by Latin American nations is $410 billion. This staggering new burden is one of the reasons why in the 1980s many of the poor nations became poorer. Their obligation to service the debt forced them to siphon cash out of the country, thereby depriving the nation of growth, and even in some cases of adequate food for their people.

The need to borrow massive sums of money arose in Brazil and elsewhere when the OPEC nations quadrupled the price of oil. Brazil, with no sources of its own for petroleum, borrowed over $100 billion to prevent a collapse of its economy, which was then thriving. Shortly thereafter, Brazil experienced staggering inflation. The OPEC nations invested their newly-acquired billions in American and European banks, which proceeded to lend them to poor nations like Mexico, the Philippines, and Chile. The consequences have been disastrous for the debtor nations. Their economies have been distorted in their efforts to pay off just the interest. Their growth rate declined, even stagnated, in the 1980s. In 1988, $43 billion was transferred to the developed world by the poor nations; this is a total perversion of the process by which underdeveloped countries should be assisted.

The debtor nations, in their efforts to meet the interest payments, have cut back on social services. The 1989 UNICEF report reveals that "it is children who are bearing the heaviest burden of debt and recession in the 1980s . . . ." There were food riots in Algeria, resulting from debt-restructuring agreements. There were disturbances and deaths in southern Jordan caused by price increases entailed in a debt-rescheduling with the IMF. Uprisings occurred in the Dominican

Republic, Egypt, and Zambia because of increases in the price of food. Argentina was required to declare a state of siege to curb violence provoked by austerity measures deemed necessary to try to service Argentina's debt of over $50 billion. More than three hundred deaths occurred in Venezuela during a week of violence that followed the imposition of austerity measures, made necessary in order to service the debt of that country.

The devastating consequences of the new massive debts include the following:

1. Living standards declined 15 percent in Latin America since the debt of $410 billion of that continent emerged.

2. Unemployment in the debtor countries increased significantly in the 1980s. In the last decade, the real wages of workers have decreased by 24 percent in Venezuela, 33 percent in Brazil and 47 percent in Mexico.

3. In the five years between 1982 and 1987, Latin American nations alone transferred $150 billion in interest to the industrialized world. This sum has been increased significantly, since the United States' borrowing to service its own debt of $2.7 trillion drives up the world's interest rates. Higher interest rates impact adversely on the amount of interest debtor nations must pay.

4. Debt problems in the sub-Saharan countries, one-tenth of the world's total, pose additional problems since these nations owe 80 percent of their debt to the World Bank and to the IMF, which are forbidden by their charters to forgive loans.

It is clear that the debt impasse poses a political threat to the stability of several newly democratic countries in Latin America. The proportion of the population living in poverty in Latin America is growing, income distribution is worsening, and diseases thought to have been eliminated have reappeared. Dissidents and antigovernment factions in Latin American countries urge that the debt, often contracted by dictators now gone from the scene, be repudiated. But such open repudiation would in all likelihood result in an economic boycott by all lending institutions in the developed world.

From the beginning of the new and crippling indebtedness of the Third World, religious leaders have spoken out asking for relief. In April 1989, the Chilean bishops noted that Chile has one of the highest debts in per capita terms (almost $2,000) and that this debt had caused an increase in unemployment, which in some areas had reached 50 percent. On July 7, 1989, the bishops of Mexico joined in a letter with the bishops of the United States to President Bush, lamenting the fact that Mexico's debt of over $100 billion was "strangling the economy." In 1987, a bishop in the Caribbean wrote to the U.S. Catholic bishops with the bold assertion that "no reading of Scripture would oblige hungry people to starve themselves to honor contractual obligations to repay rich people and institutions."

John Paul II has been deeply aware of what the new debts of the Third World have been doing to the economies of those countries and to their souls. On May 3, 1989, the Pope reviewed the doleful picture in an address in Zambia. He expressed sorrow and anguish for the many infants and children who "die every day in Africa because resources are now being swallowed up in debt repayment." He called for a "new and courageous international solidarity, a solidarity not based on self-interest, but inspired and guided by a true caring for human beings."

The Pope was echoing the 1987 words of the Pontifical Commission on Justice and Peace, and the appeals worldwide of religious and civic leaders who behold a new form of economic bondage imposed on poor nations by rich ones. Some religious leaders reminded the world of the practice extolled in the Old Testament by which in a Jubilee Year debts were forgiven and land returned.

On September 29, 1989, the Administrative Board of the U.S. Catholic Conference adopted a carefully drafted 9,000-word statement entitled "Relieving the World Debt." The document follows up on the Catholic bishops' 1987 pastoral, "Economic Justice For All." The bishops made it clear that, in their view, the norms of commutative, distributive, and social justice, which are a part of traditional Catholic social teaching, are all being violated by the new situation of massive debts in the Third World.

The U.S.C.C. statement is balanced and evenhanded. It concedes that not a little of the debt of Third World countries was assumed foolishly by incompetent or corrupt rulers, and that they "had sent billions of dollars back to the industrialized world as flight capital." The bishops do not endorse any specific plan, such as those proposed by Secretary of the Treasury Nicholas Brady or Secretary of State James Baker. But it is clear that the bishops are alarmed and angry that the United States would allow this new form of debtors' prison to arise in the world. The bishops admit the general principle that debts should be paid, but they also believe that "in many instances the presumptive obligation to repay should be overridden or modified because of the social cost imposed on the poor." The bishops conclude that "the debtor country should not be compelled to choose debt service over self-reliant development."

It is humiliating for Christians in America to have to recognize that their country in the 1970s and 1980s allowed a whole new and terrible form of economic feudalism to develop in the poorer nations of the world. An unprecedented group of absentee landlords has been set up, demanding a return of their investment, regardless of what their demands may do to the economies or the people of the debtor nations. Prior to the last generation, transnational corporations have taken advantage of people who have desperate needs for basic consumer goods. But now the lending institutions of the rich nations have imposed financial burdens of cruel dimensions on most of the poor nations of the earth. A new economic polarization is visible in Latin America. The present plight of the middle and lower classes in Latin America is a radical reversal from the sunny days of the 1960s and early 1970s, when the hemisphere's rapid economic development offered the prospect of a broad-based prosperity. Now their heavy debt burdens have triggered stagnation and inflation, adding to the misery and the hopelessness of the 60 to 80 percent of the population in Latin America whose situation is approaching the despair of sub-Saharan Africa or Bangladesh.

It is especially humiliating for American Catholics to contemplate what their country has done to Latin America in the last fifteen years. This continent, where almost one half of the world's Catholics reside, has been decimated by a modern form of feudalism. Central America has been torn apart and impoverished because some anticommunist ideologues were persuaded by the powerful in Central American countries that any change in the status quo was coming from the Communists, assisted and aided by Moscow.

In addition, the United States, in the name of unregulated capitalism and free market forces, has allowed a whole continent of 400 million people to become enslaved by debts which are strangling their economies, impoverishing their people, and stifling their aspirations.

The Catholic bishops, in their 1989 statement on Third World debt, urged "our commercial bankers, including the many who are Catholic, to understand and accept co-responsibility for the solution of this urgent and crucial problem." Pope John Paul II, in an exhortation to an audience on June 19, 1989, with members of the board of the Chase Manhattan Bank, asked them for their help on the question of the international debt, "which remains a serious threat to the peace and progress of the human family."

Religious leaders and followers in the United States have received enough information and sufficient exhortation to persuade them that their country is involved in the creation of a new form of institutionalized economic peonage. There are countless causes of this frightening worldwide malaise. If history records in the year 2050 that Christians in America sat by in silence in the 1990s and thereafter, as hundreds of millions of persons suffered because of America's heedlessness or its selfishness, humanity is not likely to think that Christians are believers who love one another because they are all loved by Jesus Christ.

CHAPTER 15

The Religious Right in the 1990s

The 1990s may be the worst decade in the history of America for believers who want to be listened to when they offer their conclusions on important legal/moral issues facing the people of the United States. Americans are still annoyed, and even angered, at the way in which the religious fundamentalists and members of the Moral Majority presented their case in the 1980s. America, by and large, wants religious groups to articulate what they feel is the moral path for America to follow. Americans do not favor the government as the principal architect of the nation's morality. But after the populist and political activities of the Religious Right in the 1980s, millions of Americans are more skeptical than they have ever been in American history of the relevance, or even the appropriateness, of intervention by religious groups in the formation of America's public morality.

An empirical 1989 study of how Americans feel about religion, by George Gallup, Jr. and Jim Castelli, entitled "The People's Religion," concludes that ten years "of increased visibility of religious leaders speaking out on political and social issues and the Jackson and Robertson campaigns have left most Americans turned off by such activity" (page 231). Although this negative view of participation by religious groups is focused on direct involvement by religious persons in the political process, it does suggest that there is a strong feeling among Americans that the churches can go too far in their advocacy of specific political reform. Indeed, the hostility to tactics like those of Reverend Jerry Falwell and the Moral Majority is intense; the only question is the extent to which a decade of high-profile televangelists and religious fundamentalists have altered the attitudes of most

Americans towards hitherto acceptable practices engaged in by religious groups to change public attitudes on a particular issue.

The Gallup-Castelli study concluded that "opposition to church involvement in politics tended to increase with age and decrease with education . . ." (page 231). But what cannot be tested at this time is any potential long-range negative effect which the Moral Majority and similar groups may have had on efforts by churches to improve the social order. That question is closely related to the future religious composition of the American people. The Gallup-Castelli book predicts that in the 1990s the evangelical Protestants will outnumber non-evangelical or mainline Protestants. The 1989 book, *America's Mainline Religion*, by Wade Clark Roof and William McKinney, asserts that the mainline Protestant churches are moving to the sidelines, to the margins of American religious life. This is one more factor that suggests that the impact of Catholics on America's public morality is likely to increase in the 1990s.

The fundamentalist Christians have always been numerous in America. Why they seemingly burst on the scene in the 1980s is not a simple issue. Reverend Falwell, who founded the Moral Majority in 1979, almost claimed that he had a revelation that he and his associates should go public, as Martin Luther King, Jr. and the Civil Rights movement had done. In his 1980 book, *Listen, America!*, Falwell summarized what he called the five major national sins—abortion, homosexuality, pornography, humanism, and the fractured family. He also made it clear that he is opposed to communism, the Equal Rights Amendment and the no-win strategy which, he says, the nation followed in Vietnam. He also denounces the SALT II treaty, the Panama Canal Agreements, busing for purposes of integration and the ban on school prayer.

What is particularly baffling to most Christians is the exaggerated use Falwell makes of the Scriptures. He claims in his book that "the Bible is absolutely infallible, without error in matters pertaining to faith and practice, as well as in areas such as geography, science, history, etc." (page 63). Falwell derives his positions directly from Scripture, employing some interpretations of individual passages which can only be characterized as bizarre.

In the 1980s, I debated and dialogued several times with Reverend Falwell on television. I could sense—and the audience could too—the anger which Reverend Falwell had at what he conceived to be the sudden moral deterioration of America. He was angry at the government for allowing a religiously-based nation to permit divorce, pornography, drugs, and especially abortion. I shared his displeasure at some of the declines in morality in America, but rejected his bullying tactics and his suffocating certainty on so many issues that are very contingent. But I felt a certain identification with Reverend Falwell, and with millions of other Americans, who almost wanted to let out a cry of anguish that some of the moral and spiritual values most precious to them were being destroyed. The Moral Majority resonated favorably to many in the Catholic community—as Reverend Falwell repeatedly noted. Catholics decry abortion, worry about pornography, stand aghast at the collapse of marriage, and want tuition tax credits for their schools. As a result, when the Moral Majority was dissolved in 1988—some would say it self-destructed—there was a certain sadness among some Catholics. It almost seemed to some observers that the secularists and the humanists had won another battle.

If Reverend Falwell and the fundamentalists sought to imitate the techniques of Dr. Martin Luther King, Jr. and his followers, they failed to understand one of Dr. King's essential messages: "Those whom we seek to change we must first love." Dr. King wrote from his jail cell in Birmingham in 1963 that we must be extremists for love. It was love, he insisted time and time again, that is the most powerful instrument for good, for change, for justice, and for peace.

The fundamentalists may well have had the same measure of love possessed by Dr. King and his colleagues, but they frequently appeared as zealots who wanted to impose their will on Americans. The Moral Majority entered the political order in ways which have not been attempted since the era when the founders of the temperance movement turned every state into "wet" or "dry." In 1980, Reverend Falwell and others went to Detroit and persuaded Republican officials to change their platform to seek the recriminalization of abortion, the granting of tuition tax credits for church-related schools, and the introduction of a constitutional amendment to allow prayer in the public schools. That direct intervention by a religious group at the highest levels of a political party was and is something that would be deemed inappropriate by almost all religious persons. It was, in the short run, apparently useful to the Republican Party in 1980, 1984, and 1988. But the long-range impact of this almost unprecedented action has yet to unfold. The changes in the Republican platform that banned abortion and pledged to work for federal aid for church-related schools presumably attracted some Catholic voters to the GOP. But these voters might well have voted the same way, even absent the new Republican commitment to work for these two objectives.

The torrent of commentary put forth in the 1980s about the new religious right seems boring and tedious today. Some of the religious personages have faded away, a few went to jail for scandals, and the whole movement seems to many as a momentary, transitory phenomenon which left few traces in the world of religion and politics. It will take at least a few years to analyze what impact the religious fundamentalists may have had during their surge in the Reagan years. They receive little gratitude or appreciation from mainline Protestants, some recognition from conservative Catholics, and not a little fear and anxiety from the Jewish community.

The fundamentalists may have left a permanent mark on American politics, in that some of their positions have become accepted by at least a slim majority in the Republican Party. The identification of religious fundamentalists in the South with the GOP has helped that party to win elections. Also involved in this area is the fact that the Democrats have not adopted a counterposition that is effective. Jim Castelli, in his 1988 book, *A Plea For Common Sense: Resolving the Clash Between Religion and Politics* puts it well:

> The Democrats have been eloquent in attacking the Republicans' partisan use of religion and warning of the dangers of identifying one party and one set of politics with the will of God. But, with rare exceptions, they have failed to offer a positive vision of the mixing of religion and politics; they have not talked about the appropriate ways in which religious individuals and institutions can be involved in political life (page 192).

Castelli concludes that "Americans deserve better than a choice between a party which panders to religion and a party which treats it like a taboo" (page 192).

It is entirely conceivable that there is building in the American psyche a repugnance for the exploitation of religion, which appeared regularly in the 1980s. The examples are numerous. In 1986, Republicans financed ads implying that the party supported "a personal relationship with Christ." The *Christian Voice* rated members of Congress from a conservative point of view, and declared that dozens of them, all practicing Christians, rated zero or close to that in their votes. And the Religious Right has frequently sought to restrict public office to "Bible-believing, born-again" Christians.

It would be very premature to suggest that the religious fundamentalists will fade away in the 1990s. They may indeed become even more obstreperous. The moral evils they highlight are real, and are possibly becoming more threatening each year. Most Americans, including many devout Christians, want to accept or settle down in an America which has given up its protests against the decay of the family, abortion, and the virtual absence of God from the discussion of public issues. This new or secularized America may be irreversible, but the religious fundamentalists—joined at least silently by millions of Americans—want to return America to the levels of morality which they witnessed and respected during most of their lifetimes. But they do not know how to act or react to what they perceive as the demoralization and the decadence all around them.

It may be that leaders and followers from these millions, unhappy over the amorality of America's posture, will form a new alliance designed to reinsert or revive some of the basic moral values which have been eliminated from America's life as a nation. These millions feel that the country has been deconsecrated and debased. They are not certain what they want their country to do, but they want things to change. These persons lash out at the availability of drugs, and badger public officials to make it possible again to feel safe on the streets, and to eliminate venality from the lives of governmental officials. But they know these are only the symptoms of the moral malaise which they sense in American life. They cringe at some two million homeless people in America, suffer because every fifth child in America lives under the poverty line, and mourn at the unabashed consumerism that dominates the lives of so many.

But what do moral and religious persons like this do to improve the morality of American life? They have few, if any, answers to that nagging question. But they know that the America they loved and admired is being changed for the worse, and that they have importunate feelings that they are guilty of some kind of wrongdoing because they are silent.

Can the millions of Americans who for countless different reasons fall into this category come together in a movement for the moral rearmament of America? The Moral Majority sought to reach some of those persons. But it failed to get much beyond the narrow constituency that brought it into being. Its appeal was too scriptural, too narrow, and too belligerent to be either a viable ecclesiastical or political movement in America. But the feelings of discontent that brought it into being are still present among countless believers and nonbelievers in America. The angst which they feel is a free-floating anxiety which defies description and evades analysis. It comes and goes like a fever or a virus. It combines a sense of shame and a feeling of guilt about what America is doing to itself, or rather what America is allowing others to do to it. It may be that this sense of apprehensiveness is the inevitable feeling of depression that comes to those who experience sudden and unexpected reversals in their lives and fortunes. Many Americans see their country in decline. They are baffled and troubled. But they do not yet possess a scenario for action. If leaders with a sense of that civil religion which has always been at the heart of American life can invent some kind of a new incarnation for that sensibility, they will have millions of Americans who will respond. The new form of civil religion, whatever it may be called, will have some of the elements of Falwell's public morality. But the anticommunist themes that were so central to the approach of the religious fundamentalists will not be appealing to Americans in the 1990s. Nor will the essentially political battles over abortion, pornography, and aid to religiously-affiliated schools. Those issues are tired and boring to millions of people. But the issues underlying them—the meaning and the dignity of life—form the core of the aspirations of all those millions who want America to be morally and spiritually better.

An obituary for the Religious Right is not timely, because in almost every generation in American life there is a new religious or moral movement designed to improve the nation's moral health. These movements reflect and repeat the Great Awakening of the eighteenth century, the abolitionist movement in the early 1800s, and the crusades for human rights and against the war in Vietnam in the 1960s and the 1970s. Americans have a built-in desire to make their country responsive to the new moral visions of its citizens. For most Americans, their government must learn and grow and become more moral. That is why the fundamentalists touched a nerve that has always been there in the American soul. People have a sense that their country is unique in world history and in the development of religion. They see their own blindness and obtuseness and secret sins, and recognize that governments experience similar falls from grace.

What new moral awakening will come to America in the 1990s? A vast number of Americans believe in God's providence over their nation. This has been a part of America's civil religion for decades. It is unclear what the idea of God's providence over a nation really means, but Americans feel that God has a very special role for the United States to play in the world. Politicians clearly rely on this idea and exploit it in order to imply their own identification with the providence which God has for America as it continues its unique pilgrimage.

Believers are not about to minimize the vague and amorphous idea of God's providence over America. It is clear to contemporary Americans that the United States had a very special role in World War II, in the formation of the United Nations, and in helping to bring about the end of the cold war after forty years of coexistence and terror. Americans somehow feel that God with his love has helped Americans with their accomplishments—events unique in the history of the world. Americans do not want to be pietistic or presumptuous about God's intentions toward their nation. But they do feel that Americans are a chosen people and that God may well have another important mission for them to accomplish in the world.

One of the clear attractions of the Moral Majority and the Religious Right was the sense they conveyed that God is trying to direct the destinies of America, but that Americans are resisting God's grace. This is an idea that is appealing to Americans who have been brought up on the idea that by nature and by grace Americans are different from other people, and that they have a special role to play in the universe. That idea will not go away. It is innate in the souls of believers and nonbelievers in America. It is hard to deny that Americans have had an enormous impact on the world; for over 200 years its moral and political ideals have tended to dominate humanity. Will this continue in the next century? The fear that it might not haunts many Americans. They feel vaguely uneasy about the economic rise of Japan, the decline in America's position in the world, and the growing speculation that the sun may be setting on the American era in world history. The end of the cold war will further complicate the mood of

Americans, since there will be no longer an opportunity to feel good because America is purportedly defending the "free world."

Is it fanciful to think that sometime—perhaps soon—the Religious Left would have a renaissance in America? Adherents of the Religious Left came together to fight against the war in Vietnam, the military involvement of the United States in Central America, and the abdication of the American government in the 1980s from its responsibilities to the poor, the blacks, the environment, and the hungry of the nation. The mainline Protestant churches, represented by the National Council of Churches, large elements of the Catholic community, and the vast majority of the Jewish groups could roughly be said to gravitate to the "Religious Left." It probably does not contribute to a helpful analysis of religious forces in America to suggest a polarization of the "Religious Right" and the "Religious Left." But if the prominence of the Religious Right is coming to an end, there has to be a contrast with its opposite. And the fact is that the "Religious Left" has been, for at least two generations, enormously influential on legal/moral issues. On domestic issues, one could say that mainstream Protestants, official Catholic groups, and most Jewish organizations have formed the controlling coalition in Washington and around the country. On civil rights, social welfare, immigration issues, and education, the loose affiliation of these groups has carried the day. On international matters the record is much less clear. This religious coalition has always been nervous about the way the United States has escalated and maintained the cold war. The Protestant-Catholic-Jewish coalition has generally, although not always, resisted U.S. military aggression—especially in Vietnam and Central America. During the 1980s, this coalition fought a rear guard action on both domestic and international issues. The 1990s open up a whole new era for this informally linked lobby of religious groups. It will have to counter the positions of the Religious Right on some issues, but the collapse of the cold war makes the 1990s an era which will be totally new in opportunities. If the churches in the 1980s fought against tired cold war cliches, in the 1990s they will be fighting for a whole new vision of what America should be to the world. If the defense budget is reduced by some $100 billion, there will be titanic struggles over which priorities should be preferred in allocating the new resources. If malnutrition and the number of refugees increase, the churches will be required to mount a new struggle for more foreign aid.

If there is any lesson to be learned from the conduct of the Religious Right, it is that churches hurt themselves if in their impatience for change, they enter too closely into the political process. Religious groups in the 1990s will be tempted to try to persuade high officials of the Democratic Party to endorse the new priorities which they will develop. Democratic officials will likewise be tempted to accept the partnership of the Religious Left in the hope of consolidating the old alliances between labor, the blacks, and the South, which traditionally formed the matrix of the Democratic Party. The temptations in both cases should be resisted. The American people may want religious bodies to speak out on moral issues, but they do not want them to form a partnership with political entities. The evidence is overwhelming that in the 1980s, Americans acquired a deepening of their conviction that churches and the clergy better serve their own purposes when they maintain a certain detachment from direct political action.

Americans are intolerant of religious personages who speak of political matters with the certitude of faith or who denounce their opponents and treat them as agents of Satan. At the same time, the majority of Americans do not want their clergy to disappear into the sacristy or the cloister. They feel a need for guidance as to which choices their nation should make.

G.K. Chesterton recognized the need of Americans for religious direction, and referred to the United States as a "nation with the soul of a church."

Americans will have more moral choices to make in the 1990s than possibly at any time in American history.

It seems clear that Americans in the 1990s will continue to be personally and profoundly religious. The Gallup-Castelli study, "The People's Religion," affirms that the "religious beliefs and practices of Americans today look very much like the beliefs and practices of the 1930s and 1940s" (page 251). Church membership and attendance are identical to what they were in the 1930s. The same percentage of Americans today believe in the afterlife and the divinity of Christ as did in the 1930s.

America may have been secularized in several significant ways. Some of the jeremiads of the Religious Right are true. But the people of America continue to believe and practice in astonishing ways.

The Gallup-Castelli study identifies 58 percent of the American people as Protestant, and 27 percent as Catholics. What can be expected in the 1990s from this coalition that makes up 85 percent of America? Have they learned anything from the blunders and the mistakes of the religious fundamentalists in the 1980s?

Obviously there will be vast disagreements among these groups of Christians. But it is important to remember that the richest nation in the history of the world, now facing one of the greatest crossroads in its history, has a religious composition of this nature. America, like every other individual pilgrim seeking to follow the correct road, has the potential of becoming a great sinner or a great saint.

CHAPTER 16

The Present Position of Catholics in America

In 1789, there were a mere 25,000 Catholics in a population of some four million Americans. In 1989, the hierarchy celebrated the bicentennial of the Catholic Church in the American republic, born in Baltimore 200 years before. Temptations to triumphalism were many. The growth of American Catholics from such humble beginnings to a group of 54 million with a vast array of institutions, has to be described as awesome. Mistakes have been made. Millions have left the church of their birth, and millions more have become materialistic to a point where, even though they may practice the Catholic faith regularly, it is hard to describe them as Christians in any meaningful sense.

What is the potential and promise of this vast, exceptionally well-educated group which makes up almost one fourth of the U.S. population? That is the haunting and daunting question as one contemplates the future of America's ideals at home and around the world. Catholics have enormous potential to call America back to its roots.

The Catholic Church, more than any other religious group in America, has retained its conviction that the natural moral law, knowable by reason without divine revelation, can make known to all persons the basic dictates of that morality which is essential if one is to live up to his destiny as an image of the Creator. This belief in the natural moral law was shared by Protestants, at least until the early days of the twentieth century. Judges and philosophers spoke of natural law as a reality known and agreed to by everyone.

But the erosion, even the disappearance, of belief in the natural law has brought it about that Catholics are almost alone in adhering to a philosophy of natural law which can trace its origin to Aristotle and the Stoics, and which has had a long and distinguished list of adherents, including Augustine, Aquinas, and some of the framers of the U.S. Constitution.

The natural law, as a body of truth knowable by reason, has seemingly vanished from the minds of jurists and philosophers in America. It was emphatically repudiated by Justice Hugo Black as an "excrescence" on the Constitution; he was reacting to the use of the idea of natural law by conservative justices who, from 1905, when *Lochner v. New York* was decided, until the late 1930s, invalidated progressive social legislation on the grounds that it assertedly violated the principles of the natural law. Those who subscribe to the natural law would respond to Justice Black that to employ the idea of natural law to sustain laissez-faire notions of freedom of contract is a misuse of a philosophical idea (which, in any case, does not yield certainties on such contingent issues as the best way to regulate market forces).

Catholic spokesmen sought to hold back the liberalization of divorce by emphasizing that the indissolubility and permanence of the marital bond is provable by natural law. There was little if any agreement with that contention from non-Catholic groups. Laws forbidding divorce that had been carried over from England, and had been the law of the land from 1630 until the 1930s vanished almost without a trace. Grounds for divorce collapsed into a simple decrial of the presence of the irreconcilable differences.

Catholic spokesmen in the 1940s and 1950s also urged the natural law as a reason why statutes forbidding the distribution of contraceptives should be retained. In that area, the argument from natural law was given even less credibility than on the question of divorce.

The central argument that Catholics now employ against abortion is the natural moral law. Catholic opponents of abortion assert as self-evident that the basic rules of natural-law justice require that the state protect the life of a fetus with the same diligence with which it safeguards the life of a newborn child. Catholics condemning abortion repeatedly assert that they are not requiring that non-Catholics follow and adhere to Catholic teaching on abortion, but that everyone simply has to recognize and accept the fact that by the law of nature itself, everyone born or unborn is entitled to protection from being destroyed.

The religious fundamentalists, who almost alone among non-

Catholic religious bodies, want to reinstate sanctions against abortion, do not officially refer to the natural law, but to the Bible or Christian tradition. Even if the fundamentalists did have a tradition of following natural law and used it in their opposition to abortion, the results would hardly be different. Those who do not want to recriminalize abortion simply do not agree with the idea of a natural moral law, knowable and binding on all human beings. To be sure, these persons might concede that there is a natural law which tells everyone that rape, robbery, and torture are immoral. But they are unpersuaded that the idea has any applicability to things like divorce or abortion. They look upon these issues as private matters to be regulated not by the state, but by the individuals involved.

Catholic spokesmen, for whom the idea of natural law continues to be self-evident, are tempted either to challenge the intellectual competence of those who reject the natural law or to assert that they are self-serving moral utilitarians. Is there some area of consensus in which the undeniably valid claims of natural-law thinking can obtain some type of acceptance by non-Catholics who, even if they are devout and practicing Christians, have not been brought up in a tradition in which the natural law had any significant role?

That is the question to which thoughtful Catholics devote their attention every day. Catholics are intensely aware that Vatican II has disapproved all forms of coercion in spiritual things. Catholics sincerely do not wish to impose their views on others. At the same time, Catholics feel that they are required as simple human beings, regardless of their religious faith, to protect those basic moral values on which the American people agreed until the recent past. As a result, Catholics are not comfortable in accepting, in the name of pluralism or privatism, the easy availability of abortion or divorce.

Should then Catholics fight on for the curbing of divorce or abortion? They have presumably given up on seeking to tighten up on the ease with which divorce can be obtained. The divorce rate among Catholics is almost as high as that of the population as a whole. The abortion rate among Catholic women is also in the range of the national average. Should then Catholics lower the decibels over abortion and concentrate on trying to reach and educate the Catholic women who each year have their share of the 1.6 million legal abortions done in America?

There are millions of Catholics who would answer "yes" to that question. Governor Mario Cuomo, in his address on abortion and the law at Notre Dame University, in 1984, put the question this way:

> I believe that legal interdicting of abortion, by either the federal government or the individual states, is not a plausible possibility, and even if it could be obtained, it wouldn't work. Given present attitudes, it would be "prohibition" revisited, legislating what couldn't be enforced and in the process creating a disrespect for law in general.

But the Catholic Church has an emerging role in America which does not allow it to confine itself to the pastoral care of its own congregants. The natural law, Catholic tradition, and an ever deeper sense of mission to preserve America's basic moral values seemingly impels Catholic leaders to speak out to the entire nation and to the world. Catholics in America have attained a new maturity, a collective self-confidence, and a feeling that in God's providence they have a new and important role to fulfill in the United States. They like to think that the years of open anti-Catholicism are over and that millions of Americans, weary of the moral drift in their nation, look for leadership from the churches. These people, furthermore, are inclined to look to the Catholic Church because its beliefs are unchanging, more traditional, and grounded in reason as well as in revelation. Non-Catholics also feel that Protestants for a long time rejected and even abused Catholics and that Catholics deserve to be heard.

The Catholic bishops for at least a generation have been active and articulate. The most recent volume recording their positions contains statements and testimony on every major legal/moral issue in the United States today. Their extensive work in taking positions and establishing priorities goes unreported in the press. One could think sometimes that the bishops have positions only on abortion and nuclear weapons. But they have faced up to all their social responsibilities and have declared their positions in impressive ways.

What level of energy should the church devote to expounding and implementing its positions on war, capitalism, Third World debt and similarly important areas of concern? The U.S. Catholic Conference promulgates its analysis and its recommendations on these issues, but how can the policies embraced in their position papers get popularized and adopted? In view of the vast potential influence available to American Catholics, it seems clear that the church should teach the nation and the world in all of the ways reasonably available. The

Catholic bishops have already sought to do that in their pastorals on nuclear war and the economy. They are striving to do something comparable with respect to a pastoral on the position of women.

Some bishops and many Catholics are disinclined to become involved in taking positions on issues on which, almost inevitably, Catholics and others will be divided. Catholics, like most Americans, would divide 60–40 on either side of issues like raising the minimum wage, the appropriate levels of funding for clean air measures, and the best way to tax wealthy persons and profitable corporations. But on the great moral issues of the day there is a broad feeling among Catholics that the moral power of the church in America is not being adequately employed to change the future of the world. In October 1989, Pope John Paul II reminded a group in Rome that in the twentieth century a few wealthy nations enjoyed prosperity unknown in the history of the world, while the vast majority of the people on earth lived in abject poverty and hopelessness. That is the type of vision which religious leaders in the developed world should be articulating.

How can the Catholic Church in America respond to that challenge? Until the recent past, church leaders did not concentrate on that question. The vast array of Catholic schools, the operation of some 250 Catholic colleges, the maintenance of hundreds of Catholic hospitals, and the creation of new parishes consumed the energies of the church. But that age is coming to a close. A period of transition is here. The continued pastoral needs of the faithful are important, but the United States now has before it the opportunity of creating a whole new universe. In the forty-three years from Yalta to Malta, the United States survived the coexistence in terror, built up massive military defenses, and taught its people to despise the Communists. Now the United States cannot avoid recognizing its responsibility, as the richest nation in the history of the world, to shape a new universe in which everyone will have access to that minimum level of decency which all human beings deserve. The United States—in alliance with other developed nations—is capable of bringing decency and dignity to the four billion people who live with poverty and despair as their daily companions. And the Catholic Church in America is close to the levers of power which, if properly employed, can open up a new era of world peace and plenty not even conceived of in the most utopian dreams of the most idealistic individuals.

What can the Catholic Church do? Whatever it does has to be done in a nation where the number of priests is declining, where the 180,000 nuns available in 1970 have declined to 110,000, and where millions of Catholics have become upwardly mobile in ways that will make them less caring for the needs of others—especially for those who reside in Asia or Africa.

It is by no means clear that Catholics will even be aware of, much less respond to, the enormous moral challenges the United States will face. Indeed, it may be that the United States will continue to withdraw into its own cocoon of self-isolation and self-indulgence. America may be tired or effete or decadent after forty years of prosperity, pleasure, and power. The challenge of Christianity may not even reach the majority of the American people; they may have trivialized religion into rituals which are performed for marriages and funerals. They may have in fact abandoned any real religious convictions, even though they may be churchgoers.

If the vast majority of Christians can be described in this way, can American Catholics rise above them and give prophetic witness to the compelling need for the United States to develop a plan to bring food, fuel, and fertilizer to the 1.2 billion people who will be added to the global village before the year 2000? There is some hope that Catholics could rise to this challenge. They would not do it alone; they would act in collaboration with believers and nonbelievers of all kinds. But the Catholic role could be one of moral and spiritual leadership. What principles would they use when they exercised leadership? Again, the question of the natural moral law arises. Could Catholics turn this idea into a vibrant and expanding approach to human nature in ways that would make it attractive and compelling to most Americans? Could Catholics combine the natural law with those elements of the Judeo-Christian tradition on which there is a consensus in the United States? Or could Catholics and others formulate some new moral idea which would persuade Americans that they have a moral mission to bring economic justice to the world?

America has been a morally powerful nation in its history. The Declaration of Independence, with its open appeal to the law of nature, began the worldwide movement for political self-determination. The United States Constitution and its Bill of Rights form the heart of the law of the more than 100 nations that have been born since 1945 from the ashes of colonialism.

The principle of federalism, the separation of powers, and the ideas of equal protection and due process have been transmitted by America into the legal codes of the world. The legal concepts that are at the heart of American democracy were the core ideas used in the United Nations Charter and in the twenty-two covenants on human rights that have emerged from the United Nations since 1948.

Can there be a new incarnation of all those moral principles as the United States beholds a whole new world with the disappearance of the cold war? In the last forty years, the Third World has acquired political rights. What it needs now is a way to go from political rights to economic rights. The developing nations need a whole new international economic order. That concept was the buzzword at the United Nations for several years. The nonaligned nations cried out for economic rights against the multinational corporations that came to their countries after the colonial powers left. The developing nations indulged in not a little rhetoric, but their constant complaint was valid: The unregulated expansion of capitalism to underdeveloped countries offered no guarantee of a just society, now or in the foreseeable future.

The United States seemed almost impervious to those cries. In the 1980s especially, America seemed to have had its back turned on the United Nations and the developing countries. One U.S. contention was that this country was spending some $300 billion each year to stop the spread of communism, and was therefore protecting the developing nations from totalitarianism. That claim sounded unpersuasive a decade ago to nations in Latin America, Africa, and Asia that were trying desperately to improve their standard of living. Today, the anticommunist position of the United States sounds totally unpersuasive.

There is, therefore, an entirely new situation confronting the United States. It is more awesome than the position of the world in 1945. At that time it seemed clear to the United States that it should revive Europe with the Marshall Plan, and rehabilitate Japan by rebuilding it into a democracy. What America did in Europe and Japan after World War II has received universal acclaim. What should the United States do now that the cold war has ended? The situation is infinitely more complicated. There are no victors and no vanquished. There are struggling former colonies of Europe plus the formidable and overwhelming presence of one-fifth of humanity in China. The situation is also unlike the scene in 1945, since it is not clear that the

United States will be a net receiver of benefits if it commits itself to help the two-thirds of humanity that lives in the world of under-developed nations.

Could Catholics in America help to determine what the United States will do as it faces the poor nations of the world crying out for help with their fundamental economic needs? Although I write in this chapter about the present position of Catholics, I obviously am not excluding the hope and possibility of significant world leadership from other groups, religious and nonreligious. Indeed, if the hoped-for leadership does come forth, it will be an amalgam and a cross section of several groups within the United States.

The problems of hungry nations and exploding populations will not be the only questions the United States will be required to face. There will be nations that will brandish their weapons against other na-tions—and the weapons will be marked "Made in U.S.A." During the cold war, the United States sold billions of dollars' worth of arms to neutral and nonaligned nations. One of the reasons given was to bring these nations into the orbit of the United States as it competed with the USSR. But those weapons are still out there—now searching for a mission. Will the weapons sold or given by the United States become a whole new source of international and regional tension and rivalry? It might well be.

Other global problems include the warming of the earth, the threats to the ozone layer, the depletion of fossil fuels, the destruction of the rain forest, and comparable problems which are so complex and fearsome that humanity generally resists hearing about them.

American Catholics are as aware of all these problems as other Americans—perhaps more so. But there seems to be lacking in the Catholic community a sense that Catholics have a special, even a unique, role in resolving these problems. Catholics are just emerging from decades during which they felt that they were, in a sense, a religious and cultural minority living somewhat as aliens in a pan-Protestant and increasingly secular country. That feeling has now all but disappeared. But there still seems to be no common feeling in the Catholic community that the formation of America's public morality and its relationship to the world depends on Catholic initiative and leadership. But Catholics—and others—realize that there is a deep hunger among Americans for a new and better vision of what their country should be, and what it should represent in the world. Americans are idealists, dreamers, visionaries. And they want to share and spread their idealism to the entire world.

Catholics are in a special and unique position to help to formulate what America will be and do in the 1990s. There are in the United States over one million living graduates of the twenty-eight Jesuit colleges and universities. There are 54,000 priests, 120,000 nuns and religious, an ever-increasing number of married deacons, and hundreds of thousands of well-informed and devout Catholic laypersons. There are, of course, thousands of highly educated and motivated non-Catholics. But by their traditions and their heritage, Catholics have a special role to play as America tries to find itself in the world after the cold war.

It is not easy to specify what Catholics could or should do for America at this time. They have the same blindness and the same astigmatism that have afflicted other Americans. But they also have a deeper and richer tradition in metaphysics and mysticism than many other Christians. They have a certainty in their convictions which other Christians do not possess. And they have a new sense of solidarity as Catholics and as Americans, with respect to the daunting responsibilities the United States faces at this moment in world history.

Could there suddenly be leaders like Lech Walesa arising out of the Catholic community in the United States? The situation in America is more complicated than the one in Poland or most other nations. American Catholics who desire to change the face of the nation's public morality must dramatize issues far less sharply defined than apartheid in South Africa or economic collapse in Poland. The issues in which the United States is involved are deep, profound, and not susceptible to any quick resolution. Nor are they solvable by neat moral principles. They must be compromised out by solutions that make no one happy.

So, what can be expected of Catholics in America? Are they the sleeping giant that might awake to startle the world? Or have they been anesthetized by wealth and consumerism so that they only want the status quo—with a few concessions for the poor and the homeless?

The pastorals of the bishops have challenged laypersons to be active on social issues related to nuclear weapons and to social justice. Some measurable movement by Catholics toward the position of their leaders has been observed. But it remains to be seen whether Catholics will produce sea change in the attitudes of Americans on these issues.

Changes in public attitudes that are traceable to religious influences are difficult to pinpoint. Significant shifts in public attitudes are usually attributable to many factors, all of which are complex in themselves. But on the other hand, religious convictions have always been powerful factors in changing policies in America. Changes with respect to slavery, civil rights, the Vietnam War, and fairness to handicapped persons are but a few of the major issues on which developments in religious thinking changed the tide of public opinion. It is seldom clear whether the clergy is leading the congregation or vice versa. Christians who are committed to their faith offer changes or reform in the social structure as an essential and inexorable part of their role in society. They are acting, they would feel, like Christ, who drove the moneychangers out of the temple. They are following the example of thousands through the centuries who felt impelled by their creed and their conscience to change what they sensed was unjust.

An example of Christians persisting in advancing their position on issues of justice is the Jesuit community at the Catholic University in San Salvador; six Jesuit professors were assassinated on November 16, 1989, because the incumbent government and the military forces authorized or allowed the removal of a powerful moral force that was in opposition to many of the policies of the government.

No one expects the heroic virtue that leads to martyrdom from American Catholics. But it is hoped that after all the extraordinary theological training which they have received in Christian philosophy and theology, they would seek to prevent their government from continuing in policies at home and abroad which cannot be reconciled with the basic norms of justice. Theoretically, the educated Catholics of America should be in the vanguard of Christians struggling to bring about a just and a good society. They have received more and better education in Christian principles than probably any generation of Catholics in the history of the Christian era. They are led by bishops who are arguably better trained and more talented than any previous generation of American bishops.

What then might be expected? The hope would be that Catholics in America would respond to the yearnings for moral leadership which are undeniably being expressed by the people of America. These citizens sense an emptiness in American life. They are deeply troubled and grieved by children starving around the world, and they know that their own nation has made several serious mistakes in the policies it has adopted over the past forty years. There is a cry of the heart coming from the American people. It is a cry that is sometimes unclear and uncertain. But it is nonetheless a cry for a moral awakening in the nation, a renewal of the finest things that America has achieved, and which, the feeling goes, America is no longer pursuing.

The religious fundamentalists and the Moral Majority touched that feeling in millions of Americans by its appeal to pro-family and pro-God sentiments. But the vast majority of Americans were not attracted on a lasting basis to the approach to America's morality advanced by the Moral Majority. They want a new vision, not one that hearkens back to an America which was presumably better because divorce, abortion, and drugs were not a problem. Americans want to feel good again about their country, and that feeling will not be restored by the hope or the illusion that religious groups can somehow bring the nation back to a mythical time when a pan-Protestant morality was accepted, and all were presumably happy and at peace.

Do Catholics have a vision and a tradition which can satisfy the yearning of Americans for a society in which they can be more proud of their church and of their country? There is a widespread feeling that Catholics do indeed have such a vision. Richard Neuhaus, in his book, *The Naked Public Square*, states in several different ways that this is the "Catholic moment" in American history. Reverend Neuhaus, a conservative Lutheran pastor, is attracted to the firm views of the Catholic tradition against divorce, abortion, and permissiveness. But many others look to the rich philosophical and theological traditions of the Catholic church and hope that these traditions in all their metaphysical and mystical splendor can be applied to the betterment of America's public morality. Such attention is flattering for Catholics. The day of the anti-Catholic screed is over. Some non-Catholic voices are openly appealing for Catholics to be forthcoming in applying their moral and social teachings to the problems of the nation.

It is a new, even a heady, moment for American Catholics. But there is a cloud, a substantial cloud, over the prospects of Catholics improving the public morality of America because, just as Catholics presumably have acquired a pulpit, the nation, disillusioned and turned off by the fundamentalists and the Moral Majority, may be far less disposed to listen to church groups. On the other hand, if Catholics form a movement on their own, separated from their churches and in informal collaboration with other Christians and non-Christians, the nation may be unusually responsive. The new group or movement would not be church-related or initiated by ecclesiastical officials. It would be a genuine grass-roots group which would be working for a moral renewal of the nation in a way that would not seek to revive, revise, or impose on anyone any religious doctrine.

Are Catholics capable of bringing about such a movement? There is strong evidence that the answer to that question is "yes." But there remains a question as to how many American Christians have been converted into Christians who perceive and accept the truly radical view Christianity has of the world. Pope John Paul II enunciated that view on October 27, 1989, when he spoke to economic and social experts in Rome in these words:

> Mankind has never known an era of prosperity even vaguely comparable to that which the world in the second half of the 20th century has come to enjoy . . . but . . . it is a prosperity that benefits but a small proportion of mankind, while leaving the majority of the world's inhabitants in a state of underdevelopment.

The church has a duty, the Pope continued, to "awaken consciences and invite them to the fact that today, like Lazarus at the door of the rich man, millions are in dire need while a great part of the world's resources are employed in areas which have little or nothing to contribute to the improvement of life on this planet."

That totally Christian view of the universe was behind the unprecedented step taken by all the religions of Canada when, on Ash Wednesday 1988, they sent a 25-page letter to the top officials in Canada deploring some of the basic positions taken by the Canadian government. The document, endorsed by the twelve leading Canadian religious bodies, including the Canadian Conference of Catholic Bishops, condemned the proposed expenditure of $10 billion for new nuclear submarines, and excoriated the government of Prime Minister Brian Mulroney for proposing military solutions to political problems.

The coming together for the first time of all of the major religious bodies of Canada could appropriately set an example for U.S. religious groups. The preparation for a joint statement has already been done. For many years Protestants, Catholics, and Jewish groups in America have been issuing statements on all the major legal/moral issues. Putting together a consensus statement would not be difficult now.

Could the Catholics of America, especially Catholic laypersons, be the architects of such an ecumenical statement? The time is surely ripe. The years between Yalta and Malta are gone; a new approach to U.S. foreign policy is desperately needed. Perhaps in God's providence the Catholic Church in America has been preparing, during its 200 years of existence in America, for this dramatic moment.

CHAPTER 17

Ten Commandments for the Churches in America

Members of churches and religious groups in America speak frequently of their frustrations in trying to cope with the multiple challenges to their energies and their aspirations. They want to pray and live quietly with their Lord. They would like to have prayers and piety in their homes and in their communities. But the thrust everywhere in the churches seems to be toward action in order to resolve some intractable problems. If some problem is partially resolved, other more impossible problems spring up. The faithful know that they cannot turn their back on these problems, but they do not want to accept a state of constant agitation about social issues as the essence of their Christian faith. They also recognize that the agitation will not subside, and indeed it may increase. No one can offer peace or tranquillity. The best that can be advanced is a state of continual alertness to issues whose resolution clearly depends on the activities of morally sensitive persons.

In order to try to form some guidelines for Christians and others as to how they should proceed, the following suggestions or "commandments" are offered. They are not in any particular order, nor do they in any way pretend to be definitive. But they do attempt to touch on those baffling dilemmas which morally aware Americans cannot avoid. And they offer ways by which all the religious bodies in America could act together to combine their moral strength for the good of the nation and the world.

i. *Faith and Justice are Inseparable.*

The principal and primordial need for churches in America is to be and become an entity that is totally theological, scriptural, and mystical. There is an iron law in Christian spirituality that no one can impart those spiritual qualities which they do not possess; sanctity and holiness can be engendered only by those who have acquired these qualities. The same iron rule applies to churches; if they are only superficially Christian, or hollow, they cannot change the hearts and lives of their congregants.

The capacity, therefore, which Christian groups have to change the public morality of a nation derives from and depends on the depth of the convictions of their members. If the participants in the activities of a church working for social justice are acting only or primarily because of humanitarian motives, they can be charged with employing, even abusing, the authority and the prestige of the church when their own motives are only political.

The assumption by the churches of causes in the temporal order almost inevitably tends to divide a church and dissipate its energies. There are formidable preexisting obstacles to the spirituality of religious groups in America; they must overcome the materialism, the avarice, and the racism of their members. American Christians face more temptations for the acquisition of wealth than any other Christians in the world. In a sense, it is a miracle that Christianity thrives as much as it does in America, amid the seductions of a society that possesses more material wealth than any previous society in the history of the world.

Tensions have always existed in the Christian community as to the appropriate level of activity on behalf of social reform. The social gospel has been almost in competition with mainline Protestants in the United States in this century. Some denominations, like the Amish, withdraw as much as they can from the distractions of secular learning and worldly pleasures. But the majority of Protestants expect that their churches will remain as places where there will be attractive liturgies and great emphasis placed on the essential otherworldliness of religion.

The tension between supernatural religion and work for social justice has become sharp in the Catholic church since Vatican II. That ecumenical council placed unprecedented emphasis on the idea that the mission of the Catholic Church must combine the preaching of faith with the promotion of justice. Those twin goals have radiated into the stated objectives of the Catholic religious orders. In two General Congregations conducted by the Jesuit order after Vatican II, the linking of the advancement of faith and the promotion of justice was clear and compelling. The Thirty-second General Congregation put it this way for the world's 25,000 Jesuits:

> The life we lead, the faith-understanding we have of it, and the personal relationship to Christ which should be at the heart of all we do are not three separate realities to which correspond three separate Apostolates. To promote justice, to proclaim the faith, and to lead others to a personal encounter with Christ are the three inseparable elements that make up the whole of our Apostolate.

The synod of Catholic bishops that met in Rome in 1971 as a follow-up to Vatican II declared that the promotion of justice is a "constitutive" part of the preaching of the faith.

The essential connection between faith and justice is now clearer in Catholic teaching than ever before. But that assurance is not always evident in Protestant preaching and practice. Indeed, the conservative critics of the National Council of Churches regularly charge that the NCC has gone outside of its Christian mission and embraced positions which are allegedly tainted with communism or socialism. Richard Neuhaus, in his book, *The Naked Public Square*, virtually harasses the NCC for its alleged departure or deviance from basic Christian teachings.

The lines between preaching and prophecy will seldom be bright. But what American Christians expect of their churches is a solid explanation of the gospel, attractive programs of religious education, and a constant reminder of the shortness of life and the length of eternity.

The fear that the churches in America are being too secularized is real, persistent, and credible. Sometimes, of course, that charge is made by persons who disagree with the message about social problems being transmitted by the churches. But it is also offered by countless persons who find in their churches petitions about questions like South Africa, Northern Ireland, and the rights of animals, but too little about creation, redemption, and how the Holy Spirit is trying to talk to all of us.

The first and the greatest of the commandments for the churches in

America is the absolute necessity of developing an intense spiritual life for all of their members. If this were done, it might be that the development of a just social order would take care of itself. If Christians loved as Christ mandated, they could change the world.

Father Pierre Teilhard de Chardin, the famed Jesuit, put it well: "Love is the most universal, formidable, and mysterious of cosmic energies."

II. *Coercion is Unchristian.*

If there is one single concept which has penetrated the consciousness of religious people in America in the recent past, it is the fact that coercion in areas of religion has no place whatsoever. All religious bodies now agree that they will not use the power of government to carry out their own sectarian purposes. The Supreme Court has already required that practice in the public schools. And the negative reaction to perceived bullying by the religious fundamentalists in the 1980s deepened the antagonism which present-day Christians in America have for any shadow of coercion or the compelled use of government to strengthen any religion, or all religions.

The Declaration on Religious Freedom promulgated by Vatican II held that "it is therefore fully in accordance with the nature of faith that in religious matters every form of coercion by men should be excluded." The Declaration also affirmed that the "search for truth . . . must be carried out in a manner that is appropriate to the dignity of the human person . . . it is by personal assent that men must adhere to the truth they have discovered."

Other religious denominations have adopted comparable renunciations of coercion. But the tendency of sincere religious leaders to insist that the government must help them to spread the truth is so traditional with Christians that believers in America must insist that they will forego "every form of coercion," as Vatican II stated so sweepingly.

Churches in America have been helped in their joint renunciation of coercion by the United States Supreme Court which has not only banned "excessive entanglement" between government and religion, but also, as a corollary of that principle, has barred any activities shared by government and religion which would likely become "politically divisive."

Many believers in America would claim that they have clearly repudiated "every form of coercion," and that this is a settled issue among the denominations. This may be true, but there are crucial questions of public morality still to be resolved in the United States and the centuries-old tendency or temptation of the churches to use social, political, or economic coercion will almost inevitably recur. The Catholic church, by its ringing renunciation of "every form of coercion" at Vatican II, set forth an ideal which may well be particularly helpful and useful in the United States.

III. *Religious Groups Need Solidarity in America*

Coordinated and collective action by all religious bodies in America on issues on which they agree would seem to be routine. But such actions are not routine. Protestant, Catholic, and Jewish bodies may have an informal de facto alliance in Washington on some issues. But the collective voice of all religious bodies is seldom heard. It was raised and heard in 1963 when some 1500 religious leaders came together in Chicago for the Conference on Race and Religion; the declaration from that assembly helped to pass the Civil Rights Act of 1964 and the Voting Rights Act of 1965.

There are theological, psychological, and emotional issues that keep religious bodies apart in America. Catholics have never joined the National Council of Churches. Some Protestants would find it difficult to cooperate with the U.S. Catholic Conference. The Leadership Conference unites 170 public interest groups related to civil rights— including all of the major religious bodies.

A combined consensus statement by most religious bodies in the United States could be set aside by the Congress just like separate statements of the various denominations are disregarded. But the urgency of making known the positions of religious groups as soon as new issues emerge is self-evident. At the present time, one has to search the denominational press to discover what even the major sects are contemplating on new public questions. The presence of a combined voice of religious bodies on issues of common agreement or common concern would be useful to everyone. It would also demonstrate that the walls of separation between Catholics and Protestants, going back to the Reformation and to the dominance in the United States of a pan-Protestant majority have crumbled. It would also constitute a way by which smaller denominations could have their voice heard either in consensus or in dissent.

The formation of a unit by which religious bodies could make their collective judgment known would be a dramatic way of announcing that America, as it opens its third century as a nation, needs the accumulated wisdom of its churches and synagogues.

IV. *The Churches and Children*

If there is any one thing on which all religions would agree it is the compelling duty of everyone to help children. The dictates of Judaism, Christianity, and Secularism agree resoundingly on the tenderness and diligence of the care that everyone should offer to children.

Especially in a nation like America, that boasts with pride that it adheres to the Judeo-Christian ethic, the plight of its children has to be deemed a scandal. In 1989, every fifth child in America lived under the poverty line—13 million out of 63 million; this is the largest number in the past fifteen years. In 1988, 500,000 American children were malnourished. The United States ranks nineteenth among industrialized nations in keeping its babies alive; each day 110 babies in America die before their first birthday.

Children in America are getting poorer while the nation gets richer. By the year 2000, one in four children—16 million youngsters—will be poor; 3 million more than in 1987. In addition, infant mortality is not decreasing. And American children are being hurt by unsafe child care.

The Select Committee on Children of the U.S. House of Representatives and the Children's Defense Fund regularly publish studies detailing the cruel neglect of America's children. It is clear that all groups of children are poorer today than they were in the 1970s.

During the presidential campaign in 1988, George Bush made a pledge to "talk, and talk, and talk until our country is working together to reach children." The rage and pain of parents and politicians who see children suffering is a moral and political force of enormous power.

Religious groups will inevitably urge that they cannot attack all of these problems unless they also take on the problems surrounding the decay of the family, unskilled persons who are unemployed, and the lack of affordable housing in urban areas. That may be true in part. But followers of Judaism and Christianity are told in dozens of ways that they must take care of refugees, the homeless, the hungry, and children. They are obliged to be good Samaritans if they want to think of themselves as good neighbors.

Religious groups continue to compile an edifying list of good works in America. It may be that religious organizations in the United States contribute more to charity than any comparable group in the history of Christianity. But the 313-page report issued in 1989 by the Children's Defense Fund demonstrates graphically that at least 13 million children in America have an acute need of help.

V. *Religious Bodies and Homosexuals in America*

In the 1980s, the clashes between homosexuals and the new religious fundamentalists dramatized a problem which many Christians probably wanted to ignore. It is unlikely that religious groups in America will agree soon, or ever, on the moral problems related to gays. This ancient problem, which apparently involves some 10 percent of the population, was "settled" in the law of a pan-Protestant America which generally made illegal any sexual relationship between male adults, even if they were consenting. A Georgia law of that nature was sustained 5–4 by the United States Supreme Court in *Bowers v. Hardwick* in 1986. Justice Byron White wrote with a measure of callousness that there is no privacy right or constitutional privilege for consenting adults to engage in homosexual conduct. At the time of the *Hardwick* decision, about one-half of the states had decriminalized homosexual conduct among consenting adults. If the 5–4 decision had gone the other way, most legal restrictions on consenting homosexual conduct probably would have disappeared. But that would not necessarily have resolved the question whether laws should be enacted to prevent discrimination against gays in employment, housing, or similar areas of activity. In 1989, some church groups opposed the adoption of such a law in San Francisco; the measure was defeated. Such a law was finally adopted in Massachusetts in 1989—after years of struggle and controversy. The law provides exemptions for church-related organizations which might have conscientious difficulties in hiring or renting to homosexuals. Wisconsin is the only other state that bans discrimination against gays. Although several municipalities provide protection for the civil rights of gays and lesbians, one can predict that in the 1990s controversies will continue as some religious groups publicly and strongly oppose legislation that forbids discrimination against gays in jobs and housing. Some Catholic bishops and most fundamentalist Christians will probably continue to use their moral, political, and ecclesiastical power to stop legislation like the new Massachusetts statute.

Another item involving clear discrimination against gays is the stated policy of the U.S. Defense Department that openly gay and lesbian students cannot be commissioned as military officers and cannot receive ROTC tuition benefits at American colleges. This is one of the several reasons why in the late 1980s, students at Yale and Harvard passed a resolution opposing the return of ROTC to campus.

Church officials have the right to declare their judgment on what they conceive to be the morality or the wisdom of a proposed law. But when they oppose legislation providing protection for the civil rights of homosexuals, they almost inevitably are using the ecclesiastical authority of their office to block the enactment of legislation which a wide variety of groups, including some religious groups, feel is appropriate and needed.

Religious groups in America worked against laws that weakened the restrictions on doing business on Sunday, allowed divorce, permitted gambling, and sanctioned abortion. Their struggles have not been successful in many of those areas. Will church groups fight to retain laws that restrict the activities and the opportunities of homosexuals?

Some religious officials may be inclined to work against any concessions to gays because of the presence of AIDS. The emergence of that tragic and mysterious disease should not prompt anyone to pronounce the totally unsubstantiated allegation that God has sent a plague. Patients with AIDS should be able to receive from church-related organizations the help that should come from groups that by their very nature are pledged to give their best efforts to the last, the lowest, and the least in society.

VI. *America's Churches and the Religions of the World*

Despite the fact that the churches of America have more international connections than almost any other organized group in the United States, they tend to be nationalistic, patriotic, and isolationist. The churches—especially the Catholic Church—have somehow been timid about reminding the country of what their fellow congregants are doing in other nations. All of this is a part of the isolation endemic to the American people. After World War II, the United States was thrust almost unwillingly into the role of a world power. The United States was the prime mover in the formation of the United Nations, an organization which, everyone judged at the time, should be located in the United States.

But in the 1950s and thereafter, the United States tired of its role as one of the moral architects of the post-war world. It forgot its newly acquired role and became the protagonist in a war to contain communism. Some of the churches acted as cheerleaders of that crusade; many others sat silently by or openly repudiated the cold war. The undeniable cruelty of the communists in Eastern Europe and the repression in the Soviet Union certainly offered substance to the idea that the United States, in God's providence, was destined to prevent the spread of godless atheism around the globe.

The world picture today is almost entirely different. Religious freedom is generally available in the USSR and Eastern Europe. China is still repressive, but the situation is startlingly different than it was at the time the United Nations was established. Churches in America should, therefore, make a complete reassessment of how the United States should proceed in the world after the cold war has ended. It is self-evident that religious and moral organizations in America have an unparalleled opportunity to shape the destiny of the world into the next century.

Proposals to reform the United Nations have been regularly advanced ever since it became clear that its structure is outdated and obsolete. It makes little sense to retain a Security Council where the five winners of World War II have permanent places. There is also a need to restructure the way by which nations vote and finance the United Nations.

As the nation looks for a new agenda, the country can have the hope that Mr. Gorbachev and other major world figures might sponsor a restructuring of the United Nations.

Amazing possibilities are opening up for the churches in America and around the world. The World Council of Churches will have new tasks thrust upon it. The Holy See will be in a position to give moral support for programs to bring development, literacy, agricultural reform, and improvements in public health to millions of deprived people.

The exciting potential for religious groups in America is almost too much to comprehend. The only question is whether the churches of America are up to an adequate response to the most stupendous challenge that has ever come to them in the 200-year history of America. Churches around the world, in collaboration with all major religious faiths, might make or support proposals for some kind of world federalism or world government. Churches contributed their share of the intellectual and spiritual energy that produced the United Nations. It is to be hoped that they have the wisdom and the courage to participate fully in the forthcoming struggle to establish some kind of a global entity which would bring justice and peace to the 6.2 billion children of God who will dwell in the universe in the year 2000.

VII. *America's Religious Bodies and Islam*

As the center of world history passes from Europe and America to the peoples of Asia and Africa, the Christian churches of the developed world have a very special obligation to try to understand and relate to the religions which two-thirds of humanity follow, such as Hinduism, Buddhism, and others. But American Christians have a compelling duty to understand what the 900 million Muslims of the world are thinking of at this time. Of special significance are the contemporary aspirations of the followers of Islamic fundamentalism.

American Christians continue to be astonishingly ignorant about the Muslim religion and Islam. The emergence of Ayatollah Ruhollah Khomeni in Iran and the detention of fifty-two Americans in 1979 and 1980 shocked America into realizing that there are millions of Muslims in Islamic countries who feel that the United States, and indeed the West are decadent, immoral, and corrupt. A book entitled *Islamic Fundamentalism* by Dilip Hero, published in 1988, details the many and profound reasons why so many in the Islamic world desire to keep Western imperialism and American materialism out of their countries. The West has forgotten that the European powers colonized many Muslim nations like Egypt, Malaysia, and Pakistan. Many Muslim religious leaders were among the forces that induced the colonial powers to withdraw from the nations they had occupied. When European culture was driven out of these countries after World War II, Islamic fundamentalists sought to restore the religious traditions which had been destroyed or suppressed during the 150 years of European occupation. A struggle of enormous proportions continues to evolve in the predominantly Muslim nations of Africa and Asia. It is quite possible that in some of these countries a pervasive anti-Western mentality will develop and take hold. In Islam there is no distinction between religion and politics. As a result, the revivalist movements designed to restore religious orthodoxy or to purify Muslim practices often seek to employ political power for religious objectives. Could there be a Holy War against the West in certain Islamic nations, or possibly over the vast region where Muslims control the political and economic life of the area? Could there emerge an Islamic common market along the lines of the European economic community? This would be, Dilip Hero suggests, "the first stage of a wide plan to draw all Muslim countries into a single economic network and thus transform Islam into a global economic system on a par with capitalism and socialism" (page 282).

The militant attitudes of some religious leaders in the Islamic world are incomprehensible to Christian leaders who have renounced all form of coercion as a means to advance their religious objectives. But the rise of fundamentalism in Islamic countries is propelled in part by the unshakable belief of Muslim leaders and followers that they are acting out the will of Allah.

It is somehow assumed that the violent wars between Christians and Muslims in past centuries could never be revived. But the fact is that there are millions of Muslims in the world—one-fifth of humanity follows the Islamic faith—who are angry at what they conceive to be the arrogance, the idolatry, and the decadence of Western nations.

If the cold war continues to fade away so that the United States cannot feel any longer that it must carry on a crusade against communism, could American leaders turn their militaristic instincts against what they would describe as the dangerous extremism of Muslim religious fanatics who have vowed to destroy America, the "Great Satan"? Even if the United States reduces its arms strength, it will still possess one of the most powerful military machines in the history of the world. Those in charge of powerful military installations have a way of seeking out targets to demonstrate the usefulness of their hardware. This is one more reason why at the end of the cold war, the churches of America should seek mightily to end the militarism which, for the first time in American history, became a part of American life in the 1950s.

VIII. *Christianity and the Rights of Women*

There is a deepening feeling among religious and nonreligious Americans that the Christian churches have for centuries been unfair to women. Until the recent past, there was an unanalyzed feeling among Christians that the churches had, over the centuries, elevated the status of women. The exaltation of Mary, the respect given to nuns, and the praise for the role of mothers were all deemed to have raised the position of women in Christian countries above that attained by women in non-Christian nations. Whatever truth may be contained in these views receives little attention or credence today. The Christian churches are widely described as unfair to women, and as almost an opponent of the liberation of women in the marketplace and in society.

The status of women in Western culture has changed more in the last twenty years than in the previous twenty centuries. The pace of changing attitudes is so furious that it is difficult to grasp and analyze the issues at any one time. The issues relate to the place of women in marriage and divorce; issues about abortion, ordination to the priesthood, and the wisdom of the Equal Rights Amendment.

The failure of the Equal Rights Amendment dramatized the confusion about the appropriate role for women in America. The proposed amendment to the U.S. Constitution was simple: "Equality of Rights under the law shall not be denied or abridged by the United States or by any state on account of sex." But church groups divided over this seemingly harmless extension of the rights already guaranteed by reason of the Equal Protection Clause of the Fourteenth Amendment. Mainline Protestant groups endorsed the ERA; the Catholic bishops made no pronouncement on it, while the fundamentalists fought vigorously against it. The greatest legal aspiration of women in the history of America was defeated; it received the ratification of only thirty-five of the thirty-eight states necessary, although it had been overwhelmingly approved by well over the two-thirds vote necessary in both houses of Congress.

It seems naive to suggest that religious groups in America could discuss the rights of women and somehow produce a consensus agreement. But some moral forces are needed to help the nation understand what it should think and do about the place of women in society. In the 1960s virtually all private church-related colleges in America became coeducational; the firm traditions of separate sex education at institutions like Dartmouth, Vassar, Williams, and Notre Dame were dropped. No one is urging that this was inappropriate; but there has been little explanation for the practice, insisted upon by the churches, of separating men and women in religiously affiliated colleges.

In the United Nations covenant for the elimination of all forms of discrimination against women, the world has for the first time made a Magna Carta on the rights which women should receive. This document, now a part of world law, is a remarkably measured statement of women's aspirations. It devotes special attention to the rights of women in developing countries, where the vast majority of women spend most of their waking hours on frequently debasing duties such as obtaining water, acquiring food, and doing farm work.

The Covenant on the Rights of Women is open for ratification by the United States Senate; if it is ratified, it would be binding on the United States, pursuant to the words of the U.S. Constitution which prescribe that every treaty becomes the "supreme law of the land."

Religious groups could use the UN Covenant on the Rights of Women as a point of departure for a national debate on a policy to which, at least theoretically, the churches could bring understanding and unity. There are, of course, all types of problems, foreseen and unforeseen. But religious groups in America have worked together on racism, refugees, war, and social problems. In the 1990s, the churches should focus on the role and rights of women in modern society.

IX. *The Primacy of Human Rights*

In the forty years of the cold war an amazing development occurred in the global explosion of interest in, and devotion to, internationally recognized human rights. The common beliefs of humanity in human rights were codified in the Universal Declaration of Human Rights adopted by the UN General Assembly on December 10, 1948. The two dozen covenants on human rights that have since emerged from the United Nations have transformed the legal system of the world by making the implementation of human rights a guarantee of international law.

This enormous expansion of international law has prompted the birth of scores of nongovernmental organizations devoted to human rights in the United States and around the world. The forerunner of these groups, Amnesty International, was born in humble circumstances in London in 1961. Since that time, it has won the Nobel Peace Prize and has altered the way in which humanity views the denial of human rights.

In the 1980s, nongovernmental American groups devoted to human rights have grown into important and influential lobbies.

Although these groups are not formally linked with religious bodies, they work closely with religiously affiliated organizations everywhere. It can be predicted with a good deal of confidence that America's interest in human rights will have a very substantial impact on U.S. foreign policy in the 1990s. The idea that human rights should be at the heart of America's foreign policy is now accepted by everyone; the only difference would be the way in which America balances its interests and its ideals in its relationship with the rest of the world.

If there is one possible area in which religious groups in America would be unified, it is in the field of the struggle for human rights. One could say that religious bodies have been fighting for human rights ever since Moses said to Pharaoh, "Let my people go." But an institutionalized, ecumenical, and broad-based commitment by all religious bodies in America to the implementation of international human rights everywhere could change the face of the earth—and change the image of religious organizations in the United States.

X. Prayer: The One Essential of All Religions

Religious people today shudder when they are reminded that through the centuries religious factions went to war and killed each other because they were allegedly heretics or schismatics or even "enemies of God." It may be that the United States went to war in Vietnam to defend the superiority of capitalism, or democracy, or even America's concept of religion. Whatever the truth of such an assertion, the common conviction of mankind today would seem to be that a war over religious differences is unthinkable.

World developments seem to support the idea that all religious groups, despite their differences, disavow war for virtually any purpose. In addition, the idea of national sovereignty is receding, the notion of a world federation of countries beyond the United Nations is thinkable, and even some thought of a global gathering of religions—broader than the World Council of Churches—is not too farfetched.

Is it opportune, then, for churches in America to propose that all of the religions of the world pray together? For some the idea may seem utopian and unrealistic. But the members of the churches of America realize that they reside in a nation whose economic and political decisions will, for better or for worse, alter the face of the earth. Prayer therefore is called for—to search for wisdom as to the just decisions to be made, and for courage and selflessness to carry them out.

Would it not be appropriate for those in America and in the developed nations of the world to seek to form some type of prayer groups with those in nations who will be directly affected by decisions made in the rich nations? Christians do not feel comfortable today sending "missionaries" to "pagan" lands to convert the "heathens." That approach to Christianity and to humanity has passed away. But ever-closer relationships between America's Christians and the majority of humanity who live in poor nations are inevitable, and highly desirable. All relationships between human beings are enhanced and improved by praying together. That is a simple truth agreed to by the adherents of every religion.

If Christians in America offer to pray with Buddhists, Muslims, Hindus, and others, the level of suspicion as to the motivation of the Americans will be high. The level of ignorance and distrust may be so profound that mutual prayer will not be attainable at this time. But American Christians would at least proclaim to the world that the essence of their faith means that, as Christ directed, they pray always.

Prayer is the essence of every religion. It is the core and the heart of Christianity. As the third millennium of Christianity approaches, the appeal and need of prayer is more imperative than at any time in 2000 years; the reason is the unprecedented abundance of moral demands on Christians because of their commanding involvement in the array of economic and political decisions which will affect the future of the human race in unbelievable ways for centuries to come.

If Christians in America pray more and involve others around the world in prayer, they will demonstrate to the world that they are not completely materialistic or totally selfish. They will exhibit faith, hope, and love. America may still continue to make the awful mistakes that arise from arrogance and affluence. But at least some Americans will have announced to the world that they try to believe in the piety their nation proclaims when it puts on all of its dollar bills the motto, "In God we trust."

CHAPTER 18

Religion and Morality: Some Ultimate Questions

It is clear from the foregoing that very hard questions have to be faced. Have some politicians and public officials, while pretending to be firm and appealing for prayer for the republic, bypassed the counsels and even the commandments shared by the religious bodies in America? Has a secularism crept into America's way of dealing with moral issues? Has the nation inadvertently or otherwise shifted away from those fundamental moral virtues on which the republic was established?

Even if the answers to most of these questions are in the affirmative, it does not follow that the leaders of government must be faulted as defectors or persons with too little faith or courage. It may be that there are too few prophets in the churches, and that the message of religious groups in America has been diluted. Preachers, like politicians, are anxious to retain their positions and are tempted to modify or mute the truth.

However the fault is to be divided, the fact remains that there is confusion and contradiction with respect to what moral tradition should be followed and enforced by the state in America.

There are many, of course, who, even though they may be personally religious, feel very uneasy about incorporating into the public morality of America any moral values which could be perceived to be sectarian or even religious. These observers are commendably sensitive to the feelings of non-Christians and nonbelievers in America. They are searching for a secular morality that will not become, in a pejorative sense, secularistic. They want a set of moral principles that will be respected by the courts and the legislatures and that will not impose values to which non-Christians or nonbelievers could object.

The source of such values is, of course, the United States Constitution and American law. In a quest for values that are not directly traceable to religion, federal and state courts—and especially the U.S. Supreme Court—have expanded the concepts of "due process," "equal protection of the laws," and "privileges and immunities" found in the Fourteenth Amendment. The vast proliferation of decisional law related to civil rights and civil liberties derives proximately from the phrases of the Constitution. But these phrases are not self-defining. "Due process" and "equal protection" are in fact two of the most elusive ideas in the vast body of Anglo-American jurisprudence. Nonetheless, they have served as depositories of the noble moral concepts that have brought equality, fairness, and justice to minorities in America. Paradoxically, the vast expansion of equal opportunities for minorities and for women came, not in the decades when the nation was adhering to a strict pan-Protestant ethos, but when significant elements of that ethos had faded away or been declared unconstitutional.

But the question keeps recurring: whose moral ideas are being utilized by the Supreme Court as that tribunal develops notions of privacy, fairness, and equality which are bringing unprecedented freedoms and new rights to millions of Americans?

One reply suggests that the Supreme Court finds its values in a secularized version of the Judeo-Christian tradition—in moral concepts which, since the days of Protestant domination, have taken on a life of their own in the consciences of Americans. There is much to be said for this approach. Americans believe strongly in and espouse vigorously the values of hard work, honesty, fairness, the pursuit of knowledge, and kindness to others. They lead lives of Christian virtue even though millions have no formal alliance with a church or do not believe that Christianity was revealed by God. Nonetheless, they have been brought up in a culture that has been penetrated by virtues which, while originally Christian or Jewish, are now sometimes identified as American.

But if the nation becomes more and more secular, could the public morality of America descend and decline into some form of authoritarianism or totalitarianism? That possibility prompted Father John Courtney Murray, S.J., to wonder and worry about the future of

America's "goodness" and the morality of its public judgments. Father Murray's proposed questioning of where America is going is analyzed in *The Search for an American Public Theology*, by Reverend Robert W. McElroy (Paulist Press, 1988). In 1950, Father Murray expressed the conviction that only believing men and women could ignite that revitalization of America which would be necessary to bring America back to the true ideals of the Western political and social tradition.

Speaking to Catholics in 1950, Father Murray stated:

> If you do not take into your hands that task, I do not know into whose hands it will fall. Or, rather, I do know. It will fall into the hands of a group, motley enough in its complexion, but whose members have at least this in common: that they are of today, wholly of today, with no roots in humanity's Christian past and no sense of continuity with it; nor gratitude for its cultural heritage; men and women whom Bertrand Russell described as "ignorant of the past, without tenderness for what is traditional, without understanding of what they are destroying." And, I may add myself, with little concept of what they are to build.

Father Murray's harsh assessment of the secularists will not be agreed to by everyone. He predicted again and again that America was on the road to secularism and that only believers could reverse that trend. He felt that Catholics, particularly, had a mission to restore America. He spoke to Catholics in these words:

> There falls upon us a major responsibility to assist in the revival, the restatement, the revitalization of the public philosophy of the United States. Upon our success in this task depends in large part, the future of our republic and our future within the republic.

Stirring rhetoric! Is it all true? It was for Father Murray and for millions of believers, Christian and non-Christian. They would agree with Father Murray, who on another occasion lamented the secularization of modern American society in these words:

> Consciously and unconsciously democracy is being transformed into the political and social organization of a great era, whose source is in the pagan darkness that always lingers, never fully clarified, in the mind of man. I mean the ancient idolatrous era of the self-sufficient man, who regards himself as sole architect of his own freedom, single author of the values that govern his life, ultimate judge of right and wrong, true and false.

This position so strongly held by Father Murray is the more remarkable because he was in many ways a minimalist in his expectations of law. As Father McElroy puts it, Murray saw the law "as protecting the public order and not as a moral blueprint for society" (page 109).

The perceptive and penetrating conclusions of Father Murray are entitled to all the respectful considerations which they continue to receive. But they were enunciated before the Second Vatican Council, before the shock waves of Vietnam and Watergate, and before the fading away of the cold war. In the new world after all of these events, what can be said with some credibility and some expectation of acceptance about the moral values which America's public leaders should embrace and follow?

The answer to that question is more uncertain and unclear than ever before in American history.

Again, the question is unavoidable: do the values of the American nation derive from Christianity; and if so, can they survive a separation from religion? The question is tormentingly difficult. With at least 90 million "unchurched" people in America, Christians and other believers are reluctant to claim that the nation has values that were or are based on the Christian tradition. There is little dispute about their desirability, but if those moral values do not depend for their origin and their validation on some connection with a spiritual force or entity different from and superior to the state, then must one concede that the government in America is proposing values which that government itself creates and validates?

One way to respond to these pressing questions is to suggest that ultimately America can live and govern itself by the norms and values that are contained in the 5,500 words of the Constitution and the laws agreed to by the representatives elected by the citizens at the local and national level. That response is somewhat satisfactory, but it still means that the government in America must be ruled only by the words of the Constitution, specific statutes on the books, and the laws created by elected officials.

Somewhere deep in the soul of America, there is a conviction that there is an unwritten law, and that the nation should follow its aspirations on moral issues even if they are not contained in the Constitution or the written laws.

In rhetoric, but also in reality, America looks to religion as the source and origin of its values. No one wants religion to be united with the government. The hope is that the government would imbibe many of its values from religion and that religion in turn would help the government in its difficult, indeed awesome, task of moderating the brutish instincts of the strong and the rich while encouraging the industry and virtue of the weak and the poor.

There is no adequate or good word to describe the relationship between government and religion in America. Some constitutional experts have recommended that the government should be benignly neutral toward religion. Others recommend a separation of religion and government—even a radical separation. Still others urge an accommodation or a partnership between the sometimes competing interests and objectives of the government and religious organizations.

The word that best describes the relationship between government and religion in America is "symbiosis." That term means the living together in an intimate way of two dissimilar organisms in a mutually beneficial relationship. Government and religion are and should be dissimilar organisms. They are, however, required to live together and that coexistence must of necessity be intimate, since the persons who belong to both the state and the churches are the same. Similarly, the relationship should be—even has to be—mutually beneficial, since the government depends upon religion for the ideals it embraces and the churches rely upon the state to bring about an orderly society in which the churches can perform their tasks.

Churches in America have been privatized so severely that it is not certain that many church authorities even want a symbiotic relationship with the government. Similarly, public officials, elected and appointed, frequently do not want any open or quiet relationship with the church which would involve any understanding that the government is expected to adopt positions consistent with those of the church.

What the contemporary relationship between government and religion should be is therefore a matter of some complexity. Absolutes are not very helpful. The issue, furthermore, is complicated by the undeniable fact that there are several agencies or institutions in American life that create moral values and seek to insert them into the public policies of the government. Public interest groups dedicated to human rights, preserving the environment, and promoting the rights of women are a powerful and permanent part of the American scene.

Some students of religion would claim that the values advanced by these groups are derived directly or indirectly from the Judeo-Christian tradition.

One thing is clear amid the babble of voices heard in America regarding the moral policies which the nation should follow: The very core of the American mystique welcomes and indeed requires that the voices of the multitudes be heard concerning what they want their nation to be and to become. Indeed, the major mistakes which the United States government has committed have arguably happened when the people were asleep or silent. Are we saying therefore that the people of America constitute a depository of the best moral thinking and traditions of American history? Although the governed can be as wrong as the government, one has to hold that in America, the voice of the people should be listened to more carefully and more continuously than the voice of the government.

This does not mean that the voice of the people is always or even generally entitled to credence; the voice of the government in America is so powerful and omnipresent that it can persuade people that certain things are good when it should be clear that they are wrong. Politicians can dominate the scene, monopolize whatever discussion is allowed, and even stigmatize those who disagree with them as un-American, dangerous, and subversive. The misuse by politicians of their positions during the cold war stigmatizing their opponents as disloyal to America, will become more notorious and scandalous as the nation begins more and more to look back at the excesses of that period of anti-Communist hysteria.

Are we saying, then, that the retention and improvement of the basic moral truths that are the core of America's soul depend upon a continual reaffirmation and refinement of those values by the people of America? That is, clearly, one of the essential components of America's public morality. But behind an alert citizenry, there has to be a number of organizations that formulate, refine, and promulgate moral standards. Churches are clearly included in these organizations. But nonreligious groups are also a part of that great web of quasi-public private organizations that exist to inform, influence, and inspire Americans as to what they should be as persons and as citizens of their country and of the world.

The United States government admits the need and value of these groups by its generous grant to all such nonprofit organizations of exemption from all federal, state, and local income taxes, and often excise and sales taxes. The state offers a vast array of police, fire, and other protection to these groups, even though they pay no taxes. The government allows them to propagandize their views, lobby legislators (if they register their identity), and criticize the government in terms as caustic as they desire. The only price they pay for tax-exempt status is a ban on endorsing candidates in local and federal elections. Is that a small or a large price to pay in return for exemption from billions of dollars in taxes?

One could argue that the nonpolitical posture of the churches enhances their credibility; they are perceived as not having a personal or political stake in the results of their advocacy. Hence, they are listened to more closely. On the other hand, it can be argued that the government, while pretending to want to maximize the influence of the nonprofit groups by granting them tax exemption has in fact hobbled them from the one overarchingly important function—endorsing and working for candidates for political office.

Whatever the ultimate truth about that problem, the present arrangement of churches and other nonprofit groups receiving tax exemption, but also being deprived of a vote in elections is not going to change. Churches, and by and large, their congregants are satisfied with the compromise arrangement. Indeed, many would resist granting the churches the right to be political. Such a role, many would feel, is fraught with danger. Indeed, Americans agree so overwhelmingly with that proposition that they recoil when a church acts in such a way that it could be construed to be endorsing a candidate—even indirectly.

Churches must therefore expect to continue their present role of taking positions on moral issues but never entering the waters of politics. That is forbidden territory. The churches hurt themselves in the eyes of believers and nonbelievers if they try to usurp what is deemed the exclusive work of the citizen: selecting the candidates to vote for.

Are the churches then semi-paralyzed in their task of making society more moral? Have they been rendered impotent? Have they been assigned—or did they settle for—a position that leaves them in a no-man's-land of neither being citizens who can vote nor corporations which can organize a political action committee and thus can give substantial campaign funds to incumbents and challengers?

In the end, one has to admit openly that there is no clear and certain plan as to what the Christian churches in America should do as they look forward to the frightening but exciting world after the year 2000. Amid terrifying temptations to be materialistic or to be indifferent to religion, Christians have to pray, fast, and struggle to try to discover what God intends that they do in a world to which God will add another billion of his sons and daughters in the next decade. The mystery of human existence—always a constant companion of Christians despite their belief in certain basic truths about man and God— will be deeper than ever before, as hundreds of millions of human beings struggle to escape starvation, homelessness, and asphyxiation from ecological disasters.

Christians have always been on pilgrimages, crusades, and troublesome journeys. To be seeking for God is endemic to the Christian experience. But Christians now face a new challenge, since in America they are at the seat of power for the developed nations. They control the forces behind Third World development, the banks, the multinational corporations, and the national and international bodies that formulate those decisions which will dictate whether millions live or die in the poor nations of the world. Christians, whether they want to or not, must make some of the fundamental decisions that will control the destiny of millions of people in the twenty-first century. It is an awesome and an inescapable responsibility. Christians should tremble in the presence of God and man as they undertake it.

Postscript

I finished this study on the relationship of religion and America's churches to the public morality of the United States before Iraq invaded Kuwait in early August 1990. It is not yet clear, and may never become clear, whether the churches had any influence on the decision regarding America's entrance into that War in the Persian Gulf.

But it *is* clear that Catholic and mainline Protestant churches in America opposed the war which the United States waged for the liberation of Kuwait. Indeed for the first time in American history, the 300 Catholic bishops and the National Council of Churches, representing mainline Protestants and some Orthodox Christians, opposed the war before it began; the churches urged the continuation of the very strict economic sanctions which the United Nations had imposed on Iraq. That advice was not followed.

Of similar historical importance is the fact that the World Council of Churches, meeting in Australia during the weeks of the war, openly and vehemently called for a cease-fire. There were some dissents by Anglican representatives, but the 3,000 delegates from all of the major Protestant and Orthodox denominations (the Catholic Church, not a member of the WCC, had observers present) boldly proclaimed that, in their view, the Gospel required that the twenty-eight nations in an armed alliance against Iraq should proclaim a cease-fire.

Catholic opposition to the war in the United States employed the seven traditional requirements for a just war. Commentators conceded that the war was properly declared, that the grievance involving the invasion of Kuwait was real, and that there was a substantial chance of victory. But critics of the war had trouble finding evidence that the other four requirements for a just war were satisfied. All possible alternatives had not been exhausted or even explored, the harm to be done could, in all probability, outweigh whatever good would be accomplished, the means to be employed could easily violate the four 1949 Geneva Conventions on the Conduct of War and the principal intention of the United States (to reserve its access to inexpensive oil) could not fulfill the requirement that the nation initiating the war have a noble and idealistic motive for its conduct.

At least two high-ranking Catholic prelates in America spoke with some approval of the war after it started. But virtually every other episcopal member of the U.S. Catholic Conference held fast to the determination of that body that the war was not justified. Many Catholics, however, were disappointed that the bishops were not more articulate and outspoken in their opposition to the war.

It is, nonetheless, remarkable that the top leaders of the 54 million Catholics and the spokesmen for some 70 million Protestants opposed the war begun by the Bush administration on January 16, 1991.

In almost every chapter of my book, I have tried to describe the position of the churches in the major legal-moral issues facing the United States. I have sought to discover whether the churches have been influential in formulating or implementing a sound moral position for the country. In some cases—for example, the growth in state-sponsored gambling—the position of the churches has clearly been set aside. In other areas, the results are mixed. It seems premature to conclude, in March 1991, that the position of the churches with respect to the War in the Persian Gulf has been completely repudiated. Any sound appraisal of the morality of America's War in the Gulf is made much more difficult by the near hysterical feeling of triumph in America over the victory in the Gulf. It seems as if the American people, in the Spring of 1991, felt deprived of almost any reason to feel good about themselves as a nation and that they seized upon the triumph over Iraq as a justification for self-adulation which, history may judge, was excessive.

As reality sets in, the alleged magnitude of the victory will diminish. Iraq was not a major military force; it had not even been able to defeat Iran in a war that lasted almost ten years. Iraq was exhausted, in many ways, when it occupied Kuwait. It had been weakened by the economic sanctions imposed by the United Nations—the toughest and tightest sanctions in the history of humanity. Consequently, the victory of the United States is not monumental; it was expected and even routine.

Persons who are anxious to improve America's public morality have new and serious threats confronting them. Will there be a tendency for the nation now to assume and assert that there is a quick military fix to some intractable problems? The nation seems to have an obsession with the idea that the syndrome over Vietnam is gone, and that the United States is now invincible. Will such oversimplified thinking be applied to other problems in the Middle East and around the world? The truth is that the United States, by its savage bombing of Iraq and Kuwait, may well have done more harm than good in the Middle East. The United States has intervened with massive military violence, has killed perhaps 100,000 people, and disrupted the economies of two nations for years to come. The United States may have inadvertently brought on a new geopolitical arrangement which may become even more turbulent and troublesome than the situation was before the unjust invasion of a tiny country like Kuwait. The United States has intervened in an unprecedented way in the complicated, centuries-old animosities and rivalries of Arab nations united only by their hostility to Israel.

The legal-moral issues confronting America's churches will, consequently, be even more complicated than the problems of this kind which have engaged the attention of the churches in the 200 years of America's existence.

Let us look, first, at some of the dangers facing persons in America who feel strongly that they should continue to measure the conduct of their nation with a moral compass.

The cries of jubilation and the yellow ribbons that dominated the mood of America, in March 1991, drowned out any consideration of the harm that was done to the people of Iraq. Will the Arab world and the 1 billion people who are Muslims across the globe look upon the carnage done in Iraq as a massacre inflicted by the United States for its own purposes—to make secure its access to oil and to prove to itself that Americans are invincible with their military might? What will the Arab and Muslim world think, in the years to come, about the decimation of Iraq? The Islamic world still resents bitterly the intervention of the colonial powers into the affairs of the oil-producing nations. But England, France, and the other nations that occupied one or more of the nations of Islam never bombed an entire nation killing a very substantial number of its citizens. It is hard to think that the memory of the massacre, carried out from the air over Iraq, will not be recalled with enmity and animosity by Arabs for generations to come. Could the military adventures of the United States in 1991, in the Persian Gulf, produce terrorist attacks against the United States and other nations?

The fact is that the "victory" of the United States in the Persian Gulf will have consequences that are unintended, unforeseen, and possibly calamitous. It is easy to theorize that the United States and its partners in war can now bring about a new era of peace in the Middle East. The fact is that the Palestinians have been further isolated because the PLO chose to go with Saddam Hussein. Israel has additional reasons to distrust the Palestinians on the West Bank and Gaza. And, the naked military power of the United States will deepen the longstanding antagonism for the United States as an ally of Israel and as a nation which is determined to control the oil supplies of the Middle East.

All of this has happened at the very time when the world had the rising hope that the 40 years of coexistence in terror was over, and that the threat of massive military competition had subsided. But now people are thinking, again, of the famous solemn warning given by President Dwight Eisenhower in his farewell to the nation on January 17, 1966.

> We must guard against the acquisition of unwarranted influence, whether sought or unsought, by the military-industrial complex. The potential for the disastrous rise of misplaced power exists and will persist.

There are other reasons to fear that the sharp and sudden escalation of violence in the world may bring not peace but the creation of new tensions or the aggravation of existing antagonisms. Will acute domestic problems in the United States such as the presence of 35 million poor people and the decaying infra-structure of the nation's bridges, schools, and highways be further neglected because the "peace dividend" has withered away? Will America, furthermore, be so involved in what it may conceive to be its new role in the world that it will allow the continued deterioration of its economic status?

One senses that the people of America, in the Spring of 1991, are obsessed with glorifying the war, arranging parades for its partici-pants, and praising the White House for its leadership in order—at least in part—to avoid thinking of the hard and intractable problems that the War in the Gulf did not resolve and which, in fact, it may have worsened.

While conceding these anxieties, there are, nonetheless, reasons to feel and to hope that America's intervention in the Middle East may be the beginning of a new and promising era for America and the world.

The first hope comes from the new activities of the United Nations. Almost for the first time in its history, the United Nations Security Council acted as it was designed to do. It imposed economic sanctions on Iraq, and gave authorization to the United States and twenty-six other nations to use force, if necessary, to expel Iraq from Kuwait. The twelve resolutions of the United Nations, concurred in by the veto-holding permanent members of the Security Council, were unprecedented in the history of the U.N. The end of the cold war made possible this development—thus opening up new and exciting possibilities of replacing the law of force by the force of law.

Perhaps the restructuring of the United Nations is the next stop. The U.N. will be 50 years old in 1995—an ideal time to reexamine and streamline its outmoded provisions. The U.N. Reform Association has the blueprint ready. The United Nations Association—an organization with significant support from church-related groups in the United States—is also ready to labor mightily to fashion the United Nations into an organization which will help the development of a new world order after the startling intervention of the United States in the Persian Gulf. It is not fanciful to think that if the United States and the USSR took the initiative in remaking the United Nations into a worldwide organization that could plan international legal and political machinery suitable for the twenty-first century, almost unbelievable things could happen.

The second development that could occur out of the War in the Gulf is the fashioning of an international criminal court. When the United States, the U.S.S.R., China, and all of the victorious allies punished the Nazis at Nuremburg, the dream and plan was to create a permanent Nuremburg. That hope—supported by an extensive body of literature over the last four decades—has not materialized. But now is the moment to revive it. The very existence of a standing international criminal tribunal to punish political despots would, in itself, constitute a substantial deterrent to dictators like Saddam Hussein.

A third possibility arising as a result of the war is the hope that the industrialized nations will stop the sale of arms to nations in the Middle East and elsewhere. In the 1980's, Iraq was able to purchase arms worth more than $48 billion—from the Soviet Union, France, and other countries. If these sales had been stopped early on, there would have been no need for the war that brought such tragic and destabilizing results.

In a recent year, the entire world spent more than $900 billion in arms and armies. If the United States and its allies in the Gulf pledged their collective determination to keep arms out of the Middle East, they would create a peace for that area of the world that could be lasting.

A fourth hope from the war centers on Israel. For over 40 years, the United States has been the friend and ally of Israel; America has given more aid and support to Israel than any other nation in the world. No one wants to interrupt that solidarity. But Israel needs outside help to break the stubbornness of the most right-wing government that has ever controlled Israel. The Camp David Accords, brokered by President Carter in 1979, have to be revived or modified in some form. One has the hope that somehow—in God's mysterious providence—a way to bring peace to the people of Israel could finally emerge from the horrors and devastation of the war against Iraq.

The mission of the churches in American history has been clear and consistent. From the beginning of the nation, organized religion in America has always spoken out about moral issues that confront the country. It seems fair to say that in America the citizens clearly do not want the churches to dictate the country's public morality. At the same time, the people of America welcome views about moral issues from every source. Those who live in the United States do not want the government formulating moral positions for the country. The ethics and the morals of the nation should come from persons and organizations outside of the government. One of those agencies is organized religion in America. The views and vision of organized religion have always been listened to, heeded, and not infrequently followed.

In the world after the war with Iraq, the ethical dilemmas which the United States will have to face will be more agonizing than any the nation has faced in its first 200 years of existence. As a result, the churches will have a new and more complicated role to play. That role may be more crucial to the nation and to the world than anyone can possibly imagine at this time.

Index